FROM THE HILL

TO THE MOUNT

FROM THE **HILL**

TO THE **MOUNT**

Richard G. Hirsch

THE ZIONIST LIBRARY

Publishing House of the
World Zionist Organization

gefen
publishing house בית הוצאה לאור

JERUSALEM ♦ NEW YORK

Published by:
Gefen Publishing House Ltd.
And
The Zionist Library
Publishing House of the World Zionist Organization
P.O.B 92, Jerusalem, 91000

Typesetting: Marzel A.S. – Jerusalem
Cover Design: Studio Paz, Jerusalem

1 3 5 7 9 8 6 4 2

Gefen Publishing House
POB 36004, Jerusalem 91360, Israel
972-2-538-0247 • isragefe@netvision.net.il

Gefen Books
12 New Street Hewlett, NY 11557, USA
516-295-2805 • gefenbooks@compuserve.com

www.israelbooks.com

Printed in Israel

Send for our free catalogue

ISBN 965-229-243-5

Library of Congress Cataloging-in-Publication Data:
Hirsch, Richard G.
From the hill to the mount: a reform Zionist quest/ Richard G. Hirsch
Includes Index

1. Hirsch, Richard G.   2. Rabbis—United States—Biography.   3. Reform Judaism—United
States—History—20th century.   4. Zionism and Judaism.   5. Israel and the Diaspora.   I. Title
BM755.H477 A3 2000 • 296.8'.341'092—dc21 • CIP Number : 00-055127

Contents

FROM THE HILL TO THE MOUNT

The Hill

"We have built no national temples but the Capitol;*
we consult no common oracle but the Constitution."

Statement of Rufus Choate,
Congressman and Senator from Massachusetts
U.S. House of Representatives, 1833

The Mount

Come, let us go up to the MOUNT of the Lord,
To the House of the God of Jacob;
That He may instruct us in His ways,
And that we may walk in His paths,
For out of Zion shall go forth the Law,
The word of the Lord from Jerusalem.

(Isaiah 2:3)

---

* The Capitol, symbol of American democracy, built on Capitol Hill in Washington, D.C., houses the Congress of the United States of America.

To Bella

פיה פתחה בחכמה
ותורת חסד על לשונה

"She opens her mouth with wisdom
And the law of kindness is on her tongue."

(Proverbs 31:26)

and

To our children and grandchildren

בזכות בנים אבותיהם מתכבדים

"Through the merit of children
Their parents are honored."

(Tanhuma Vayikra 5)

Acknowledgements

The idea for this book came from a respected friend, Professor Moshe Davis, founder of the Institute of Contemporary Jewry at the Hebrew University in Jerusalem. Professor Davis convinced me to record the material contained herein for historical purposes. He enlisted a mutual friend, Priscilla Fishman, to serve as the first editor. Tragically, both passed away in the early stages of my work. I express appreciation for their initiative זכרונם לברכה "May their memory be for blessing."

I am especially grateful to Dan Leon. With incisive skill, he collated the material, and edited and polished the ideological section of the book. Through our cooperation, we have renewed an old friendship, and collaborated harmoniously in this project.

Special thanks are extended to Amos Yovel, Director of the publishing house of the World Zionist Organization ("the Zionist Library"), Ilan Greenfield, Director of Gefen Publishing Company and cherished friend Eli Eyal, member of the World Zionist Organization Executive, for their helpfulness throughout. Zoe Keren, my long-suffering secretary, typed the manuscript. Her reward is that she will not have to read the published text.

Good friends contributed to a fund to assist in the publication of the book, among them: Austin and Nani Beutel, Harvey and Ruth Cohen, Betty Golomb, Morton and Leah Kemper, Robert and Audrey Morris, Charles and Elaine Petschek, Sir Sigmund and Lady Hazel Sternberg.

Throughout my professional career I have been fortunate to work with countless leaders, both professional and lay, who have been full partners in all our endeavors. Space does not permit me to mention all their names. For fear of alienating some, I will mention none. They know who they are and they should be aware of how much I appreciate the privilege of working as a team to achieve shared goals.

The Midrash teaches that when God created the universe, He purposely made everything incomplete. Instead of making bread grow out of the earth, God made wheat grow, so that human beings would have to bake the wheat into bread. Instead of making bricks grow out of the earth, God made the earth of clay, so that human beings would bake the clay into bricks. Why? So that all humanity would become God's partner in the work of creation.

The positions of public responsibility I have held have instilled in me the conviction that, together with my colleagues, our task is to bake the bread and the bricks, to nourish and to build; and thereby to serve as God's partner in the sacred task of creating a better humanity and a better Jewish people.

Introduction

I shall never forget the first time I learned how to use a microscope. The teacher held up a colorful cloth. She asked the class, "What do you see?" We responded, "A beautiful pattern." Then she instructed us to place the cloth under the microscope. "Now what do you see?" "Holes." The teacher said, "I don't know how much science you will learn from me, but perhaps you will learn a lesson about life. Don't look for the holes. Stand back. Try to get perspective. Look for the beautiful patterns in life."

This work is an attempt to search for perspective in my life, to seek to discover a multi-colored pattern. The book consists of two basic sections. The first is autobiographical in character, but I do not intend to write a biography, as the genre is normally defined. Rather than a comprehensive chronological recounting of my life, I have highlighted a few formative personal experiences which have both motivated me and molded my views. The second and longer section consists of excerpts from my writings and public statements which project the development of my views and convictions.

From the Hill to the Mount — A tale of two cities

I was privileged to serve in two leadership positions within the movement of Progressive Judaism (also known in different parts of the world as Reform or Liberal Judaism). I was the Founding Director of the North American Reform movement's Religious Action Center in Washington and served there from 1962 until 1973. In 1973, I became the Executive Director of the World Union for Progressive Judaism and was instrumental in moving its international headquarters to Jerusalem. I served in this latter position until July, 1999, at which time I became Honorary Life President of the world movement.

Since 1972, I have been a member of the World Zionist Organization Executive and a member of the Board of Governors and the Executive of the Jewish Agency for Israel. I have held a number of elected offices, among them:

Chairman of the Zionist General Council (1987-1992) and President of the 33rd World Zionist Congress (December, 1997). Since that Congress, I have worked in a full-time capacity as the Co-Chairman of the Jewish Agency Commission of the Department of the Former Soviet Union and Eastern Europe.

I have never considered my responsibilities as jobs, but rather as missions, as opportunities to weave new patterns of Jewish identity and responsibility through shaping policy and building institutions.

During the last four decades of my half-century in the rabbinate I have lived in Washington and Jerusalem. To a very real extent, therefore, my life has been a "tale of two cities," one the capital of America and the other the capital of the Jewish people. In Washington, I spent many hours on Capitol Hill testifying and lobbying on behalf of Jewish social concerns. Working on "the Hill," as it is called in American political parlance, served as an excellent preparation for my work in Israel. Just as "the Hill" symbolizes the American democratic process, Mount Zion symbolizes the Zionist movement which created the State of Israel. Hence, the title of the book: *From the Hill to the Mount: A Reform Zionist Quest*.

In reviewing my career, I have discovered certain strands which were common both to the Washington and the Jerusalem experiences. It is gratifying to note that in the course of time these strands in my life have been interwoven into the fabric of Progressive Judaism and of the Zionist movement. I list some of these strands here as an introduction to what follows.

Strand I

I reject the notion that there is a dichotomy between universalism and particularism in Judaism. When the Religious Action Center was established, it was ostensibly associated with the universalist thrust in Judaism. It was our mandate to broaden Jewish social concerns to issues beyond what were considered at the time the vested interests of the Jewish community: anti-Semitism, church-state issues, and Israel. Conversely, efforts to support Israel economically and politically and to build a liberal movement in Israel were considered a reflection of the particularist thrust in Judaism.

When after the Six Day War I proposed that the American Reform Movement embark on a major effort in Israel, some of my closest colleagues saw a conflict of interest between my work in Washington and Jerusalem. They referred to the inherent tension in Judaism between universalism and particularism. For me, there was no inconsistency. Helping to establish our kibbutzim in the Arava desert, founded on a blend of the social ideals of both Judaism and democracy, was the most universalist task in which I was ever engaged. Working in Washington in the war against poverty in the 1960's was to bring to bear the distinctive particularist approach of Judaism on contemporary socio-economic issues. I have never been willing to compartmentalize my ideology or my actions. Therefore, the motivations for my work in Washington and Jerusalem were of one piece.

Strand II

For Reform Judaism to impact on its members, on society and on the Jewish people, it must engage in *collective* action. Long before the Religious Action Center, American Jews as individuals had been at the forefront of social justice issues. But the synagogue as an institution was quiescent and irrelevant to the primary issues confronting American society. The Center, projecting Jewish values to the center stage, enabled Jews as Jews, and in the name of Judaism, to become key actors in the drama of American democracy.

Similarly, in regard to Israel, long before the establishment of the State, Reform rabbis as *individuals* were among the foremost leaders of American Zionism. But the *movement* was non-Zionist, and in danger of becoming peripheral and marginalized. I am convinced that the most consequential decision the Reform/Progressive movement made in the last half of the twentieth century was the resolve to take decisive action to build a movement in Israel. In one fell swoop, we catapulted ourselves as a movement to the center stage of world Jewry and declared our intention to play a primary constructive role in the drama of restoring Jewish peoplehood in the setting where Jewish destiny will ultimately be determined.

For Reform Judaism to move to Washington was to become a full and equal partner in the American dream. For Reform Judaism to move to Jerusalem was to become a full and equal partner in the Jewish dream. Full partners cannot be silent partners. Equal partners not only demand equal rights; they also assume equal responsibility.

Strand III

In every effort to break new ground and to effect change, controversy ensues. In keeping with Pirkei Avot, כל מחלקת שהיא לשם שמים סופה להתקיים "Every controversy for the sake of heaven will in the end lead to a permanent result." I have always welcomed ideological controversy as the essential ingredient for social progress. Therefore, I define controversy over social issues as "salutary public education."

Both the establishment of the Religious Action Center and the move of the World Union for Progressive Judaism to Israel generated intense conflict within the movement. In the final analysis these conflicts, however bitter, were constructive. They highlighted the historic significance of the respective decisions and, once a democratic decision was taken, stimulated the incentive for effective implementation.

Strand IV

אהבת ישראל: כל ישראל ערבים זה בזה. "Love of the Jewish people" and "all Jews assume responsibility for one another." To be a Jew is to be wedded to the collectivity called the Jewish people. Judaism has given the world its fundamental ideological foundations. The Exodus from Egypt gave the world the concept of human freedom; Sinai, ethical law; biblical tradition, historical purpose leading to the messianic hope for peace and brotherhood. But we continue to contribute to the world even more than spiritual values and ennobling ideals. We contribute the Jewish people itself. Other religions have created symbols of faith, sacred objects, sacraments, cathedrals and monuments of stone. We have given the world an enduring symbol, what Tolstoy described as, "the emblem of eternity." What is that emblem? Again, in the words of Tolstoy, "the Jew is everlasting as is eternity itself."

We Jews, as individuals, are human like all other humans. We are born, we grow, we love, we hate, we are fallible, we sin, we die. But the Jewish people lives on as the symbol of God in human history. We are the *Am Olam* — the people of eternity. The Jewish people is our monument. That is why the State of Israel is so central. The world instinctively recognizes that if this people, the perennial victim of mankind's evil impulses, can return to its land, restore its sovereignty, revivify its language and culture, absorb Jews from seventy divergent cultures, and, we pray, establish enduring peace with its neighbors, then is there not hope for all humankind?

That is why what happens to world Jewry is so central. That is why the miracle of Soviet Jewry is so inspiring. The "Jews of silence," suffering under forced assimilation for over seventy years, are returning openly and with pride to their Jewish identity. And that is why Progressive Judaism is so vital. We are a major force for preservation of *Am Yisrael* around the world. We stand firmly on fertile ground, one foot in innovative fulfillment of Jewish tradition and the other in a constructive response to the secular world. Ours is a prerequisite message for Jewish survival. We synthesize faith, people, Torah, land, history and modernity.

It has been a privilege to serve on the cutting edge of crucial issues confronting American and world Jewry, the State of Israel and the liberal religious movements in Jewish life. My residence may have moved from Washington — the capital — to Jerusalem — the Mount — but my life is a tale of one people. For this I am grateful.

FORMATIVE EXPERIENCES

DEFINING MOMENTS

The oratorical contest

I do not recall exactly when or how the drama of the Jewish people's return to Zion became a motivating factor in my life. I do know that as a child in religious school I did enjoy going to after-school Hebrew classes at our Conservative synagogue, unlike the majority of my friends, for whom attendance at Hebrew school was an obligation imposed by parents. For some reason, I found myself welcoming the opportunity to learn the Hebrew language, though I must also admit that because of the methodology, the environment and other factors common to Hebrew school in those days, in actuality I learned very little.

At the synagogue I became an active member of Young Judea, a national youth organization whose purpose was to educate youth on Zionism. I read as much as I could on the subject. When it was announced that there would be an oratorical contest for National Young Judea, I entered, even though I was only thirteen years old. I won the citywide contest of the Young Judea chapters in Cleveland. This made me eligible to participate in the national oratorical contest, which was held in Baltimore in June 1940.

I prepared for the national contest with great diligence. I remember that I kept changing the text, even until the last moment before I rose to speak. While delivering my talk, I came to a passage which I had written just before the contest started. I suddenly forgot the new words which I thought I had memorized. I recall that there was a painful silence in the middle of my presentation (which to me seemed like an eternity. I assume that it must have been only a few seconds). I finally recalled what I intended to say and continued with my talk to its conclusion. The chief judge announced that I had won the first prize. Among other comments, she commended me for my presence of mind. She said, "When the streetcar passed by outside, you demonstrated tremendous composure by pausing until the noise died down." In truth, fate favored me, for I had not been aware of any streetcar.

I returned to a hero's welcome. My mother, father and brother Jay, met me at the train station. Jay, ten years old at the time, had composed a big sign which he held up at the train terminal "Welcome home, champ." My mother kept the sign which we still have.

A number of articles celebrating my winning the prize appeared in both the Jewish and general press. I remember being interviewed by a newspaper reporter who asked, "What do you want to be when you grow up?" I gave some non-committal answer. I recall him saying words to the effect, "Perhaps you will consider becoming a rabbi like the famous Rabbi Abba Hillel Silver" (the Cleveland rabbi who was renowned as a foremost leader of the American Zionist movement). I remember responding "I guess I might consider that." However, the newspaper clippings of the time noted that I wanted to be a rabbi. From that time on my career objective was set.

That fall, I received a call from Rabbi Silver's office noting that the Zionist community was proud that a Clevelander had won the National Oratorical Contest and inviting me to deliver the talk at the opening meeting of the Cleveland Zionist Federation. A huge crowd was in attendance. I recall that in addition to Rabbi Silver himself, leading national Zionist leaders participated. I was asked to come to Rabbi Silver's study before the commencement of the meeting.

The year 1940 was the presidential year when Wendell Willkie had been nominated by the Republicans to run against Franklin D. Roosevelt who was running for a third term. Several days prior to the meeting, Rabbi Silver had announced in public his support of Wendell Willkie, provoking a storm within the Jewish community, both locally and nationally. Roosevelt was considered the best friend American Jews had ever had in the White House and was idolized as a great hero of the Jewish community, to the point where he could do no wrong. To this day, I recall my grandmother, whose English was limited, listening to Roosevelt's "fireside chats" on the radio. She would gaze with great concentration as if divine words were being revealed from on high. It was only many years later, following Roosevelt's death, that American Jewry became aware of his faults. We now know that Roosevelt did not go out of his way to save the Jews of Europe, or attempt to prevent some of the horrors of the Holocaust.

That evening in his defense Rabbi Silver warned his colleagues to be wary of all political leaders. Their first concern, said he, is to be reelected. They are subject to much pressure on many complex issues. Jews cannot afford to take for granted any politician's stance on any issue. Not all liberal politicians automatically adopt pro-Jewish positions and not all conservatives invariably oppose vested Jewish interests. Responsible Jewish leadership must exercise political pressure on all elected representatives.

His second lesson was that it is in the Jewish interest that prominent Jews be seen as supporting all legitimate political views, regardless of political party affiliation. Silver stressed again and again that it was not good policy for Jews to be considered as having been in the back pocket of Roosevelt. Roosevelt's cognizance of his overwhelming support from Jews had diminished the potential impact of Jewish lobbying efforts on behalf of Jewish causes.

The points made by Silver were later reinforced by my own Washington experience. Jewish interests and general liberal interests are not always identical. Indeed, the more complex the general social issues, the more complex become issues of Jewish vested interest. Justice Louis Brandeis taught that there is no contradiction between being a good Jew and a good American. Therefore, the best way to be a good American is to advocate Jewish interests, knowing full well that these interests may be at odds with the social perspective of those politicians with whose ideas and values we generally concur.

Rabbinic studies

In 1944 I enrolled in a joint program of university and rabbinic studies. Since I had finished high school one year early, I was eighteen years old when I entered the Hebrew Union College as a freshman in the rabbinic program and as a sophomore at the University of Cincinnati.

In those days the College was very small. Only forty-two students were in residence. Some of the senior students had been sent to serve pulpits whose rabbis had entered the chaplaincy during World War II. Most of the students lived in the dormitory and only a very few were married.

Eight students entered with me. Some had been Yeshiva students and some had already served in the military in World War II. From the very beginning, those who had studied in a Yeshiva had a theoretical advantage. They knew Hebrew and Talmud and were infused with knowledge of tradition. However, some of the students with Orthodox backgrounds were in rebellion against Orthodoxy. I found it ironic that some students from Eastern European Yeshiva origins became the great defenders of classical German Reform Judaism, whereas many like me who had come from Conservative or Reform backgrounds found ourselves in search of more tradition.

Many of the professors were foreign born. Some had been rescued from Europe before the war through the efforts of the Hebrew Union College and the World Union for Progressive Judaism. I felt considerable discomfort at the fact that by my definition, only a few members of the faculty were Zionists. I was astounded that the trauma of the Holocaust had not transformed the entire faculty, or for that matter the entire student body, into Zionists.

In 1949 I decided to take a leave of absence from my studies in Cincinnati in order to study in Israel. The State had been established in May 1948 and immediately became embroiled in the War of Independence. Its fate was hanging by a thread and I felt the compulsion to be there, to share the burden and the exhilaration of creating a newborn state. Until that time, no student had left the College as an under-graduate with the request to study in Israel and receive credit for the studies. I felt it was essential for me to go as soon as possible and not to wait until after ordination.

When the word got around among the student body and the faculty, many tried to discourage me from going. In addition to the interruption of studies, there was the factor of security. The war was over, but the cease-fire arrangements were fragile. Nevertheless, despite the reluctance of the faculty and the severe misgivings of my family, I proceeded to make plans to take a year's leave of absence.

Sojourn in Israel — 1949-1950

The year in Israel was an opportunity to experience Zionism in action. During the course of the summer, I worked on kibbutzim, undertaking a variety of assignments, laying irrigation pipes, washing dishes, waiting on tables, spreading manure on the fields, cleaning out the dairy barns and the chicken coops and working in the fields and orchards.

I spent hours long into the night discussing kibbutz ideology and the dynamic impact of the kibbutz movement on society. I became convinced that the kibbutz movement was a distinctive contribution to societal organization, blending socio-economic ideals with Jewish values and that the movement could only have succeeded in a Jewish milieu.

I contended, to no avail at the time, that if the socialist founders would have viewed their movement as a *reform of* Jewish tradition rather than as a *rebellion against* Jewish tradition, they would have adopted a more constructive attitude toward Judaism. Even in those early days, I advocated that the kibbutz's communal structure provided an ideal setting for creative and innovative experiences in observance of the Sabbath and holidays and the Jewish life cycle.

Twenty years later, as we began to develop our kibbutz movement in Israel, we established the closest working relationship with the kibbutz movement leadership. I was delighted to learn that many individual kibbutzim and the movement as a whole was indeed devoting greater attention than previously to creative renewal of Jewish tradition and development of programmatic materials for encouraging the process.

Toward the end of the summer, I left the kibbutz and took up residence in Jerusalem. The ulpan system had not yet been developed. With the aid of a private teacher and fellow university students, I spent day and night studying Hebrew. By the time the Hebrew University began, I was able to understand most of the lectures. I felt privileged to study with some of the most illustrious scholars in the field of Jewish Studies: Professors Martin Buber, Ernst Simon, Hugo Bergman, Benjamin Mazar, Julius Guttman, and Simon Halkin.

The student body at the time was less than 2,000, among whom were approximately 50 students from overseas. No real provision had been made to accommodate these students, so we organized a foreign students association, from whose recommendations the large-scale programs for overseas students were later to emerge.

In the course of the year, I traveled extensively over the country, even making my way to Eilat, officially out of bounds at the time to civilians, I went in the company of two fellow students who were officers in the army. I worked for a month on archaeological excavations at Bet Yerah, a Canaanite settlement on the southern shores of the Kinneret whose deity was a moon god. Visiting the historical sites brought the Bible and Jewish history to life, even as the State of Israel with its absorption of waves of new immigrants was bringing the Jewish people to life.

Every Shabbat and holiday I attended services at a different synagogue, making a systematic effort to visit as many of the variegated ethnic oriented ones as possible. The vast differences in liturgy and custom reaffirmed the pluralistic character of Jewish worship.

By the time the academic year was over, I had become fairly fluent in Hebrew and felt thoroughly integrated into Israeli society. Yet whenever I was asked, and at the time it was the most frequently asked question, "Do you plan on coming on aliyah?" I gave the pat response, "No, what would a Reform rabbi do in Israel?"

The return to America

Shortly before I was scheduled to return from the sojourn in Israel, I received a telegram asking me to serve as head counselor of the National Young Judea Camp for the summer of 1950. The camp staff had either spent time in Israel or were thoroughly imbued with Zionist ideology. Most of the staff were active leaders within the Conservative movement. The fact that I was asked to serve as head counselor, even though I was about to become a Reform rabbi, corroborated my hypothesis, namely that if the Reform movement involved itself in Israel and Zionist matters, it too could take a leadership role and stand as equals with the other religious movements in Jewish life.

The Hebrew language was an essential tool for leadership. I viewed knowledge and use of modern Hebrew as a prerequisite to integrating Reform Judaism in *Klal Yisrael*. My ability to speak Hebrew fluently was a factor in negating the allegation that the Reform movement was heading in an assimilationist direction. Achad Ha'am had written, "Even more than the Jewish people preserved the Sabbath, the Sabbath has preserved the Jewish people." Paraphrasing him, we could claim that even more than the Jewish people has preserved the Hebrew language, the Hebrew language has preserved the Jewish people.

On my return to Cincinnati, I passed the oral and written exams given by the faculty and received academic credit for the year. In subsequent years many other students made the same sojourn, although initially the College refused to give credit to returning students. However, by the early 1970's the College recognized the enrichment potential of a sojourn in Israel and, therefore, made the year in Israel program a mandatory part of its curriculum. Ever since, every student studying for the Reform rabbinate, cantorate or Jewish education degree is obligated to spend the first year in Israel. The College has developed a magnificent campus and a program of training Israelis for the Israeli rabbinate. To its credit, therefore, the College has made a vital contribution to "Zionizing"

American Reform Judaism and to developing the Progressive movement in Israel.

I soon experienced a culture shock. For most of my colleagues, the State of Israel was not on the front burner. I helped to organize the Young People's Division of the UJA-Federation in Cincinnati and was asked to serve as Chairman of the UJA collections for the Hebrew Union College student body and faculty. I went through some difficult moments in discovering that many students and faculty were not prepared to give to the UJA fundraising campaigns in accord with their capacity. I considered the opportunity to raise funds as an educational process. It was in those days that I began to develop my philosophy of fund-raising. There is a rabbinic saying, אדם ניכר בכוסו, בכיסו ובכעסו. It is a clever alliterative phrase, indicating that a person is known for his cup (by the way he holds his liquor) by his pocket (how, why and for what he spends his money) and his temperament (what gets him excited, what animates him). It was then also that I developed a prime motivation for fund-raising, also based on words of the Sages, יותר ממה שהעגל רוצה לינוק פרה רוצה להניק. "Even more than the calf needs to nurse from the mother cow, the mother cow needs to give the milk." I tried to convey to my colleagues that the process of giving funds is essential, not only because our people needed the money for immigration and absorption, but because the act of giving our own resources is an expression of our own sense of identity as responsible Jews.

The senior sermon

As part of the curriculum, every senior student was obliged to deliver a sermon at the Sabbath services. Mine became the subject of controversy, severely criticized by some and praised by others. The sermon, delivered when I was 24 years old, presages the ideological commitments and institutional directions which were to characterize my career. Excerpts from the sermon, presented on Shabbat, November 18, 1950 in the chapel of the Hebrew Union College, follow:

> Political Zionist movements in the United States today are in decline. While the Zionist *organizations* may survive, the American Zionist *movement* is in a coma. A movement must be vibrant, dynamic, captivate its members with prophet-like zeal and, above all, preach a distinctive mission. None of these qualities can be attributed to American Zionism. The sudden disinterest in Zionist organizations is due not only to the fact that their activities appear anti-climactic, but also to the American Jews' realization, perhaps in many instances subconscious, that the mission of so-called American Zionism is not distinctive, that it is no different from the mission of the so-called non-Zionists.
>
> Most Jewish religious movements recognize the revolution that has occurred, but have refused to reckon with the resulting developments. They have seen the truth, but not the consequences. This applies to Reform Judaism in particular.
>
> Reform Judaism has displayed neither the foresight nor the courage to concede that there no longer is a dichotomy between Zionism and Judaism. It has been unwilling to grant that almost everything included under the generic term "Zionism" is by very definition an integral part of Judaism, inextricably associated with our concept of the peoplehood of Israel.

In the American Jewish community today, the phenomena of anti-Zionism, non-Zionism, and pro-Zionism can no longer exist. Today there is only Judaism. Whether Reform wills it or not, the fate of the State of Israel is in its hands, just as in many respects its own fate will be determined by developments in the State of Israel. Just as the period of the second Jewish Commonwealth is now the heritage of the entire Jewish people, so everything that constitutes Israel today, the spiritual and the mundane, the degrading and the uplifting, is the personal possession of all Jews, the living history of the entire Jewish people.

Because the Zionist organizations are in decline, it now becomes the responsibility of the religious movements which, more than any secular group, understand the true essence of Jewish life, to assume the lead. Reform Judaism preaches that it is a universal religion with a message for all humankind; yet it is content to fulfill its mission concept and satisfy its conscience by *preaching* a message to Israel, by passing resolutions. In practice, this approach is neither realistic nor constructive. Any liberal movement that does develop in Israel will evolve from the needs of the particular Israeli environment, and will therefore bear little resemblance to American Reform Judaism.

If Reform Judaism wants to influence Israel, and we have every privilege and duty to do so, then let us as a religious movement not only give moral support to Zionist undertakings. Let us enter actively into the work of revitalizing the Jewish state. Let us include as part of our general Jewish education program what today is known as Zionist education. Let us inspire our members with the need for American aliyah and *halutziut* (immigration and pioneering).

Once Reform Judaism articulates in deeds the close relationship between Israel and American Jewry, then it will find that what was originally intended as service to Israel has in turn, increased the strength and significance of Reform

Judaism in America. The difficult burdens of family
responsibility will bring the rich blessings of family love.

The fundamental thesis that Zionism had to be incorporated into Reform
Judaism and that, therefore, Reform Judaism and Zionism were inextricable
was, to say the least, a radical new theory for most of my colleagues. Rabbi Leo
Baeck, then teaching at the Hebrew Union College, sat me down after the
sermon in the back of the chapel and explained to me why my hypothesis of total
integration between Zionism and Reform Judaism was faulty. I must confess
that until that discussion, I would never have suspected that Leo Baeck, whom I
loved and admired for his character, courage and learning, was not a committed
Zionist. It was inconceivable to me that he who had endured the trauma of the
Holocaust, and who, indeed, had become a living symbol of Jewish
perseverance, would not be a staunch advocate of the establishment of the
Jewish State. Because I respected Leo Baeck so much, the sudden confrontation
with the reality that even the saintly Leo Baeck was not a political Zionist,
highlighted for me the fact that Reform Judaism had not come to terms with the
full consequences of the Zionist movement and the establishment of the Jewish
State. The negative reactions to my sermon only reinforced the conviction that
on these issues the Reform movement had a long way to go. For weeks after
delivering the sermon, I was engaged in continuous debate. This only
exacerbated my sense of dissonance with colleagues on the issue of Zionism.

THE CONGREGATIONAL RABBINATE

I spent five creative years as a congregational rabbi, serving from 1951-1953 as assistant rabbi at Temple Emanuel in Chicago, Illinois, and from 1953-1956 as co-rabbi at Temple Emanuel in Denver, Colorado.

In the congregational rabbinate, I discovered that many congregants tended to look upon the rabbi as a *"kappara,"* a *"vicarious atonement,"* who is assigned to lead the Jewish life that the congregants either do not know how to live or do not want to live. Too many rabbis, either willingly or reluctantly, accept the role of *"kappara."* The effective rabbi will make demands of his congregation. He will aspire to set higher standards of Jewish learning and living than the congregation is willing to set for itself. He will cause others to listen to him, because he knows how to be a good listener. He will help others to engage in a search for spiritual values, because he himself is always in search.

The rabbi understands that his ultimate task is to be a teacher of Judaism. *Talmud Torah,* the study of Torah, is not only to acquire knowledge, but to attain wisdom. The goal is not only to accumulate facts, but to inculcate values, not only to sharpen minds, but to shape a *"mentsch"* (a human being). Education is not apart from life, but a part of life. As is written in the Midrash Tehilim (119:44): כל מי שאוהב את התורה אינו אוהב אלא החיים. "Whoever loves the Torah loves life." The Jew does not live in order to learn. He learns in order to live.

Early in my rabbinical experience, I learned the true meaning of the Salanter "rebbe's" dictum: רב שאין חולקין עליו בקהילתו אינו בגדר רב ורב המפחד מפניהם אינו בגדר אדם. "A rabbi whose congregation does not disagree with him is not a rabbi, and a rabbi who is afraid of his congregation is not a man."

A worthy rabbi gives his congregants ample opportunity to disagree with him, because he is never afraid of differing with his congregants. He speaks his mind and challenges his congregants to speak theirs. Unlike the businessman, at the end of the day he cannot calculate profits and losses. He never knows how many lives he has influenced and how many human sparks he has ignited. He deals with the most intangible, yet the most concrete components of the human being — the mind, the heart and the soul.

Through the rabbinate a person can fulfill the rabbinic dictum of שכר מצוה מצוה. "The reward of a good deed is the deed itself." The rabbi's rewards are real, because in the process he experiences personal growth. To teach others is to educate oneself. To advocate a code of conduct for others is to discipline oneself. The rabbi meets fellow Jews at the altar of eternal verities and in that eternal light the rabbi's life is illumined.

The Talmud teaches us: לא מקומו של אדם מכבדו אלא אדם מכבד את מקומו. "It is not the position which honors the person, but the person who gives honor to the position" (Taanit 21b). A good rabbi enhances the title rabbi.

BELLA

I began these recollections by selecting formative experiences in my life. Without any question, the most formative has been my marriage to Bella. By 1954, having been in Denver for a year, I had met every single Jewish woman in town. Cupid threw many darts at me, but none of them hit the target. Then Bella came into my life.

Temple Emanuel in Denver had its own summer camp in the Rocky Mountains. As director of the camp, I selected as counselors those who could contribute to the Jewish dimensions of the programming. One staff person I had difficulty in recruiting was a nurse. Camp was about to open, and we were getting desperate. Then the chairman of our camp medical committee phoned to tell me he had met an attractive young nurse from Israel who was visiting with her cousins in Denver. He thought that she could not only serve as the nurse of the camp, but would also be able to teach Israeli dancing and songs. I immediately invited the nurse for an interview.

Bella told me that she had come to the States on a six-month visitor's visa and was expecting to leave Denver in a week to travel around the country before her return to Israel in early September. She was reared in Zlatoust, Russia, a city in the Ural Mountains close to the Siberian border, and was trained as a nurse there. Bella's two older sisters had married two Polish Jewish refugees. When in 1946 the Soviet Union permitted non-Russians to emigrate, the brothers-in-law had taken their wives, Bella's mother, her younger brother, and herself as their dependents. For two years they had lived in displaced persons camps, the last place being Bergen-Belsen. Bella had signed up as a nurse to fight with the Hagana (the predecessor of the Israel Defense Forces), had left Marseilles on an illegal immigrant ship and landed in Israel on May 14, 1948, the day the State was established. Her ship was the first to enter the independent Jewish state. After arriving in Israel, she went immediately to the front lines, spent two years in the army and since then had been working as a nurse in the Tel Aviv area.

When I offered her the position as nurse at our camp, Bella was reluctant to interrupt her travels. However, I convinced her that she could enrich the values of American Jewish children and would herself enjoy an extraordinary educational experience.

So Bella came to camp. She made an invaluable contribution and soon became the best-liked person on the staff. During the pre-camp staff orientation sessions, we asked the counselors to clean the cabins, which had not been used all winter long. Most of the counselors came from well-to-do homes and had never had a mop in their hands before. Bella showed them how to mop Israeli style and the cabins were cleaned in a jiffy. The counselors even came to tell me how much they enjoyed it.

Because Bella had grown up in the Ural Mountains, she loved the rich vegetation and animal life of the Rocky Mountain region. One day as I was walking near the woods at the edge of the camp, I heard a woman's voice singing a lilting melody. I followed the music drifting from the trees and soon discovered Bella picking wild mushrooms. Smitten by her charm, I jokingly compared her to the sirens of Greek mythology.

During the course of the summer, Bella and I developed a close friendship. She sat at the head table with me, and we conversed in Hebrew. We would take walks at night and had ample opportunity to get to know each other. However, since Bella did not leave the camp during the entire season, we never had a formal date. None of the counselors even suspected that we had a special relationship.

Camp closed on Sunday. Tuesday, we flew to Miami, and the following Sunday, September 5, 1954 were married in the home of my parents.

A life partner

We returned from our honeymoon three days before Rosh Hashanah. For the first time, Bella discovered that she had become the "rebbetzin" (rabbi's wife) of a large congregation of over 1,200 families. Until that time, she had never been in a synagogue in her life. In Zlatoust, Russia, there was no synagogue, and in Israel she was among the 80% of the population who define themselves as secular. Therefore, what occasion did she have to enter a synagogue? Yet, by marrying me, she was "ordained" to become a full-fledged rebbetzin responsible for fulfilling all the obligations and duties of her office.

Somehow she made it through the high holiday period. Her popularity with the children and counselors at camp stood her in good stead. Everyone in the congregation was thrilled with the love affair between the rabbi and the nurse from Israel. And Bella very quickly became an active and effective rebbetzin.

Bella and I were blessed with four children, born one after the other in three and a-half years. From the day of their birth Hebrew was the language of the home. Our children, now all grown, all professionals, all with their own families, continue to perpetuate our Jewish and social values. They have enabled us to fulfill the rabbinic dictum: ברא מזכה אבא, אבא לא מזכה ברא. "A child confers merit on the parent, the parent does not confer merit on the child" (Sanhedrin 104a).

Throughout my public career Bella has been a full partner. The development of the movements in Israel and in the Former Soviet Union was facilitated by her active participation. Through our partnership in marriage and work, I have fulfilled the precept: ראה חיים עם אישה אשר אהבת כל ימי חיי הבלך אשר נתן לך תחת השמש כל ימי הבלך כי הוא חלקך בחיים. "Enjoy life with the wife you love all the fleeting days of life which have been granted to you under the sun, for that is your portion in life" (Ecclesiastes 9:9).

EXPERIENCES IN SOCIAL ACTION

In 1956 at age 29, I was appointed Director of the Chicago Federation and the Great Lakes Council of the Union of American Hebrew Congregations. I was responsible for coordinating the activities of the Reform movement in Chicago and the Mid-West. I was involved in every aspect of the work, from camping and youth to organizing new congregations. Television was fast becoming a prime means of communication. A commercial company agreed to sponsor the first prime time religious TV program featuring a Protestant minister, a Catholic priest, and a rabbi. I was selected as the rabbi. The programs were widely publicized within the community at large, so that I became well-known throughout greater Chicago.

Justified criticism

Chicago was beset with complex demographic urban problems. The University of Chicago, a foremost center of learning, was in danger of being overrun by the rapidly spreading slum areas. Urban planners had developed the first serious urban renewal program in the country. Rather than transfer the physical premises of the massive University of Chicago campus, it was decided to make a serious effort to develop an inter-racial community. The plan, designated as the Hyde Park-Kenwood urban renewal program, envisaged the investment of vast sums to renew the public facilities and communal services, to improve the public education system, and to make a serious effort to develop high-level integrated housing for an inter-racial community. I responded to the plan enthusiastically, believing it to be in keeping with democratic and Jewish ideals of racial and social equality. Also, if the forced exodus of synagogues and Jewish communal institutions could be halted, then Jewish life would be more secure.

The Chicago City Council held hearings on the plan. Both the Chicago Council of Churches (Protestant) and the Catholic Archdiocese, which had engaged professional staff to study the plan and its ramifications, were asked to testify. In order to have tri-faith testimony, I was asked to testify on behalf of the Jewish community. I was given only one day's notice. Until that moment, I had not read the detailed proposals of the plan nor did I possess expert knowledge of the complex economic and social issues involved. With no time to prepare properly, I composed a brief statement wherein I quoted from biblical sources, using passages such as "woe to you who sell the poor for a pair of shoes," and "unless the Lord build the house, they labor in vain who build it; unless the Lord watches over the city, the watchman keeps vigil in vain."

In contrast to the expert testimony of the Protestant and Catholic spokesmen, my presentation was platitudinous and unsubstantiated by factual knowledge. To make matters worse, a well-known liberal city councilman, himself a Jew, ripped into me for the presumptuousness of preaching the Bible rather than relating to the specifics of the plan.

The criticism of my testimony hit the Chicago press. The leaders of the Chicago Federation were appalled. A special meeting of the officers was convened. I was bombarded with questions. Why had I spoken without the organizations I represented having adopted a position on the plan? What was the propriety of religious institutions testifying on an urban renewal program? Why had I been so poorly prepared?

No one could have been more critical of me than I was of myself. If our leaders were embarrassed, I was humiliated. For days I fretted about how I had failed to fulfill my leadership responsibilities. However, in retrospect the experience was constructive. I considered the criticism justified and was determined to make amends by becoming knowledgeable on the subject. I read widely and met with leading experts in the field. Together with the Catholic and Protestant churches, the Chicago Federation of the UAHC sponsored a series of citywide conferences. Subsequently, I wrote a book entitled *Judaism and Cities in Crisis*. Over the years I was invited to lecture throughout the country. My work with interreligious and interracial groups whetted my appetite for social activism. It provided essential preparatory experiences for the position I was to assume in Washington.

Founding the Religious Action Center

During the 1950's, under the leadership of Rabbi Maurice N. Eisendrath, President of the Union of American Hebrew Congregations, ardent advocate of social justice, and two key staff members, Rabbi Eugene Lipman and Albert Vorspan, the Reform movement developed its social justice programs. Lipman and Vorspan wrote a book, *Justice and Judaism*, which recommended ways for the synagogue to involve its membership in social concerns. A national Commission on Social Action was established and congregations were urged to form social action committees.

In 1959 Kivie Kaplan, a wealthy and liberal Reform leader from Boston, who also served as President of the National Association for the Advancement of Colored People (NAACP) contributed funds to purchase a building in Washington to house the Social Action Center of Reform Judaism. When the proposal was introduced to the Biennial Convention of the Union in 1959, an acrimonious debate developed in the plenary session. Among the arguments used by the opponents were the following: "religion should not intervene in politics;" "when I join a synagogue, I join to pray and not to express a position on current political issues." One distinguished rabbi declared: "We don't need any young whipper-snapper rabbi in Washington to speak on behalf of our congregations."

The Convention determined that the proposal would be discussed within the movement for two years and that a final decision would be made at the following Biennial Convention to be held in Washington in 1961.

I was asked to become the young whipper-snapper rabbi and to serve as the founding director of the Center, if the Union approved the plan. The controversy raged for two years within the movement. Some congregations withdrew, others threatened to withdraw. It was not until the Biennial Convention of 1961 that the Union made the affirmative decision to found the Social Action Center. (I recommended that the name be changed from *Social Action* to *Religious Action* on the grounds that *Religious* action would be both more descriptive and more palatable.)

During the two years between the Biennials, I and other staff traveled the country in an effort to persuade congregations to give approval. One Shabbat I was in Cleveland speaking before a large congregation in Fairmount Temple. I was introduced by the chairman of the Social Action Committee, a prominent lawyer whom I had known. I started talking about how it was essential that we Jews, both as individuals and collectively, engage in social action. At the time, unlike today, very few Jews were in Congress. I began to wax emotional (as I sometimes do), "Jews should be up front as Jews. Why aren't there more Jewish congressmen? Why aren't there more Jewish senators?" Suddenly, out of the corner of my eye, I saw the chairman of the evening. I burst out spontaneously, "Why shouldn't there be a Senator Howard Metzenbaum of the State of Ohio?" The congregation broke out in applause. Ten years later, Howard Metzenbaum became Senator.

Many years later after he had retired, Senator Metzenbaum wrote me the following letter:

> I will never forget the man who first nominated me for the United States Senate. It was at a time when running for the Senate was the furthest thing from my mind. I knew (or thought I knew) that it was unattainable. I was aware of the fact that no Jew had ever been elected to high public office in the state of Ohio. I don't remember the exact date, but I remember I was sitting in the congregation — you had the audience spellbound. Out of the blue, as you were talking about the obligations and the need to be involved, there came from your lips words to the effect that "a Howard Metzenbaum could and should be in the United States Senate." I was both shocked and pleased. It took the voters of Ohio a little while to accommodate your prediction, but they eventually got around to it and I served 19 very happy and eventful years in the Senate. Without your prediction from "on high," it probably never would have happened.

I have often wished that some of my other ideas would have been implemented so easily.

The proposal to establish the Religious Action Center was approved overwhelmingly at the Biennial Convention in November 1961. I walked into the Religious Action Center on February 1, 1962. The large four storey building, formerly an embassy on Massachusetts Avenue, was empty. I was determined to make the facility a center for like-minded groups. Within a short period of time the building was filled with our own staff and with a variegated mix of social action organizations, including the Leadership Conference on Civil Rights, the Citizens Crusade Against Poverty and the United Negro College Fund.

At the dedication in November 1962, I projected my vision of the goals and program objectives of the Center.

> The fundamental division in American religious life is not between the faiths, but within each faith, between true religion and religiosity, between those who are activated by, and those who are apathetic to, religious ideals, between those who relate religion to life and those who use religion to escape from life.
>
> By establishing our Religious Action Center, we affirm the covenant made by Reform Judaism. The founders of our movement declared that Judaism's moral laws were eternal while the ritual laws were evanescent. How tragic it would be if we, who claim to perpetuate their spirit, were to exclude the prophetic message from Prophetic Judaism. Shall we continue to debate a guide for ritual observance without at the same time debating guides for moral behavior and standards for society? Is there to be a Reform Jewish viewpoint on breaking the glass at weddings and not a Reform Jewish viewpoint on breaking the pattern of racial prejudice? Shall our congregations devote their energies to increasing membership dues and not to increasing concern for world peace? Shall we seek new means of attracting to the synagogue those who *do not* attend and not seek new means of having an impact on the lives of those who *do* attend? Shall we, who bitterly resented the silence of most of the churches of Nazi Germany, ourselves remain silent in the face of injustice and inequity in our society?
>
> *To demand the right to preach to society without becoming involved in the society to whom we preach is to act irresponsibly.* To issue commands from above, like Roman emperors, without entering the arena to become gladiators in

the struggle for righteousness, is to remove religion from society.

We recognize that there are many unresolved questions concerning the proper function of religious groups in public affairs. There are risks involved in what we have done and in what we propose to do. There is an element of presumptuousness whenever any one or any group ventures forth to speak *to* others, to speak *for* others, to speak for the right, "as God gives us to see the right." But we live in an era of cataclysmic social change. The fate of our society and our world are determined by the decisions made by men. Whether we will it or not, we participate in those decisions. Either we participate consciously and responsibly, or we participate by silence and acquiescence. We intend to participate consciously and, we trust, responsibly.

THE CIVIL RIGHTS REVOLUTION

During my years in Washington our Center dealt with a host of public concerns: among them: church-state, public housing, welfare, migrant labor, economic policy, foreign policy, civil rights, Israel and Soviet Jewry. We testified before Senate and House committees, convened conferences, organized intensive training programs for Jewish and Christian clergy, and issued publications and background papers.

By far the most dramatic developments related to the civil rights crises of the 1960's. The umbrella coordinating body of all the civil rights groups was the Leadership Conference on Civil Rights. As I was active in the organization and participated in the process of preparing the legislative proposals for the United States Congress, I invited the Conference to house its offices in the Religious Action Center. I take pride in knowing that much of the civil rights legislation of the 1960's was drafted in our Center and that our Conference Room was the setting for the major deliberations dealing with civil rights issues.

The Supreme Court decision of 1954 banning "separate but equal" public education had set in motion some societal changes, but the pace was slow and the changes inadequate. It took Martin Luther King to give impetus to the civil rights legislation. A devotee of Mahatma Gandhi's non-violent approach, he recognized that massive passive protest was the way to initiate radical change.

In actuality, a panoply of groups contributed to the civil rights changes of the 1960's. Reading from left to right on the political spectrum were the following civil rights organizations: The Student Non-Violent Coordinating Committee (SNCC), the Committee on Racial Equality (CORE), the Southern Christian Leadership Conference, the National Association for the Advancement of Colored People (NAACP) and the National Urban League. I came to know the leaders of these organizations personally and discovered that in essence the black community was no different from the Jewish community. They differed from each other in projecting both strategies and objectives. There was great competitiveness among the leaders for personal status and prestige. They wrestled with each other for public notoriety and political influence.

In addition to the civil rights groups, many labor groups, civil liberties, and national religious organizations made invaluable contributions to the struggle. I was especially proud of the commitment and effectiveness of Jewish communal agencies and religious movements organized in the framework of the National Community Relations Advisory Council (today called the Jewish Council for Public Affairs).

I relearned the lesson which I had learned in other civic controversies: No individual and no organization is omniscient and no one has a monopoly on *the* solution. Unlike diseases attacking the human body, for which miraculous cures can be discovered, societal ills have no panacea. Therefore, the task of the social activist is to work through broad coalitions of like-minded citizens. Divergent organizational positions and conflicting ideologies all contribute to advancing the social justice objectives of the democratic process.

Martin Luther King and the other civil rights leaders were frequent visitors to the Religious Action Center. I invited Martin Luther King to use my office and the Center's facilities whenever he was in Washington.

The March on Washington, August 28, 1963

When Martin Luther King first proposed his March on Washington, many Congressmen and liberal public figures objected. Some worried that the March could lead to violence. Others believed that the interruption of life in Washington would be counter-productive. In reality, many people were not sure of Martin Luther King's motives and did not necessarily want to be identified with his tactics.

The social action leadership of the Reform movement decided that we had to make a positive judgment and urged our colleagues to participate with full energy and commitment. Our Center became the headquarters for the Jewish participation in the March. Contrary to all the ominous predictions, the March on Washington proved to be a watershed historic event. It became the setting for Martin Luther King's remarkable "I have a dream" oration.

It was because of Martin Luther King that I delivered what I consider, immodestly, to be the finest oration of my career.

Demonstrating in Selma, Alabama

Selma, Alabama, a small city in the deep South, whose population was equally divided between blacks and whites, became a focal point for the battle for voting rights. In March, 1965, Martin Luther King organized a march of local black citizens to the county courthouse to register to vote. The sheriff, a hard-bitten segregationist, organized a posse of volunteer deputies, many of them members of the Ku Klux Klan, to prevent them from entering the courthouse. When the blacks pressed forward, the sheriff's men beat the blacks brutally, dispersing the marchers as the white townspeople cheered. The public media gave full coverage to the crisis.

Early the next morning I received a call from a clergyman who was an active staff member of the Washington Council of Churches. He told me that during the night Martin Luther King had issued a call to clergy of all faiths to join him in Selma to demonstrate their support. They had reserved fifteen places on a plane, departing Washington in the early afternoon. They had already recruited thirteen Protestant clergymen and one Catholic priest and wanted to know if I would be willing to go representing the Jewish clergy. It was considered extremely dangerous. Several people had already been killed. I called Bella at home. I explained the circumstances to her and told her how essential it was that at least one Jew be present. I asked her if she would agree to let me go, understanding full well that the conditions were potentially life threatening. She immediately responded, as she always has, that I had to do my duty and she encouraged me to go.

When we arrived at Selma, we were taken immediately to the black church where the demonstration was being held. Thousands of people were gathered outside and the church itself was packed to the rafters. We were led to the pulpit where Martin Luther King was addressing the crowd. When he finished, he came up to me and said, "Dick, you're next." Totally unprepared, I offered only three thoughts, but the talk lasted almost half an hour. How was that possible?

I decided that I would speak the words of the Midrash. My first thought: "Jewish tradition teaches us that when God created man, he created only one man. Why? Our rabbinic sages responded, 'So that no man would ever be able to say, my father is better than your father.'" I was interrupted with a huge ovation, stomping, people singing "Hallelujah, Brother — you give it to them, rabbi." The applause lasted close to ten minutes.

I then gave my second thought: "According to Jewish tradition, God created man using dust from the four corners of the earth. Why? So that no person would ever be able to say, 'the place from which I come is better than the place from which you come.'" Again, an overwhelming burst of applause, and shouting "hallelujah, hallelujah." Martin Luther King quieted the audience.

Then I delivered my third sentence: "When God created man, he used every color of dust. Why? So that no man would ever be able to say, 'the color of my skin is better than the color of your skin.'" Again, thunderous applause which lasted for many minutes. I then gave a closing thought, wishing success for the just cause and sat down. Never in my life have I experienced such exaltation and gratification from an audience. I was pleased that the application of Jewish tradition to a burning current issue had such impact.

Sleeping with a Bishop

After the church demonstration, we convened several meetings with Martin Luther King and other leaders to discuss strategy and then went to sleep. The clergy who had come were assigned rooms in homes of the local people. One of my friends who had come on the plane from Washington was Bishop John Wesley Lord, the Methodist Bishop of Greater Washington. Since we knew each other well, we volunteered to go together to the home of our host, a middle-aged woman who lived in one room in a slum area of the town. She had one double bed which she assigned to Bishop Lord and myself. She herself had prepared blankets to sleep on the floor. Even though Bishop Lord and I protested, saying that she should sleep in the bed and we would sleep on the floor, she refused. So, out of respect for her, we took the bed and spent the night together.

When we awoke in the morning, we became aware that a dozen newspaper reporters were standing outside. They had heard that the rabbi and the bishop had slept together in the same bed and found it a compelling human-interest story. The reporters asked, "Rabbi, how did it feel to sleep with a bishop?" I responded, "I knew that sooner or later I would sleep with the Lord, but never in my wildest dreams did I imagine that I would sleep with a bishop." That comment appeared in several newspapers.

On our return from Washington, we were asked to meet with President Lyndon B. Johnson at the White House. We conveyed to him our conviction that the primary way to resolve these conflicts was through the legislative process. We urged him to pursue ever more vigorously civil rights legislation. To his credit, President Johnson did give highest priority to the passage of the legislation. It was especially helpful that the President whose origins were in the South was an ardent advocate of civil rights.

Eulogizing Martin Luther King

Martin Luther King was assassinated on April 4, 1968. The Jewish community of Greater Washington convened a memorial service on April 7, 1968 attended by over two thousand people. Because of my closeness to Martin Luther King, I was asked to deliver the eulogy. Excerpts follow:

צדיק אחד מעמיד את העולם על יסודו. "One righteous man keeps the world standing firmly on its foundation."

Martin Luther King was the righteous man of our generation. Before he came to bless us with his life, our sensitivity to moral issues had been dulled by the indulgences of prosperity. Our vision of a national purpose had been dimmed by the bright glare of self-righteous affluence. Prejudice, discrimination, poverty, ignorance paraded openly in the land, but we saw them not. We heard them not.

Then Martin Luther King entered our world. He came with a heart large for compassion, feet strong for marching, and a voice golden for inspiration. And he came with a black skin, the very color of which made all poverty more visible and all injustice more conspicuous.

צדיק בא לעולם טובה באה לעולם. "When a righteous man comes into the world, goodness comes into the world." He brought with him the message of goodness, of righteousness.

He made us look at ourselves in the light of eternity. He made us stand firm on our foundations. He showed us the gap between America's promise and America's fulfillment. He would not let us forget that there were human beings who were being treated less than human. From bus to waiting room to lunchroom to hotel room to voting booth to slum house to ghetto school to university campus to employment offices, he confronted us with the America we had refused to believe existed.

He shattered our illusions, but he restored our dream — the American dream. He helped us to see that our fundamental goal was not to make the world safe for democracy, but rather to make democracy safe for the world. And in so doing, he became our conscience. His pulpit was the street, his congregation all mankind, and his message universal.

And that is why he was struck down. The forces of hatred always seek to destroy our noblest symbols. But they seek in vain. The Pharaohs, the Inquisitors, the Hitlers, the Oswalds, the assassins never learn that the symbol is more than a man's body. It is a man's life, his work, his deeds, his values. The destruction of the body only serves to enhance the value of the spirit. The wanton taking of life only generates new life for the forces of good. The symbol in death becomes more than the symbol in life. It assumes a new life, a new mission of its own. Freed from the frailties of the human body, it soars to new heights of influence. As history has preserved the מעשים טובים, (the good works) of the martyrs of all generations, so will it enshrine this martyr, this symbol of humanity felled by inhumanity.

Martin Luther King would have us build a society which will know that man's spiritual needs cannot be isolated from his material needs, that the real blight of our time is not poverty, but the nation which tolerates poverty, not unemployment, but the nation which passively accepts human stultification, not the impassioned racist, but the dispassionate average man who sits as a spectator high above the arena of life.

He would have us build a society which seeks protection not in armored cars, but in the impenetrable armor of justice, a society where men know that not to quell riots but to fulfill rights is their ultimate purpose, and not to cool the ghetto, but to transform it is their ultimate challenge.

Dr. King would also speak to us here assembled as Jews. For he was steeped in the knowledge of our Bible, inspired by our perseverance through history, and guided by the convictions of our prophets. In his last address, he talked of having been to the mountaintop, and like Moses, having seen the Promised Land. He hinted, perhaps in some kind of premonition, that he had shown the way, but that he might never be privileged to enter.

There is a remarkable affinity between the fate, the history, and the goals of Negro and Jew. The Jewish experience in Egypt set the stage for human freedom. Whenever and wherever men struggle to free themselves from the yoke of bondage, the drama of redemption of the Hebrew slaves from Egypt is reenacted.

But if in our contemporary reenactment, the Negroes are the children of Israel and Martin Luther King is their Moses, then we the Jews of America are confronted with a major question. Who are we? What role do we play? How can a Jew hear the word "ghetto" and not experience a special wince of pain? How can a Jew say, as all too many have said to me recently, "I am through with supporting the civil rights cause," or as someone said to me yesterday, "The civil rights movement died with Martin Luther King."

The civil rights movement was not the personal possession of Martin Luther King. The civil rights movement does not belong to Negroes alone. It belongs to all who make it their cause. Let no one try to take the civil rights movement away from us. Let no Jew try to read us out of the civil rights movement. We do not engage in social action to help others. We engage in it to help ourselves, to fulfill the dictates of Jewish ethics, to live the lessons of our history.

This Friday, with the commencement of Passover, we shall relive the most important lesson of our history — God destroys the evil society and redeems the enslaved. Not our fathers alone in some distant past, but each of us in the present is a slave so long as any person is enslaved in body or mind or soul.

The cause to which Martin Luther King dedicated his life did not end with his death. It was ennobled by his death, as it was advanced by his life. As we sit around our tables this Passover, he will be there with us. He has bridged for us a distance of more than 3,000 years. The Moses of the Negro has invested the Moses of the Jew with new meaning, just as the plight of the Negro has given new understanding to the eternal task of the Jewish people — לתקן עולם במלכות שדי. "To perfect the world under the kingdom of God."

THE SIX DAY WAR

Impact on Christian-Jewish relations

In its own way, the Six Day War of 1967 had a greater impact on the relationship of world Jewry to Israel than the creation of the State itself. Had the State not been established in 1948, it is questionable whether it would have been established at all. But, once it had been established, it had become a symbol of hope for the renewal of Jewish peoplehood. The threat of extinction mobilized American Jewry. Washington became the focal arena for action.

I had forged close cooperative relations with Washington representatives of the respective religious groups engaged in work similar to mine at the Religious Action Center. We often testified jointly before Senate and congressional committees. The rationale for our joint social action was that we were bringing to bear the moral imperatives of our Judeo-Christian heritage. Therefore, it was only natural that when the Middle East crisis erupted, I would go to these same colleagues, brothers in spirit, and expect their support to pressure the United States and the United Nations to take action in defense of Israel.

What could be a more clear-cut moral issue than the right of the State of Israel to exist? And who would respond to the issue with greater empathy than the Christian churches, which in recent years had become so sensitized to moral issues in general, and to the sin of anti-Jewish hatred in particular?

But to my dismay and bewilderment, the Christian leadership responded with silence or expressions of neutrality. The major Protestant denominations, the National Council of Churches, and the US Catholic Conference issued pallid calls of impartial objectivity and prayers for peace.

Their arguments boiled down to five points: (1) establishing the State of Israel was an unfortunate "political compromise," devised as a necessary haven for persecuted Jews, but generating "injustice to Arabs;" (2) the war waged by the Arab states against the creation of the State of Israel was an understandable, albeit regrettable, reaction to the "political compromise"; (3) for liberals who de-emphasized nationalism, the creation of the new State appeared as anachronistic; (4) solutions to conflict between nation-states must be sought only through the United Nations, for its status would otherwise be denigrated. (This argument should have been seen as fallacious when the Security Council debates demonstrated that the Arab states and Russia were opposed to any UN action in lifting the Egyptian blockade of the Gulf of Aqaba); (5) what the Jews perceived to be a clear-cut *moral* issue was considered by the established Christian churches to be another complex *political* issue.

The relations between Jewish and Christian organizations were so fractured during the Six-Day War that an interreligious conference was convened in the Fall of 1967 to try to repair the damage. I was asked to deliver a paper presenting the Jewish perspective. I spoke frankly to my Christian colleagues. A distinguished Protestant clergyman, with whom I had worked closely, was evidently quite astounded by the sharpness of my criticism. He responded in kind, "Dick, I always thought you Jews were the prototype of the universal man. Now I see you are only tribal particularists."

The Problem of peoplehood

In retrospect, it seems that liberal Christians had accepted Jews, because during the post World War II period Jews had become more like them. Jewish identity, originally defined as *ethnic* had tended to be defined as *religious*. In an age of liberalism, such Jews, who are differentiated from Christians only by religious belief, are easily integrated into society. However, when Jews demonstrate, as they did in the Six-Day War, that they are a people and that the people in the land of Israel have created a Jewish State, the image of the Jew reverted to what it had been in earlier generations: the "atavistic" impulses of Jews propelled them toward peoplehood. Conversely, the fundamentalist Christians, who all along had believed that the Jews were a chosen *people*, rejoiced over the victory of Israel. They welcomed the proof that the Jews in the land of Israel were capable of acting as an independent nation. Thus, the Six Day War marked a watershed in Jewish-Christian relations. The victory reinforced the image of the

Jews as the eternal *people*. The fundamentalist Christians, in keeping with their theology, viewed the return of the Jewish people to Israel and the strengthening of Jewish sovereignty as a harbinger of the second advent of the Messiah. Many liberal Christians looked upon the victory as a retrogression; the Jews had forsaken their universalist aspirations and reverted to their nationalist origins.

At the time the Vatican had refused to recognize the State. In 1964, Pope Paul VI had visited Israel, but referred to it as "the Holy Land," purposely refraining from pronouncing the words "State of Israel" and refusing to meet with any Israeli official. Yet, concurrently the Church had begun to revise its attitude toward the Jews. It absolved contemporary Jews of complicity in the New Testament's portrayal of the crucifixion, and advocated the purging of anti-Semitic church liturgical and educational materials. Turning to my Catholic colleagues, I expressed appreciation for the continuing revisions in church teachings about the Jews, but I insisted that the Catholic Church would never be able to establish the proper relations with the Jewish people until it changed its policy toward the State of Israel. "We Jews have earned the right to define ourselves. We define ourselves as a people. The Jewish people has in turn created a Jewish state. The State is our symbol of hope. So until the church officially recognizes the State of Israel, Christians and Jews will never have optimal relations."

Fortunately, with the passage of the years, Christian attitudes toward the State of Israel have evolved. In 1993, the Vatican recognized the State of Israel, and diplomatic relations were established. In 2000, Pope John Paul II made an historic pilgrimage to the Jewish State, meeting officially with its elected leaders, confessing Church sins of omission and commission toward the Jews, and calling on Christians and Jews together "to make courageous efforts to remove all forms of prejudice." His bold initiative symbolized a new era in Christian-Jewish relationships.

Nonetheless, I continue to insist that Christian policies are to be judged not only by attitudes toward Jews living in their own societies nor by reinterpretation of Christian theology toward Jews, but by positions taken by Christian groups in relation to the State of Israel as the symbol of Jewish peoplehood.

Impact on Reform Judaism

My criticism of the Christian world led to criticism of Reform Judaism. If I demanded recognition of the State by Christians, did I not have an even greater obligation to demand full recognition of the State by Reform Jews? I was convinced that Reform Judaism had defaulted in its relationship to the Jewish State. To be sure, the great leaders of American Zionism had been Reform rabbis. Abba Hillel Silver and Stephen S. Wise, both of whom were Reform rabbis, had become the primary spokesmen for American Zionism in their generation. Indeed, Abba Hillel Silver had presented the case for the establishment of a Jewish State on behalf of the Jewish Agency before the United Nations. Stephen Wise had served as President of the Zionist Organization of America and Chairman of the United Palestine Appeal. Yet, in effect, both men had acted as individuals, independent of the Reform movement. In the case of Abba Hillel Silver, his congregation was non-Zionist, and his Zionist activity, while earning respect for him within the entire Jewish community, had not significantly affected his own congregation.

I began to conjecture: what would have been the impact of Reform Judaism in Israel had the Zionist leaders who were Reform organized the equivalent of Mizrachi, the Orthodox Zionist movement? The Orthodox Zionists had always been a minority within Orthodox circles. Yet, the organization of Mizrachi had set the pattern for Orthodox participation in the Zionist movement. They had built their institutions and developed their programs as an integral part of the pre-state Jewish society. They had mobilized from within their ranks a significant aliyah of Orthodox Zionists to Israel. They had become a force to be reckoned with and were an integral part of the leadership of the state-in-waiting. When the State was declared, Mizrachi was represented in the cabinet in positions of major responsibility, and was entitled to government funds for support of their Orthodox institutions.

None of the Reform or Conservative leadership active in Zionist circles ever seriously thought about founding a party of liberal Jews within the Zionist movement. Had they done so, even acting as a minority within their own movements, the religious streams would have been a factor in the Zionist movement and subsequently within the State of Israel. Had the liberal movements built institutions in Israel and participated fully in its public life, as had the Orthodox, then we in our generation would not have to play "catch-up ball." Was it too late to do so now? Surely, the major task was to come to terms institutionally, ideologically, and programmatically with the trauma we had just endured with the Six Day War.

What is feasible?

I drafted a proposal for the September, 1967 meeting of the Executive staff of the Union of American Hebrew Congregations. I proposed that we set up a Commission on Israel and that Israel committees be established in each congregation. The proposal stressed the urgency of building a movement in Israel, with detailed recommendations for creating new institutions and programs both in Israel and America.

I drew a pie of the budget of the Union of American Hebrew Congregations. It had many slices, but nowhere was there a slice for Israel. At the time a main theme in Washington political circles was the "reallocation of national resources." I recommended that we "reallocate our national *Reform Jewish* resources" and take a major slice out of the existing budget for Israel. The support which I had begun to receive evaporated quickly when the members of the staff realized that according to my plan each of their respective budgets would be reduced.

I saw that my grand vision was in danger of being grounded even before it began to fly. So, I quickly made a proposal which in retrospect may have been an historical mistake. I told my colleagues that I was so convinced that my proposals represented an idea whose time had come, that I personally would assume responsibility for raising funds outside the regular operating budget of the Union of American Hebrew Congregations and that until such time as we had funds for a full-time professional director, I would volunteer to serve as the Director of the Commission on Israel, in addition to my work at the Religious Action Center. (Subsequently, I also agreed to serve as the Chairman of the World Union for Progressive Judaism's Commission on Israel.) Once my colleagues recognized that it was possible to establish the Israel Commission without affecting the budget of the Union as a whole, or of its respective departments, the mood switched again and there was an overwhelming endorsement of the proposals.

Why do I say that I may have made an historical mistake? Because from that time forward the mobilization of funds to engage in the work of developing a movement in Israel and around the world was not considered an integral part of the obligation of the American Reform movement. First priority belonged to the American institutions, to the Union of American Hebrew Congregations and the Hebrew Union College — Jewish Institute of Religion and their programs in America. What happened to Reform Judaism in Israel and elsewhere was of far lower priority. This was contrary at the time to the fundraising priorities of local federations, the United Jewish Appeal and other American institutions associated with Israel. Their fundraising campaigns featured aliyah to Israel and development of Israel's institutions as major objectives. By raising funds outside the regular fundraising structure, the American Reform movement was declaring to its own members that Israel and world Jewry were of secondary import. It was my contention then, as it is now, that the development of Progressive Judaism in Israel and around the world was of no less importance to American Jewry than the development of American Judaism itself.

I was sent on a mission to Israel in order to return with recommendations for the UAHC Biennial. I met with the leadership of our fledgling movement and leaders of political parties, educational institutions, the Jewish Agency, representatives of the kibbutz movement, and intellectual and religious leaders. I returned with many new proposals and a sense that if the Reform movement acted with vigor, we would be able to embark on a new historic venture.

We drafted a resolution for the UAHC Biennial in November, 1967. The resolution contains the following plank:

We authorize the Board of Trustees of the UAHC to create a National Committee on Israel, among whose purposes shall be: to advance, in cooperation with the World Union for Progressive Judaism, the cause of Progressive Judaism in Israel, to support existing congregations and to create new congregations; to initiate a camp program in Israel and to encourage the development of adult programs, including, if feasible, settlements under the auspices of Progressive Judaism; to conduct vigorous campaigns to strengthen our relations with the people of Israel and to educate our members and the community at large on issues involving Israel; and to encourage the formation of corresponding committees in every region and congregation. In order to finance this work, the Committee is hereby authorized to solicit from the entire constituency of American Reform Judaism, as a voluntary offering, one dollar per year per person — man, woman, and child.

In retrospect, two aspects of the discussion within the Resolutions Committee of the Biennial Convention appear amusing. The original resolution contained a sentence on aliyah, to the effect that individual Reform Jews should consider, as a legitimate objective of Jewish fulfillment, the option of going on aliyah. The smaller resolutions committee which met first to discuss the proposed resolution eliminated the world "aliyah" and suggested as a replacement the phrase, "we should encourage stays of extended duration in Israel." When this diluted formulation reached the larger resolutions committee, they decided to eliminate the subject altogether. In those days, even "stays of extended duration" were considered too extreme.

In the original proposal, I recommended that we establish a Progressive kibbutz in Israel. One member of the committee said, "Kibbutz, that sounds radical. Let's call it a collective settlement." Another member said, "Collective settlement, that sounds even more radical. Let's just call it a settlement." A third person said, "Is it not presumptuous for us to announce to the world that we are going to establish a settlement? It may not even be feasible." I suggested that in that case we should insert the words "if feasible." That explains why the words "if feasible," appear in the resolution. Years later, of course, we proved that it was feasible to establish a kibbutz founded by a splendid blend of young activists from Israel and abroad. Also, we demonstrated that with the proper orientation, fairly significant numbers of young people and adults will come on aliyah.

THE WORLD UNION FOR PROGRESSIVE JUDAISM

Changing course

The Six Day War changed the course of the World Union for Progressive Judaism. Until the Six Day War, its main objective was considered to be the spread of Progressive Judaism around the world. Immediately prior to World War II, the World Union had been instrumental in rescuing rabbis and rabbinical students from Fascist Germany. Funds were raised to send rabbis to far-flung countries to establish movements which were then to become self-sustaining. Thus, the World Union had helped to establish movements in Australia, New Zealand, South Africa, and Latin America. The World Union had convened international conferences every two years in Europe, most often in London or on the continent. The international conferences dealt primarily with theological issues. Learned papers were read by distinguished rabbis. These same rabbis comprised the leadership of the World Union. The annual income of the World Union was minimal, coming primarily from small contributions raised from among a handful of loyal supporters.

The international convention of the World Union in 1968 was scheduled for Amsterdam. A few of us in leadership positions contended that in the aftermath of the Six Day War, it was inconceivable for the World Union to convene in any city other than Jerusalem. After considerable lobbying among the international leadership, it was agreed that the venue would be shifted to Jerusalem for July 1968. The objective of the conference would be to express solidarity with the Jews of Israel and to lay the groundwork for a reinvigorated effort to develop a significant Progressive movement in Israel.

Over 400 delegates attended the conference in Jerusalem, the first of many conventions of the movement held in Israel. The local planning committee unwittingly created an international incident which became the focal point of the convention. It sent a letter to the Minister of Religious Affairs asking for permission to hold a worship service at the Western Wall with men and women praying together side by side. The Minister of Religious Affairs refused permission. We refused to go to any place but the praying area of the Wall. Despite meetings with Prime Minister Levi Eshkol, Jerusalem Mayor Teddy Kollek and other high level intermediaries, the two sides were not reconciled. The result was that there was no prayer at the Western Wall. This incident was the first of many conflicts waged around a site which should serve as a symbol of national unity perpetuating the sacred character of the holy city. Ever since that incident, the Wall, all too frequently, has become the scene of divisiveness and controversy.

The convention adopted a statement calling for full equal rights for Progressive Judaism in Israel. For the first time, Progressive Judaism took a firm position on religion-state issues while meeting in Jerusalem. It was a harbinger of developments to come.

A working Sabbatical

The experiences during the summer of 1968 whetted our appetites to spend an extended period in Israel. Because I had a Sabbatical coming in any case, Bella and I decided that we would spend the 1969-70 year in Israel. We thought it would be valuable for the children. Although they were fluent in Hebrew, we knew that a year in Israel would help enrich their Hebrew language skills. We also thought that it would be an opportunity for us to help advance the Israel Movement for Progressive Judaism.

During the year, I worked closely with the lay and rabbinic leadership of the movement. We formulated a plan for development of the movement, established new congregations, and agreed that World Union program funds would be funneled through a national budget administered by Israelis. Until that time, the entire decision-making process took place at the World Union office in New York. If we were to develop an indigenous Israeli movement, it was essential to generate local initiatives and responsibility.

Babylon and Jerusalem

Among other initiatives, we established the first official movement contacts with the World Zionist Organization and the Jewish Agency. In an article in the Jerusalem Post of December 31, 1969, I rejected the predominant American Jewish view known as the Babylon-Jerusalem hypothesis. The common perception at the time was that America was analogous to ancient Babylon, a great independent center whose wealth, status, influence, vitality and creativity would be a source of support and stimulus to the center in Jerusalem. I dismissed the "two-foci" approach, namely that the two centers of world Jewry — Israel and America — were of equal status and importance. Instead, I wrote that "Israel is the 'Broadway' of the Jewish people — the major stage for the enactment of the Jewish drama, and at best the American stage is the setting for the 'road show.'" In a public lecture given around the same time, I described the relationship thus: "Israel is Broadway; America is off-Broadway."

The article was reproduced and disseminated to the entire rabbinical and lay leadership of the American Reform movement. I received numerous critical letters objecting to my deprecation of American Jewry. I countered that no slur was intended. I was merely projecting the reality as I saw it, a reality with which eventually American Jewry would come to terms over the next generation or so. Once both American and Israeli Jewry recognized the centrality of Israel, then the desired action would follow. The article proposed what in effect, thirty years later, became known as the Birthright program: a project to send vast numbers of Diaspora Jewish youth to Israel. Excerpts of what I wrote:

> "What is required is a radical new approach to Diaspora Jewish education, the creation of new institutions, either independent or related to existing institutions, that will serve as academic centers of high standard for tens of thousands of Jewish youth from abroad, one that will provide opportunities for enriched experiences in Jewish living.
>
> The same resources that American Jews have made available to build housing for new immigrants to Israel or for Israeli academic institutions, should be made available to

preserve and intensify the Jewishness of their own sons and daughters. And the consequences for aliyah and the establishment of closer ties between the two communities are manifest. The Jews of America must learn to relate to Israel as an integral part of their life. And the Jews of Israel must so order the priorities of the State that it becomes a great campus of Jewish life and learning, serving the needs of the entire Jewish people."

The article that was so criticized by my American colleagues was read enthusiastically by Louis Pincus and Leon Dulzin, Chairman and Treasurer respectively of the Jewish Agency — World Zionist Organization. They asked my counsel as to how best to strengthen the Zionist movements in America and reinforce the ties between American Jewry and Israel. I predicted that the Diaspora Zionist movements would continue the slide to ineffectiveness and that the synagogue movements would become the principal framework for Jewish identity. Therefore, it was essential to draw closer to the synagogue movements that represented the preservative forces of Jewish life for the future.

The Zionist Executive

Prior to our return to Washington in June 1970, Pincus and Dulzin proposed to appoint me to the American Section of the World Zionist Organization Executive. In an effort to strengthen the American Zionist movement and its relationship to the religious streams, they had appointed three rabbis who were representative of Orthodox, Conservative, and Reform Judaism. (They distinguished between *representing* and *representative of*. The Zionist movement selected the person and not the religious stream. Therefore, the appointment would be on an *ad personam* basis.) I accepted with enthusiasm and began to sit on the American Section. I was formally elected at the World Zionist Congress of 1972.

Re-evaluating the mission of the World Union for Progressive Judaism

Initially, I had no intention of making aliyah with the family. Bella and I were pleased with our life in Washington. The children were all doing exceptionally well in school. The Religious Action Center was developing into an institution of significance and influence. I never thought seriously that I should be the person to assume responsibility for the World Union in Israel. True, I was fluent in Hebrew, but I believed that a person with a rich background in Jewish learning, particularly knowledge of the Talmud and rabbinic sources, should head up the World Union.

It was essential to have someone of stature and competence organize the work of the movement in Israel. After discussing the issue with the leaders of the World Union, I approached three distinguished rabbis and suggested to each in turn that they consider early retirement and move to Jerusalem to assume responsibility for the World Union. After due deliberation, all three were unwilling to undertake the assignment. When I reported to the World Union leadership that I was unable to find anyone, they began to pressure me. I responded that I was not prepared to go, nor did I feel that it would be in the best interests of the movement if I were sent.

Concurrent with the search for a leader were two other developments. The land adjacent to the Hebrew Union College in Jerusalem became available. When David Ben Gurion was Prime Minister, he had given a long-term lease of land near the King David Hotel to Nelson Glueck, President of the Hebrew Union College. The College had erected an architecturally beautiful building which served as an academic and archaeological center. The land between the College and the King David hotel, a twelve dunam (three acre) plot, was undeveloped. In February 1971, we learned that plans for development of the plot had fallen through. A delegation representing the College, the World Union, and the Union of American Hebrew Congregations met with Prime

Minister Golda Meir and Finance Minister Pinhas Sapir. We prevailed upon them to give the College a long-term lease for the vacant land. The College, the Union and the World Union then proceeded to draw plans for the erection of a World Education Center for Progressive Judaism — a joint undertaking of the entire movement.

At the time, we had also begun to discuss affiliation with the World Zionist Organization and the Jewish Agency for Israel.

The pieces had begun to fall in place: the proposal to transfer the headquarters of the World Union, the affiliation with the WZO-Jewish Agency for Israel, and the development of a world center in the heart of Jerusalem. It was clear that the movement was developing a new thrust.

The prospect of once again, as in the case of the Religious Action Center, serving on the cutting-edge for the Reform movement, became more and more attractive. Moreover, I began to realize that if I did not assume responsibility for moving the international headquarters to Israel, the move might never take place. So, after long hours of deliberation with Bella, we decided to accept the responsibility. I insisted, to begin with, that if the movement was serious, we would require overwhelming approval of the idea by all the institutional arms of the movement and also significant financial support.

If not now, when?

The announcement of the move was made with great fanfare at the UAHC Biennial in November 1971. However, the matter of financing the move was never satisfactorily resolved. Several months after the public announcement, the officers of the World Union asked to meet with me. They expressed concern that no acceptable solution had been found to the funding problem. Since I had demonstrated a capacity to raise funds, they recommended that we postpone the decision to move the international headquarters to Jerusalem for several years and that instead I should function out of the New York office as the Executive Director mobilizing financial support in the United States. I responded that postponing the decision would only encourage those who were already opposed to the move. The challenge was to root Reform Judaism in

Israel. This could only be done by a dramatic symbolic act, which I was prepared to lead in Jerusalem. I summed up my position with the dictum of the Ethics of the Fathers: אם לא עכשו, אימתי — "If not now, when?"

However, I had no intention of leaving Washington to move to New York. The officers spent some time trying to persuade me to the contrary. It became clear during the course of the discussion that the leaders had already made the decision that the move should be postponed. I, thereby, reluctantly informed them that I was withdrawing my commitment to become the Executive Director of the World Union. I told them that it was a sad day for me personally and I believed would eventually be considered as a default by Reform Judaism, a failure to take advantage of an historic opportunity to make a mark on the Jewish people, as well as on Reform Judaism. The officers asked me to leave the room while they deliberated for an hour. When I returned, they informed me that they had agreed to go ahead with the move to Jerusalem.

THE WORLD ZIONIST ORGANIZATION

Affiliation of the World Union

Through my active participation in the meetings of the Zionist Executive, I had established good working relationships with Louis Pincus and Leon Dulzin. When I informed them that we were planning to move to Israel to direct the transfer of the World Union to Jerusalem, they pointed out that the forthcoming move presented the WZO with a real quandary. On one hand, I had been appointed to the Zionist Executive to sit on the Executive in America. On the other hand, for a member of the Executive to be forced to resign because he came on aliyah projected a message contrary to Zionist principles.

I informed them that I knew of a way out of their dilemma. In any case, among the leadership of the Reform movement we had begun to talk about the possibility of the World Union affiliating with the WZO as an international organization. (A number of international organizations, the Women's International Zionist Organization — WIZO, the World Maccabi Union and the World Sephardi Federation, were already affiliated.) Affiliation of the World Union for Progressive Judaism as an international organization would represent a significant achievement for both Progressive Judaism and the Zionist movement. In that case, I would sit on the Executive as a representative of the movement in Jerusalem, and another Reform Jew would sit on the Executive in New York. I cautioned them that it would require an extended educational process, but I expressed confidence that the international movement would eventually endorse the idea. So, despite my coming on aliyah, I remained a member of the Zionist Executive.

In reality, the recommendation to affiliate with the World Zionist Organization did provoke significant opposition. The WZO had developed a reputation of being controlled by the political parties of the State. Our leadership who were aware of the inner workings of the organization were reluctant to participate in the volatile, party-oriented, contentious meetings of the World Zionist Congress and the Zionist federations around the world. Even at that time, some recognized that the real force in the Jewish world was not the WZO, but the Jewish Agency for Israel.

Our leaders asked, "Why can we not join the Jewish Agency, without going through the process of the WZO?" However, there was no framework in which to do this. To the critics who opposed our entering the WZO on grounds that the political process was corrupting and that our principles would be compromised by our participation, I responded that the WZO, with all of its faults, was the most comprehensive, representative and democratic organization of world Jewry. Therefore, we were obligated to join it, and through joining the WZO would play a role in the Jewish Agency. To move the headquarters to Jerusalem and not to affiliate with the World Zionist Organization was equivalent to leading the bride to the *huppah* and refusing to put the ring on her finger.

After intense debate, the International Convention of the World Union meeting in London in March 1974, approved the decision in principle to affiliate with the WZO. The negotiations between the World Union and the WZO were extensive, because it was clear to all that the affiliation of the world Reform movement would set a precedent for the Conservative and Orthodox synagogue movements, which in due course also affiliated.

A good marriage

At the annual meeting of the WZO Zionist General Council convened on January 5, 1976, the WZO constitution was revised and the terms of affiliation approved. The World Union for Progressive Judaism was formally accepted into membership of the WZO.

Yitzhak Navon, later elected President of the State of Israel, was then the Chairman of the Zionist General Council. He welcomed the affiliation as an historic event. He spoke frankly about the significant changes taking place within the Reform movement and the revision of its attitudes toward Zionism and *halacha*. He referred with approval to the distinctive contributions of the Reform movement, highlighting the concepts of mission and social justice. He urged the State of Israel and the Zionist movement to open the gates wide for all those who urge a return to Jewish values and who act for the general social good of the Jewish people.

Mr. Navon then called on me to give a formal response, excerpts of which follow:

> "May Zion rejoice in the ingathering of her children." These words resound in every marriage ceremony. On behalf of the worldwide family of Reform Judaism, I welcome all who have come to participate in this marriage ceremony between the groom, the World Zionist Organization, and the bride, the World Union for Progressive Judaism.
>
> We have agreed to the marriage terms, we have signed the marriage contract and we have declared to one and all that everything is valid and binding. The match is a good one. In the past the couple's relationship was often stormy. Detractors claim that the family of the bride intended to negate the Jewish heritage and even to propel Jews away from their Judaism. But those who know our history are aware that the opposite was true. The early founders of the Reform movement were motivated by the desire to bring those who had become indifferent or alienated back to their Jewish roots.
>
> Like every reformist trend, our movement evolved ideas which subsequently proved false, but we know that "where repenters stand, even the completely righteous have no place." No teacher is more effective or cruel than History. The tenets of Zionism were validated. Therefore, let our in-laws judge the bride not by her ideas in the distant past, but by her aspirations and by her deeds. We have recognized the fact that "not the study *about* Zion, but the deed *in* Zion" is primary.
>
> For us, Zionism is an authentic expression of Jewish faith. Just as the people of Israel and the State of Israel are inseparable, so are Zionism and Judaism integral. Just as we commit ourselves to full participation in the constant process of renewing Judaism in the Jewish State, so do we insist on full recognition as a religious movement in Israel. Parenthetically,

is it too much to hope that this marriage ceremony will not be the last one in which a Reform rabbi will participate in the State of Israel?

We make a covenant with our fellow sons of the covenant. May we labor as one to fulfill the vision of the prophet Isaiah (Isaiah 62):

"For Zion's sake I will not hold my peace and for Jerusalem's sake I will not rest, until her triumph go forth as brightness. Thou shalt be called, my delight is in her, and thy land shall be espoused. For as a young man espouses a virgin, so shall thy sons espouse thee. *And as the bridegroom rejoices over the bride, so shall thy God rejoice over thee.*"*

---

* Translation of Excerpts from the Addresses, Debates and Resolutions of the Zionist General Council, Jerusalem, January 1976.

Founding ARZA — resolutions on pluralism

Within a year of the WUPJ's formal affiliation with the WZO, it had become clear that the affiliation did not provide the level of participation we had expected. In affiliating as an international organization we agreed that we would not participate in the electoral process and would not expect any of our representatives to hold political office in the WZO. However, as we participated in the WZO meetings, our representatives felt that in order to reflect the full strength of Reform Judaism around the world, we should think in terms of establishing a Zionist party comprising individual members who sign the Jerusalem Program and participate in the elections.

In May 1977, Menachem Begin was swept into power through a coalition of the Likud, Dash and the National Religious Party. Among the coalition understandings was a call by the National Religious Party for amending the Law of Return to exclude recognition by the State of Israel of conversions performed abroad by non-Orthodox rabbis.

The need for a public platform

How could the Reform movement counter these developments? We had no political influence within the Knesset and no intention of establishing a political party of our own to run in the Knesset elections. The only framework within which we could make our voice heard on political issues confronting the State of Israel was within the WZO. By establishing a Zionist political movement abroad, we would at least have a platform in Israel and the Jewish world from which to express ourselves.

We viewed the establishment of ARZA, Association of Reform Zionists of America, and subsequently of the International Federation of Reform and Progressive Religious Zionists called ARZENU, as consistent with the commitment we had made to the leaders of the WZO upon the affiliation of the

WUPJ to encourage individual Reform Jews to become members of the Zionist movement. How were they going to join the Zionist movement? It was unlikely that they would join the local Zionist federations or other political groupings. ARZA, our own Zionist movement in the Diaspora, would provide the necessary framework. ARZA was formally launched at the UAHC Biennial in 1977.

In 1978 the ARZA leadership immediately set to work to organize for the elections. 9,000 individual members were recruited and when the elections for the World Zionist Congress took place in the United States, 11,000 people voted for the ARZA list. This gave ARZA nine mandates to the 29th World Zionist Congress, meeting in Jerusalem in February 1978.

A stormy Congress

Our leadership determined that we press for passage of Congress resolutions on two major issues: the status of the Reform and Conservative movements in Israel; and equitable funding for our Zionist programs.

The Congress procedures required that resolutions be formulated in advance and presented to the committees of the Congress. We prepared four separate resolutions for four relevant committees and worked diligently within each committee for their adoption. We agreed that our primary focus would be in the Committee on Jewish Education in the Diaspora. Our proposed resolution was defeated within the committee. However, the Congress rules provided for a *votum separatum* (a resolution which had been defeated within the committee could be presented to the plenum for a vote, if the sponsors of the resolution announced their intention to do so in advance in the committee). Since our resolution did not pass in the committee, we presented a *votum separatum* in the plenary session. When the resolution was presented, the delegates from Mizrachi and Herut tried to prevent the vote from taking place. They stormed the microphone, claiming that the WZO constitution did not permit religious issues to be debated at the Congress. Nevertheless, a vote was called and the resolution was adopted. The Mizrachi and Herut delegates then claimed that they had not received a copy of the resolution in writing. The session was adjourned and another vote scheduled for the afternoon. This time the delegates received the resolution in writing. The resolution was again adopted.

The Mizrachi and Herut delegates left the hall in anger and returned shortly thereafter, forming a snake-dance and singing *"utzo etza v'tufar."* (Your counsel shall be voided.) The delegates who supported the resolution in turn formed their own snake-dance, singing *"hinei ma tov uma naim,"* (how good and how pleasant it is for brothers to dwell together in unity). When the two snake-dance groups met head on, fighting erupted. Planted pots on the stage were thrown and a general melee ensued. After intensive efforts, order was restored and the second resolution went to the floor and was adopted. The texts of the two resolutions follow:

> 61. The Congress confirms that all departments, authorities and programs of the WZO in Israel will be managed in accordance with the principle of equal status and identical treatment for every religious movement which is affiliated with the WZO, and for every Jew, regardless of his origin or his religious or ideological identification. Programs of a religious and educational character shall represent the pluralism which characterizes Jewish life throughout the world. The Congress calls upon the State of Israel, as the homeland of the Jewish people, to put into practice the principle of assuring full rights, including equal recognition, for all rabbis, and equal assistance to all the trends in Judaism.

> 63. The WZO shall aid and assist the religious and ideological currents in their educational activities, so that the pluralism existing in Jewish life in Israel and the Diaspora is reflected. Jewish education shall emphasize the humanistic and moral values contained in Jewish culture and heritage.

After the two resolutions were adopted, the Mizrachi delegates left the plenary session in protest, declaring their intention to appeal the resolutions to the

Zionist court and threatening to leave the Zionist movement unless the two resolutions were withdrawn.

We convened a meeting of our caucus together with some of our allies from other parties. Leaders of the parties which supported us urged us to withdraw the two resolutions which had not yet come to the floor, on grounds that an historic victory had been attained. For the first time, resolutions advocating religious pluralism in Israel and equal rights for all rabbis had been adopted. To continue to pass the additional resolutions would represent over-kill. Our caucus voted to withdraw the remaining resolutions. We so informed the Chairman who reconvened the plenary session. I was called upon to address the plenary. My brief extemporaneous speech follows:

> "I address my remarks to the members of Mizrachi who are here, and ask you to convey them to all members of Mizrachi who are not present.
>
> איזהו מכובד? המכבד את הבריות. "Who is honored? He who honors his fellow man." We respect and honor our colleagues in Mizrachi; we want them to honor and respect us.
>
> Some people have congratulated us for a "tremendous victory." We do not characterize what happened in terms of partisan victory and defeat. The resolution that was adopted was not a defeat for Orthodoxy. It was a victory for full participation in the Zionist cause by all movements in Judaism.
>
> Orthodox Judaism in general and the Mizrachi Zionist movement in particular have made invaluable contributions to the preservation of Jewish life and the upbuilding of Zion. We applaud Mizrachi for its accomplishments. We appreciate you showing the way to Conservative and Reform Judaism. Had we been active in the Zionist movement, as you were, fifty or seventy-five years ago, the State of Israel and the condition of the Jewish people, and the positions of our respective movements would have been radically different. The State of Israel would have been enhanced and the Jewish people enriched.
>
> Our insistence on equal status in the World Zionist

Organization strengthens the sense of participation and
commitment of significant segments of world Jewry in the
majestic drama of national rebirth. There cannot be full
participation in a democratic process if some elements believe
they are second-class citizens. So our joining the Zionist
movement and asking for equal status is good for Zionism. It
will encourage a vast increase in the ranks of Zionist
membership and supporters. It will inject a more intensive
Zionist dimension in Jewish life throughout the world. And
ultimately, even if you members of Mizrachi do not accept it
now, in time we hope you will realize that it is good also for
Mizrachi.

We have much in common with Mizrachi, in one sense
more in common with you than with any other movement in the
Zionist family. We have a common enemy: our enemy is Jewish
ignorance and assimilation. We have a common objective: our
objective is to inculcate in all Jews a perception of being
Jewishly rooted in our religious sources. We share a common
conviction: for Zionism to endure and the Jewish people to
exist, our Jewish religious heritage must be perpetuated.

You can help us. You can guide us. עשה לך רב וקנה לך חבר.
"Provide for yourself a teacher and acquire a friend" (Ethics
of the Fathers). You have been our teachers. We ask you to
remain our friends, united by the common bond of Zion.
הקב״ה ישראל ואורייתא חד הוא. "God, Israel, and Torah are one"
(Zohar). Through our combined efforts, God, Torah, the people of
Israel, and the Land of Israel shall remain one.*

The public media declared the passage of the resolutions and the debate which
ensued to be the highlight of the Congress. I have included the above remarks in
full, because they reflect the position which we in the Reform movement have
adopted. Even as we demand our full rights, we extend our hands in respect and
friendship to Orthodoxy.

---

* Hebrew Protocol of the 29th Zionist Congress, pp. 284-285.

Reorganizing the WZO and the Jewish Agency

After years of participation in the World Zionist Organization and the Jewish Agency for Israel, it became obvious that the national institutions of world Jewry were in need of radical restructuring. In 1992 I wrote an article entitled *The Israel-Diaspora Connection: Reorganizing World Jewry to Meet the Needs of the 21st Century*. The article, distributed broadly, provoked significant discussion. A number of seminars to discuss its ramifications were convened in which representatives of all the movements within the WZO and public figures participated. As a consequence, I was asked to serve as Chairman of the *WZO Committee for Redesign and Reorganization of the World Zionist Organization and its Link to the Jewish Agency*. The Committee met regularly during a two year period. Its final report was approved by the Zionist General Council in June of 1996. Subsequently, the Jewish Agency adopted the general outlines of the plan which today provides the base of operations for both the Jewish Agency and the World Zionist Organization.

Among the arguments for advocating reorganization were the following:

1. Changing organizational conditions

Over the years the organizational structures have assumed different forms in order to meet changing conditions. Following the Balfour Declaration of 1917 and World War I, the World Zionist Organization leadership recognized that they needed the support of the total Jewish community in order to achieve their objectives. At the time, heated ideological conflicts divided world Jewry. The majority of Jews in western democratic lands were opposed to Zionism.

The Zionists, very much a minority, were desperate for the financial and political support of Jewish leadership in the West, particularly in the United States. Therefore, the Jewish Agency was created in 1929 as a roof organization for cooperation between Zionists and non-Zionists. The worldwide depression intervened, the ideological controversies persisted, and the plans of the founders were never implemented. In effect, until the establishment of the State, the WZO assumed full responsibility for the Jewish Agency. The executive of the WZO also served as the executive of the Jewish Agency.

Following World War II, Ben Gurion, then chief executive of both the Agency and the WZO, decided that it was essential to mobilize the support of the non-Zionist philanthropists. He began to propound the hypothesis that in the era of the Jewish State, the only true Zionists were those who lived in Israel. All others were friends and supporters of Israel. With the establishment of the State, he advocated the disbanding of the WZO. Even though the WZO rejected the Ben Gurion proposals, its status and influence were significantly diminished. In Israel, its pre-state functions were taken over by the government. In the Diaspora, most of its functions were assumed by the non-Zionists. New fundraising mechanisms were created which transferred responsibility from the Zionist establishment to the philanthropic establishment.

The Six Day War ushered in a new era of cooperation. The threat of annihilation and the subsequent miraculous victory mobilized the entire Jewish world and created a new condition which required that the covenant between Israel and the Diaspora be strengthened in a new working arrangement, designated as the reconstituted Jewish Agency.

The new Agency was restructured along the same lines as the original Jewish Agency, with parity between the WZO and its philanthropic partners in the Diaspora, the United Israel Appeal in the United States and the Keren Hayesod in the rest of the Diaspora. A program for delineation of functions was approved, with the Jewish Agency assuming responsibility for aliyah and absorption, settlement and other pragmatic tasks in Israel and the WZO assuming responsibility for educational and organizational tasks in the Diaspora.

2. The fading of clear-cut ideological differences among the partners

Today the Jewish State is both an indisputable fact and the prime factor of Jewish life. The controversies of today relate to ideological perceptions of what is in the best interests of the Jewish people and the Jewish State. These controversies are reflected in issues concerning budget priorities of the world Jewish polity. How should the Jewish people spend the funds it mobilizes? How much should stay in local communities and for what purposes? How much should go to Israel and for what purposes? How much should go to Jews elsewhere and for what purposes? For example, regarding Soviet Jews, should we concentrate our human and material resources on aliyah, or should we invest funds to encourage Jews to develop their own indigenous institutions and programs in the former Soviet Union?

The issues of funding reflect the ongoing conflicts between those who give priority to nation-building and those who give priority to preserving Jewish life wherever Jews live. However, unlike the confrontations of the past, the positions adopted on these kinds of controversies are unrelated to whether or not a person is a card-carrying Zionist, or whether a person lives in Israel or the Diaspora. As for the argument over Zionism, no respectable Jewish leader today would declare himself anti-Zionist or non-Zionist.

3. The mission and programs of the Jewish Agency and the WZO are indistinguishable.

To retain the existing frameworks is to retain the anomaly that the WZO programs are intended to serve Diaspora Jewry and the Agency programs are intended for Israel. No programming for the Diaspora can be efficacious unless it involves Diaspora Jews at every level, even as no programming for Israel can be effective without the involvement of Israelis in every aspect of policy formulation and implementation.

Therefore, the present structure based on a partnership between Zionists and non-Zionists is no longer relevant or viable. The organizational structure of the Jewish Agency in the twenty-first century should be based on an enduring partnership between Israel and the Diaspora. Without building ties to Israel, the Diaspora would lose its sense of purpose, its source of inspiration and its resource for experiencing Jewish peoplehood. Without the Diaspora, Israel would cease to be the spiritual center of a world people and civilization and would become a nation like all other nations. The partnership between Israel and the Diaspora reinforces the unique character of one people, united by the obligations of mutual responsibility and the sense of interdependent destiny.

The mission of the organization should be not only to build and strengthen the state and assume responsibility for aliyah, but also to strengthen world Jewry. The first fifty years of the twentieth century were devoted to establishing the Jewish state. The last fifty years of the twentieth century were devoted to aliyah and strengthening the Jewish state. The next fifty years of the twenty-first century should be devoted to preserving and strengthening world Jewry through the vehicle of the State of Israel.

If in the past Jewish energies flowed from the Diaspora to Israel, in the future they will flow from both directions, as Israel and the Diaspora sustain each other. The institutions which represent and service world Jewry should be reorganized to reflect the new reality. Duplication and competitiveness inject divisiveness and waste precious assets. Responsible Jewish leadership should give serious consideration to a realignment of Jewish organizational structures, including organizations such as the World Jewish Congress, the Jewish Agency for Israel, the World Zionist Organization and the American Jewish Joint Distribution Committee. At the very minimum, frameworks to pool and coordinate the human and material resources of these organizations should be established.

"RISE UP AND BUILD!"

When I assumed professional responsibility for the World Union in 1973, it was administered by a director and a secretary in a one and a half room office of the Union of American Hebrew Congregations building in New York. The leadership group consisted of a handful of distinguished rabbis and lay leaders in the New York area. They were all very dedicated to the work of the World Union. However, all held other full-time positions to which they devoted their primary loyalty. To their credit, they had managed to keep the World Union afloat on a shoestring budget (in 1972 the total income was $78,000) by appealing to friends, congregants, sisterhoods and other affiliated institutions for funding of special projects, often on an emergency basis.

When the World Union decided to move its headquarters to Jerusalem, it was obligated to transform itself from a small coordinating agency to a large operating agency. As a coordinating agency, the World Union did not need major funding, but once we made the decision to build a movement in Israel, we needed a major increase in financial support. This required a radical change in the leadership base of the organization. It was essential to bring laymen into leadership roles. Unlike busy rabbis, laymen would be able to devote time and give of their own financial resources. Laymen would bring a more business-like approach to the organizational objectives and would attract other lay people to work on behalf of the organization. To build a significant organization, it was essential to raise significant funds. Once it became clear that the funding would not come from the national institutions of the American movement, it was essential to develop independent sources of funding. The capacity to develop funding in turn would be predicated on setting attractive funding goals and projects.

In order to attract lay leadership, it was essential that they see firsthand the activities in which the World Union was engaged. Therefore, among our first priorities was to organize missions to countries served by the World Union. We organized trips to Latin America, to Australia and New Zealand, to South Africa, to Europe and beginning in 1988 to the Soviet Union. The drama of the World

Union had to be told on site with firsthand experiences. Potential donors had to understand that by contributing to the programs and institutions of the World Union, they were advancing a vital cause for perpetuation of the Jewish heritage.

If lay people are given challenges of demonstrable historic significance, they will give generously of their resources. Those who have managed to accumulate wealth want to use it for meaningful purposes. They have already demonstrated that they can make a living for themselves. Now the next challenge is to make a life, to contribute to a cause which advances their aspirations for the Jewish people.

Israel represented the ultimate challenge. It was essential to inspire the movement with a sense of mission. A commentary on Leviticus 19:23 set the tone.

כי תבואו אל הארץ ונטעתם. "When you come into the land, you shall plant." The Tanhuma (Kedoshim 8) interprets the verse: אמר להם הקב"ה לישראל: אף על פי שתמצאו אותה מלאה כל טוב לא תאמרו נשב ולא ניטע אלא הוו זהירין בנטיעות. "God said to Israel: Though you find it full of every good thing, do not say: Let us dwell there and plant nothing; but busy yourselves with planting."

Over and over again I preached the message: Our task is to root ourselves in the soil and the soul of the Jewish people. Unless we root ourselves in the soil, we cannot root ourselves in the soul.

To build a movement in Israel required a commitment to develop professional and lay leadership and to establish institutions and programs. The test for success was to establish movements, institutions and programs which were replicable throughout the country.

The first institution put on the drawing boards was the World Education Center for Progressive Judaism on the campus of the Hebrew Union College. From the outset, an enduring partnership was forged between Professor Alfred Gottschalk, President of the College, and myself. We were ably served by Richard Scheuer, farsighted Chairman of the College's Jerusalem Committee (later Chairman of the College-Institute Board), who was instrumental in selecting as architect the world renowned Moshe Safdie. Together, we shared a vision. The Center and the activities to be conducted therein had to make a statement — to the Israel public, to world Jewry and to our own movement. Our rabbinic sages had declared that "Jerusalem is the center of the universe." We were privileged to develop the land that was in "the center of the center." Therefore, we were taking initiative to demonstrate that Progressive Judaism would enhance the beauty of Jerusalem and enrich the cultural and spiritual dimensions of Israeli life.

The project was frustrated by governmental procrastination and fund-raising problems. Whereas the initial grant of land was made in 1971, we did not receive the official lease until 1978. Whereas the Minister of Finance had originally promised that the Treasury would match dollar for dollar with contributions from overseas, the government withdrew its offer after the Yom Kippur War. Recognizing the financial crisis, we accepted the government's position with understanding.

The proposal to erect a youth hostel-cultural center met with considerable internal opposition. At the time, the World Union was in severe financial straits and was finding it difficult to meet the payroll of its rabbis and professional staff. The explanation that it was easier to raise funds for capital construction than for operating budgets was not comprehended by some of the critics.

Today, the criticisms have dissipated as the movement takes pride in what has been achieved. The magnificent campus — the College's library, archaeological museum and academic center and the World Union's hostel and cultural centers, Beit Shmuel and Mercaz Shimshon — teems with a multiplicity of creative learning experiences for students, nursery school children, youth and adults. Visitors strolling through the Center are overwhelmed by the aesthetic character of the buildings and the pulse of the cultural and educational programs.

The success of the World Educational Center inspired the movement to erect synagogue-community centers in Tel Aviv (Beit Daniel), Haifa (Or Hadash), and Jerusalem (Kol Haneshama). Other building projects are under construction in Raanana (Mercaz Samueli) and Mevasseret Tzion, and new projects are planned for Yaffo, Ramat Hasharon, Modiin and other localities.

Israel's educational system is compartmentalized into three basic national frameworks: government schools, government religious schools, and independent ultra-Orthodox schools. In the late 1960's, the World Union determined that it was essential to establish educational programs which integrated secular education with a liberal religious education. A partnership relationship was forged with the Leo Baeck School in Haifa to further that objective. Subsequently, a national system of integrated secular and religious education called Tali was established through the initiative of Conservative rabbis (Tali is a Hebrew acronym for "intensified Jewish studies curriculum"). The Israel Movement for Progressive Judaism has established a Tali school in Jerusalem and is planning to expand its network of schools elsewhere in Israel. Nursery schools and kindergartens are sprouting throughout the country. The Leo Baeck Educational Center, recognized as one of the finest schools in the country, is expanding its superb facilities to include an Israel-Diaspora Youth Center. The movement has determined that the inculcation of values through formal and informal educational programs is of highest priority. Highly successful Israel experience programs have been developed for high school and college youth from abroad by the National Federation of Temple Youth and Netzer Olami, the international Progressive Zionist Youth movement.

In cooperation with the United Kibbutz Movement, the Jewish Agency for Israel, the Jewish National Fund and the Israel government, the movement has established three settlements: Kibbutz Yahel, founded in 1976, Kibbutz Lotan, founded in 1983, both located in the Arava north of Eilat, and Har Halutz, a free enterprise community in the Galilee. These settlements, integrating graduates of the Israeli Progressive Youth movement with Progressive youth movements from abroad, have succeeded in blending the social idealism of kibbutz ideology with the spiritual and cultural values and observances of Progressive Judaism. They have literally put Progressive Judaism "on the map" of Israel and continue to provide the entire movement with inspiring models of the *halutzic* pioneering spirit characteristic of Israel.

Responding to the need to establish an Israeli movement, the Hebrew Union College-Jewish Institute of Religion established an Israeli rabbinic training program, with the first rabbi being ordained in 1980. Since then many Israeli rabbis have graduated and many others are in study programs. The spiritual leadership of the movement is today in the hands of Israeli-reared and Israeli-trained rabbis, a harbinger of the expanding development of an indigenous Israel Progressive movement.

In 1987, the movement established the Israel Religious Action Center to serve as its public and legal advocacy arm. Sponsored by ARZA (today ARZA-

WORLD UNION, North America), the Israel Religious Action Center focuses on its mission of advancing the cause of religious freedom, pluralism, social justice and civil liberties for all. Its legal staff has won several landmark Supreme Court rulings and has helped defend the rights of new immigrants. Its high profile and professional expertise have kept the religion-state issues in the forefront of public discussion in Israel and the Diaspora.

The Israel Movement for Progressive Judaism (IMPJ) has developed education, community development, camp, youth, young adult and other program departments. It is governed by a democratically elected National Council and Executive Committee responsible for guiding the movement and stimulating its creative growth.

MARAM (the Israel Council of Progressive Rabbis) is responsible for giving guidance to innovative development of liturgy and oversees the operation of a Beit Din (rabbinic court) for issues of *Ishut* (personal status), including conversion. It works in close collaboration with the IMPJ.

When Ezra and Nehemiah returned from Babylonian exile, they issued a clarion call to rebuild the Temple in Jerusalem. נקום ובנינו ויחזקו ידיהם לטובה. "Let us rise up and let us build, so they strengthened their hands for the good work" (Nehemiah 2:18). The World Union and the Israel Movement for Progressive Judaism are committed to adopting the call of Nehemiah as their motto. We shall continue to strengthen our hands for the good work. "Let us rise up and let us build."

A story told about Christopher Wren, the famous architect of St. Paul's Cathedral in London, illustrates the vision I have tried to project. One day the architect walked by the building under construction and noticed three brick-layers at work. He asked the first what he was doing. The man responded, "I'm laying bricks." He asked the second person, who replied, "I'm building a wall." The third worker stood up, and with a sense of immense pride, declared, "I, sir, am erecting a cathedral to the Almighty."

Progressive Judaism in Israel is motivated by the conviction that we are striving to create a unique society in a land sanctified by the Jewish people's historic encounter with the divine. That conviction elevates our purpose and enhances our aspiration.

SOVIET JEWRY

In 1998, I was elected co-chairman of the Jewish Agency's Commission of the Department for the Former Soviet Union, the Baltic States and Eastern Europe. When we convened a meeting with the senior staff of the department, they asked when I first became interested in the issue of Soviet Jewry. I responded that it was in 1954. "1954?" they exclaimed! "In those days almost no one was interested in Soviet Jewry." I replied, "I know, but I fell passionately in love with one Soviet Jew, the woman who became my wife, and ever since I have been passionately committed to Soviet Jewry."

In the early 1960's, American and world Jewry began to mobilize a campaign on behalf of Soviet Jewry. The American Jewish National Conference on Soviet Jewry was established as an umbrella group of all Jewish national organizations and local Jewish community councils. I was involved from the very beginning in the organizational process. The Religious Action Center served as the representative of the Conference in Washington. From this vantagepoint, I participated in the policy formulation of the National Conference on Soviet Jewry and developed close personal and professional relationships with the Israelis who worked for *Lishkat Hakesher*, the special liaison bureau attached to the Prime Minister's Office, responsible for the struggle on behalf of Soviet Jewry.

1969 — Experiencing the Miracle Firsthand

After the Six Day War, when relations between the USSR and Israel were severed, it became essential for world Jewry to maintain contact with the first sparks of reawakening Jewish consciousness. *Lishkat Hakesher* asked Bella and me to travel to the USSR. We were an ideal couple. Bella had retained her total fluency in Russian and I had become a knowledgeable activist. The leaders of *Lishkat Hakesher* urged us to go on a mission for them to Moscow, Leningrad and Riga. We arranged to go in the Fall of 1969 from before Sukkot until after

Simchat Torah. In those days, the only way to travel in the USSR was through Intourist, the official government tourist agency. We took the official tourist car and guide during the mornings, but during the afternoons and evenings we wandered around on our own.

When we were briefed before the trip, we had asked for the names, addresses, and phone numbers of Jews whom we might meet. We were astounded when our "briefers" informed us that they had no names or addresses available. "Then how in heaven's name will we meet Jews?" we queried in surprise. They told us, "Don't worry. With your Jewish "panim" (physiognomy) and your wife's Russian language facility and western clothes, the Jews will find you." Find us they did; we met hundreds of Jews, in museums, theaters, market places, stores, homes, on the metro and buses and in general wherever we were.

The following are excerpts of Hebrew articles I wrote for the weekend magazine of the Israeli daily *Maariv*, following the trip:

Simchat Torah

My wife and I timed our visit to the USSR to be able to witness Soviet Jewish youth demonstrating their will to be Jews on the festival of Simchat Torah — the once-a-year phenomenon of singing and dancing in the streets outside the synagogues. When we emerged from our hotel, bound for the Moscow synagogue, the city was being pelted by a bitter cold hailstorm. We were heartbroken, believing that the street celebration would have to be canceled.

Not so. Archipov Street, on which the Moscow synagogue is located, was packed, from one end to the other, with a crowd estimated at over 20,000 persons. There they were, young Soviet Jews for the most part, singing Hebrew and Yiddish songs, laughing, pushing and shoving for dancing space — oblivious to the foul weather. We were caught up and swept along in the whirl.

A university student, out of breath after a fast hora, brushed by us and we struck up a conversation over the roar of celebrants. "Why are you here?" we asked. "To show the world that the Jewish people still lives," he replied, panting. "Why is that so important to you?" we pressed him. Gulping for air, he said: "The Soviet government insists upon stamping my identity card 'evrei' ["Hebrew" or "Jew"], so it must be very important to them that I remain a Jew, even though they go to great lengths to deprive me of ways to express myself as a Jew. And if it is important to those who hate Jews, then should it not be important to me? And should I not make every effort to find out what it means to be a Jew and to live as a Jew with pride?"

In all of Russia there is not one Jewish school for the study of the Hebrew language or of the Jewish heritage. Yet we conversed in Hebrew with young Jews who gather once a week clandestinely in the woods or a private home, pull out Hebrew readers and teach each other Hebrew. Leon Uris' book, *Exodus*, which is banned in Russia, has been translated into Russian by hand, photocopied, and widely circulated.

We met young Jews who wear a Star of David in their lapels and proudly call themselves Zionists, a term which is an anathema in their society. One teenager took out his wallet and carefully unfolded what he called his most precious possession — a tattered Israeli travel brochure.

The Six-Day War Impact

The Six-Day War was a traumatic experience for the Jews of Russia, as it was for Jews all over the world. But the plight of the Russian Jews was especially poignant. For they knew that their government was in great measure responsible for the war and had supplied the arms which were being used against Israel. A number of young people told us that the Israeli victory marked an historic turning point for Russian Jewry, because the Russian people, who still remembered Jews as weaklings led to mass slaughter by the Nazis, could now see that Jews could fight courageously and win against overwhelming odds.

An engineer confided to us that he worked in a tank plant.

"You American Jews make your contribution to Israel through financial assistance to immigrants. The tanks I help produce made their way to Egypt and Syria, then in the war they were captured by the Israeli armed forces. My contribution is even greater than yours."

While waiting for our guide in the lobby of our hotel, a young man recognized us as Jewish and began a conversation with us. Both he and his wife were professionals, they had a three-year-old daughter, and they were anxious to preserve their Jewish identity, but he had no Jewish education. He took out his identification card, showed us the word "Evrei" (Jew) and his first name "Moise" [Moses]. He said to my wife, "Would you have your husband, the rabbi, do me a favor? I know that Moses was a great Jew, but that's all I know. Would you please have him tell me the full story of the man whose name I bear?" I then proceeded to relate the story of Moses and the Exodus from Egypt, very much as I had done countless times to children in the kindergarten of religious school. When I had finished, tears of gratitude welled up in his eyes and all three of us wept. He thanked us profusely. "At last now I have something Jewish to transmit to my child."

The first direct contact with Soviet Jews reinforced the exhilaration of experiencing the miracles of Jewish survival. For over half a century Soviet Jews had been uprooted from their heritage by forced assimilation and victimized by vicious anti-Semitism. Yet, the spark of Jewish identity had been ignited anew. I considered the reawakened Jewish national consciousness of Soviet Jewry to be a corroboration of the Zionist mission. And I was determined to be part of it.

Introducing Progressive Judaism to the Former Soviet Union (FSU)

In 1987, a key policy maker in Soviet Jewish affairs suggested that we travel again to the USSR. He projected that under Mikhail Gorbachev, Jews would soon be permitted to leave and those who wished to remain would be able to practice their Jewishness more openly. However, he predicted that significant numbers would remain behind. He described in detail the substantial efforts undertaken by the *Habad* movement, which had miraculously activated thousands of adherents throughout the USSR. However, said he, it was unlikely that Soviet Jews, reared in the atheist milieu of communism, would suddenly become *Habad Hassidim* in massive numbers. Therefore, he urged us to explore the potential for development of liberal expressions of Judaism for those who would remain.

So, in 1987 Bella and I went to the Soviet Union again. In contrast to the previous visit, we were given names, phone numbers and addresses of activist Jews, some of whom had been refuseniks, some of whom had been "prisoners of Zion." We met with persons who were desperate to go on aliyah and with others who believed it would be possible to lead a Jewish life in the USSR.

We became convinced that under the new revolutionary approach of Gorbachev, sooner or later the communist regime would be overturned. Even though neither we, nor anyone else for that matter, were able to prognosticate the speed with which the Soviet Union would fracture into independent republics, we did come to believe that not only would Soviet Jews be permitted to leave, but that eventually restrictions prohibiting study and observance of Judaism would be removed. We contended that it was our responsibility to keep the Jews alive wherever they were. Even though a major objective should be aliyah, nevertheless, if they did not remain Jews, they would never even be candidates for aliyah. We described the virtues and benefits of Progressive Judaism to a number of young intellectuals and persons in search of their Jewish roots. We recounted the importance of worship and home observance of the Sabbath, holidays and life-cycle events. We encouraged the organization of discussion groups. And on our return, we began to educate our world movement to assume responsibility for the development of Progressive Judaism in the USSR.

In March 1988, immediately following the World Union Convention in Jerusalem, we led a delegation of some 40 leaders of the World Union to the USSR. The contact with fellow Jews who were eager to recover their Jewish identity was contagious. I had long contended that the struggle for Soviet Jewry would do more for world Jewry than world Jewry would do for it. To be given the opportunity to help Soviet Jews regain Jewish consciousness instilled a sense of purpose in Diaspora Jewry. The mission members were so inspired by the opportunity that at the closing evaluation session every participant made a commitment to contribute toward a fund for developing Progressive Judaism in the Soviet Union.

Among other decisions, we recognized that it was essential to create a groundswell within our world movement. In December, 1989, we convened in London to establish an international commission on Progressive Judaism in the Soviet Union. We began to spell out a rationale, a program and a framework for mobilizing the funding.

In April 1990, we led another mission of leaders to the USSR, prior to the Convention of the World Union for Progressive Judaism in London in May, 1990. By this time, the first Progressive Jewish Congregation, Hineini, had been established in Moscow. The highlight of our mission was welcoming the new congregation into membership of the World Union. We invited the chairman of the congregation to travel with us to London to participate in the World Union Convention. His very presence electrified the convention. At the Shabbat morning service the entire congregation was brought to tears as he read the Ten Commandments in Russian in front of the Ark. We had opened a new frontier for Progressive Judaism.

Facing Divergent Options

The phenomenon of a reawakened Soviet Jewry provoked sharp differences on issues of world Jewish public policy. Because of my responsibilities in the Jewish Agency and in the World Union, I was directly involved in the policy debates.

Neshira — The "Drop-out" problem

In the early 1970's the USSR permitted a limited number of Jews to leave, but refused permission for direct flights to Israel. Vienna became a transfer center. Many Jews, leaving the Soviet Union ostensibly to immigrate to Israel, decided in Vienna not to proceed to Israel and instead to apply for visas to the United States and other countries. Two reception areas were established in the Italian towns of Ostia and Ladispoli where Jews waiting for visas were sustained by the American Jewish Joint Distribution Committee, the Jewish Agency and other organizations. The policy question arose: should Soviet Jews have "freedom of choice?" The phrase "freedom of choice" was interpreted to mean that if Soviet Jews did not want to go to Israel, the world Jewish community was obligated to finance their transfer to any country which permitted them to enter. HIAS (the Hebrew Immigrant Aid Society) assumed responsibility for transporting them to the United States and the local American federations encouraged their resettlement through assistance programs. The Satmer anti-Zionist sect did everything possible to keep them from coming to Israel. The United States government policy permitted a significant number of Soviet Jews to come to the United States. The resettlement program was attractive to local Jewish federations. It gave them a cause, both Jewish and humanitarian.

I espoused the position that there was a fundamental difference between repatriation to Israel and resettlement in the Diaspora. I considered the phrase "freedom of choice" a misnomer. To be sure, we should fight for the right of every Jew to live in freedom wherever he or she wants. But the issue here was not only "freedom of choice" for the individual. The issue here was the rights of the Jews *as a people*, as a *collectivity*, to live in freedom and security. *As a people* we have made a "free choice" — to build and strengthen the Jewish state. We do not have the option of building two Jewish states, each with a flag of its own color, one called the "goldene medina" (America), and the other called the "blue-white medina" (Israel). We are one people. That people has one state. The people and the state together should have one policy. I contended that since world Jewry would always be limited in the amount of funds it could mobilize, priority should be given to furthering the cause of Jewish peoplehood. There is a basic distinction between a Soviet Jew immigrating to Bat Yam, Israel and a Soviet Jew immigrating to Brighton Beach, New York. The Jew in Brighton Beach lives as an individual citizen. The Jew in Israel contributes to the well-being and preservation of the entire people.

After the Yom Kippur War, the controversy over "freedom of choice" became moot. By the time emigration was resumed in full force in 1989, the shrillness of the debate was modulated.

Soviet Jews continue to go to countries other than Israel. A sizable community has developed in Germany, and the United States continues to welcome Soviet immigrants.

However, from the perspective of perpetuation of Jewish peoplehood, Israel continues to be the preferable destination. The *Olim* from the FSU have transformed Israeli society. Despite some severe problems of social adjustment among individuals, the Soviet aliyah has enriched Israeli society in every realm: the economy, sciences, hi-tech, culture and politics. Israel has been enhanced through its strivings to fulfill the ancient Amidah prayer: שא נס לקבץ גלויותינו וקבצנו יחד מארבע כנפות הארץ. "Raise high the banner to gather our dispersed ones from the ends of the earth."

Aliyah or Renewal in the FSU?

When the aliyah resumed in 1989, another issue arose: should Jewish organizations place emphasis on aliyah or on helping Soviet Jews establish their own indigenous institutions in the Former Soviet Union? Initially, the policy of the Jewish Agency and the State was oriented exclusively to aliyah. It was their conviction that the economic and political conditions in the FSU, including both overt and latent anti-Semitism, do not warrant major investments of human and material resources in stabilizing Jewish life in the FSU. According to demographic statistics available to the Agency at the beginning of the twenty-first century, the number of persons in the FSU eligible for aliyah is approximately one million. Many of them are elderly, impoverished and sickly. Recent aliyah to Israel has tended to come from the outlying areas. For those who stay in the FSU, an in-migration pattern has set in, whereby Jews tend to leave the smaller communities and move to a few major metropolitan areas.

The policy of the American Jewish Joint Distribution Committee and a multiplicity of Jewish religious and educational organizations is that every effort must be made to build up the potential for continuity of Jewish life in places of residence.

The Joint has established an excellent social service support system and encouraged cultural programs, libraries, Hillel activities and community centers. The Jewish Agency and *Lishkat Hakesher* sustain a network of schools, *ulpanim*, camps and youth programs.

The Jewish Agency has embarked on an intensive program of Enhancing Jewish Identity. The Agency and the Government of Israel have established a joint commission to cooperate in the effort to "Judaize" and "Zionize" all those eligible for aliyah and those who have already settled in Israel.

If given a preference, I would advocate that every effort be made to encourage aliyah for as many as possible. However, despite the Aliyah of almost one million Soviet Jews in the 1990's, for years to come Soviet Jewry will comprise the second largest Jewish population in the Diapora, next to American Jewry. We have an obligation not only to assure their physical well being, but also to sustain their cultural and spiritual survival.

The World Union for Progressive Judaism has embarked on an Operation Renewal program which incorporates the organization of new congregations and study groups, camping programs, publication of educational and liturgical materials, and training of para-professional leaders. Several Russian born Reform rabbis are serving in the FSU and we hope to establish a full rabbinic training program in Moscow. The rapid expansion in the FSU, despite insufficient funding and lack of Russian-speaking professional staff, attests to the potential receptivity of the message of Progressive Judaism.

Over the years I have been overwhelmingly impressed by the devotion of *Habad* and other Orthodox movements in establishing Jewish schools, reopening synagogues and encouraging a return to an Orthodox religious life. However, the Jews of the FSU, having been reared in a communist anti-religious milieu, will not respond to Orthodox Judaism in vast numbers. The path of Progressive Judaism does appeal to a critical mass in search of a relevant expression of Jewish identity.

Soviet Jewry — Symbol of Hope

The unfolding saga of Soviet Jewry highlights the distinctive character of Jewish identity. We Jews function in a kind of science-fiction time machine. We are the only people who relive the past in the present and who live in the present for the future.

The classic instance of the Jewish science-fiction time machine is the Passover *Seder*. The *Haggadah* flips the switch: בכל דור ודור חייב אדם לראות את עצמו כאלו הוא יצא ממצרים. "In every generation every person is obligated to look upon himself as if he had come forth from Egypt." In every generation every Jew tastes the bitterness of all human slavery and savors the sweetness of all human freedom. In every generation the redemption of humankind begins with the redemption of the Jew.

The struggle for Soviet Jewry became the harbinger of the freedom struggle for all peoples in Eastern Europe. It dramatized the inequities of communism, demonstrated the vulnerability of antiquated political structures, and inspired the pursuit of civil liberties for all citizens.

The successful campaign for Soviet Jewry precipitated the freedom march of oppressed Soviet nationalities across the Red Sea of communism towards their promised lands of independence. When the modern Pharaohs of Eastern Europe permitted Jews to repatriate to Israel and to renew their Jewish heritage, the strivings toward democracy in the Former Soviet Union became more credible in the eyes of the western world.

The Midrash teaches: "As the myrtle is sweet to him who smells it but bitter to him who bites into it, so Israel brings prosperity to the nation which grants them kindness, and depression to the nation which afflicts them with evil" (Esther Rabbah 6:5). Jewish destiny is inextricable from the human condition. In the words of Leo Baeck, "Judaism cannot conceive of mankind without itself, or of itself without mankind."

For Jews, the past and the future are as much a reality as the present. Where the Jews are, there is history; where there is history, there is a future; and where there is a future, there is hope.

"COMING IN AND GOING FORTH"

In reviewing my career, I am reminded of the Mishna in Berachot 9:4: הנכנס לכרך מתפלל שתים, אחת בכניסתו ואחת ביציאתו. "He who enters into a town should pray twice, once on his coming in and once on his going forth." Ben Azzai adds: *"Twice is not enough. He should pray four times. Twice on coming in and twice on going forth. On both occasions he should offer two prayers."* נותן הודאה על שעבר וצועק על העתיד. "He should offer thanks for what has happened and he should make supplication for what is still to come."

Like Ben Azzai, I express gratitude for what has been and offer prayers of hope for what will yet be. I have been privileged to work with hundreds of colleagues, both lay and professional. We have attracted to leadership positions persons of dedication and integrity with whom I have shared both aspirations and frustrations. I feel blessed to have been associated with these colleagues and to have had the opportunity of carving out new frontiers of the spirit in shared efforts with them.

What can we anticipate in Israel "going forth" to the future? Until recently, most secular Israelis have believed that the controversies over religious rights for non-Orthodox movements are an Israel-Diaspora issue, not an internal issue. Each time a new crisis erupts, the secular Israeli politicians suddenly rediscover America. They would prefer not to antagonize Diaspora Jewry, unless, of course, their Orthodox coalition partners threaten to dissolve the government, in which case at best a committee is formed to diffuse the issue. They then give the liberal religious movements platitudinous counsel. If you would only bring half a million immigrants, better yet a million *olim*, *you* could change the situation. Their reasoning is reminiscent of the words placed in the mouth of the wicked son in the Passover *Haggadah*. He is accused of saying *you* and not *we*. The problem, say they, is *yours*, not *ours*. We are sympathetic to *your* problem, but please understand that defending our party stance on the peace issues takes precedence over all else. In the final analysis, don't expect us to jeopardize peace and security over issues of secondary import to us.

In 1999, an historic breakthrough took place. Over 50,000 people participated in a public demonstration against the massive ultra-Orthodox assault on the Supreme Court, the bastion of democracy. In conjunction with the demonstration, Amos Oz, A.B. Yehoshua, David Grossman and other well known authors and public figures signed a manifesto. They declared that in the Reform and Conservative movements they see the potential for "a new dynamic Israeli Judaism which will renew our spiritual and cultural landscape." They called on Israelis to affiliate with the Reform and Conservative movements in the hundreds of thousands. In the words of A.B. Yehoshua, "to stand with the Reform and Conservative movements is to defend ourselves."

That is the thrust of the breakthrough. When they support rights for liberal Judaism, Israelis are not doing us any favors. *They* need liberal Judaism. Just as the struggle on behalf of Soviet Jewry accelerated the attainment of democratic rights for all peoples in the USSR, just as the struggle for racial equality in America advanced the pursuit of democratic rights for all citizens, so support of liberal Judaism is essential for the well-being of Israeli society. To guarantee rights for all streams of Judaism is to guarantee the preservation of Israeli democracy for the entire society, just as to deprive liberal Judaism of fundamental rights will inevitably weaken the democratic institutions of Israeli society. Liberal Judaism is an idea whose time has come. But not only for liberal Jews, for all society.

In order for a nation to guarantee freedom *of* religion, it must first guarantee freedom *from* religion. Because the State of Israel has so far been unable to guarantee freedom *from* religion, it has been unable to guarantee freedom *of* religion for all Jews.

The only solution appears to be some form of separation of religion and state. Since the *halacha*, as interpreted by the rabbinate, is incapable of meeting the special needs of all citizens in a complex democratic society, the Orthodox rabbinate cannot be entrusted with exclusive control over issues such as marriage, divorce, abortion, conversion, burial, and medical ethics. Until such time as the state can meet the human needs through setting up alternate civil frameworks, the Religion-State issues will continue to fester as an open wound. The courts and the Knesset will continue to be a boxing ring, where opponents will punch, jab and spar with each other. In this ongoing fight, there will be no permanent winners. There will only be permanent losers. Judaism will lose its

President Lyndon B. Johnson presenting a pen with which he signed the Civil Rights Act of 1966, in appreciation of the author's efforts on behalf of the legislation.

Following the assassination of President John F. Kennedy, the Synagogue Council of America, the umbrella body of Orthodox, Conservative and Reform religious organizations, bestowed a posthumous award on the President. The presentation was made to the President's brother, Senator Edward (Ted) Kennedy in 1964.
Left to right: Rabbi Uri Miller, President, Synagogue Council of America; Senator Ted Kennedy (Massachusetts); Senator Abraham Ribacoff (Connecticut); the author.

The Religious Action Center organized the Jewish participation for the historic March on Washington, August 28, 1963. The morning of the March, key civil rights leadership met at the Center.

Left to right: Bishop Stephen Gill Spotswood, African Methodist Episcopal Church and leader in the Southern Christian Leadership Conference (chaired by Martin Luther King); Reverend Whitney Young, President, National Urban League; the author; leaders of the National Federation of Temple Youth (the student in the rear is today Rabbi Mark L. Winer, West London Synagogue, Great Britain).

In front of the Religious Action Center in Washington, D.C. (1965)
First row — left to right: Marvin Braiterman, RAC Counsel and Director of Education and Research; Kivie Kaplan, donor of the building and President of the NAACP (the National Association for the Advancement of Colored People); Emily Kaplan; the author.
Second row — staff of the Center, among them: Elimelich Ram, Director of the Jewish Agency Department of Aliyah and Klitah in the Washington area (housed in the RAC) and Israeli TV news reporter; Rabbi Richard Sternberger.
The Religious Action Center represented the National Conference for Soviet Jewry in Washington and was the first agency to post a sign demanding Freedom for Soviet Jewry.

Tri-faith testimony on the Civil Rights legislation of 1966 was presented jointly.
Left to right: Congressman Emanuel Celler, Chairman, House Judiciary Committee; the author,
representing the Synagogue Council of America; Dr. Benjamin F. Payton, Executive Director,
Commission on Religion and Race, National Council of Churches; Father John F. Cronin,
representing the U.S. Catholic Conference.

The Religious Action Center initiated a Washington Seminar for Theological students in cooperation with the Divinity School at Harvard University. Vice President of the United States, Hubert H. Humphrey, addressed the faculty and student body. July, 1966.
Left to right:
Vice President Hubert H. Humphrey; Dr. Herbert L. Long, Dean of Students, Harvard Divinity School; the author.

In February 1968 the author was instrumental in organizing an anti-Vietnam War protest in Washington D.C. The demonstrators marched from a church on Capitol Hill to Arlington Cemetery. Leading clergy participated. Pictured here; left to right: Reverend Martin Luther King, Jr.; Reverend Ralph Abernathy, both of the Southern Christian Leadership Conference; Rabbi Maurice N. Eisendrath, President, Union of American Hebrew Congregations; Rabbi Abraham Joshua Heschel. The Torah, originally in the possession of Rabbi Isaac Mayer Wise, the founder of Reform Judaism in America, was given to President John F. Kennedy at the Dedication of the Religious Action Center in December, 1962, and was kept in an Ark at the Religious Action Center for many years until it was transferred to the Kennedy Library in Boston.

The Central Conference of American Rabbis convened its annual convention for the first time in Israel in 1970. The delegation welcomes former Prime Minister David Ben Gurion, who addressed the convention.

From left to right: Professor Ezra Spicehandler, Dean of the Jerusalem School, Hebrew Union College — Jewish Institute of Religion; David Ben Gurion; Rabbi Roland Gittelsohn (CCAR President and subsequently first President of ARZA); Rabbi Alexander M. Schindler (Vice President of the Union of American Hebrew Congregations and subsequently President); the author; Rabbi Harold Saperstein (Chairman of the North American Board of the WUPJ).

The author was elected President of the 33rd World Zionist Congress in Jerusalem in December, 1997. After he guided the Congress to grant full voting rights to the youth delegates, they came to the stage to express appreciation.

Professor Mordecai M. Kaplan, the founder of Reconstructionism, was honored at a luncheon in the Knesset on the occasion of his 95th birthday in 1976.

After the respective speakers had heaped praise on Professor Kaplan, he responded: "This is indeed an historic, unprecedented occasion. This is the first time in my life I have reached 95 years of age." From left to right: Professor Mordecai M. Kaplan; the author; Rabbi Ludwig Nadelmann, Executive Director, Jewish Reconstructionist Federation; Moshe Kol, Minister of Tourism, State of Israel. In 1990, the Jewish Reconstructionist Federation affiliated with the World Union for Progressive Judaism. The two movements have been cooperating in building one joint movement in Israel.

The first Israeli Progressive Jewish Congregation, Har-El, was established in 1958 in Jerusalem. The author came to Israel in the summer of 1958 as the leader of the first National Federation of Temple Youth Tour to Israel. He and Rabbi Herbert Weiner presented Torah scrolls to the congregation on behalf of the World Union for Progressive Judaism.
From left to right: Rabbi Herbert Weiner; the author; Shalom Ben Chorin and Dr. Y.L. Benor, founders of Har El congregation.

integrity. The Jewish state will lose its effectiveness as the unifying force in Jewish life.

Through the courts Progressive Judaism has been a prime catalyst for the defense against religious coercion. We should continue efforts to pursue rights through the judicial and legislative frameworks. However, let us be under no illusions. Religious belief, knowledge, commitment and observance cannot be legislated or adjudicated. Even if we should achieve some form of separation, even if we should win some rights through the courts and the Knesset, this would not necessarily lead to greater inculcation of Jewish knowledge and values or to greater observance of Jewish tradition among the secular Israelis.

The ultimate goal is to impact on those individuals in search who have begun to discover that secularism and nationalism are inadequate alternatives to fundamentalist Orthodoxy. This is where the liberal religious movements enter. We project a viable option of a Judaism which is relevant, egalitarian, aesthetic and moral. We proclaim that in Judaism laws and ritual observance are inseparable from the ethical code. The root meaning of the word *halacha* is "to walk," to go forward, to progress. In its very essence *halacha* is progressive.

To retain the spirit of Judaism, the *halacha* should not send forth a cloud of darkness, obfuscating the path through life, but ignite a pillar of enlightenment to illuminate life's purposeful goals.

To keep the Sabbath holy, it should not degenerate into a day of stone-casting and castigation, but rather inspire Jews to capture a glimpse of eternal harmony in the world, the community and the home.

To claim that our biblical forefathers were cartographers divinely appointed to set Israel's geographical boundaries for all time, is not to preserve, but to pervert Judaism.

To categorize Israeli political leaders who "seek peace and pursue it" as enemies of the people — and in the name of God, no less, is to desecrate God's name.

As Jews, we aspire not to a *Pax Romana*, a peace imposed by military might from on high, but to a *Sh'lom Emet*, a peace of truth among equals.

In the sentence after the passage I quoted from the Mishna (Berachot 9:4) we are taught: חייב אדם לברך על הרעה כשם שמברך על הטובה. *"We are obliged to offer a blessing for the bad even as we offer a blessing for the good."* The secret of Jewish survival is our capacity to bless all of life, both the bad and the good. Indeed, we have learned how to transform the bad into the good. Even in the ashes of devastation, we have discovered the seeds of redemption.

So, what is the blessing for the future? That we Jews believe in the future. We believe in the future of the Jewish State. We believe in the future of *Am Yisrael*. We believe in the future of Judaism, and we believe in the future of Progressive Judaism.

The Jewish spirit is epitomized by the prophet Jeremiah:

כי אנכי ידעתי את המחשבות אשר אנכי חושב עליכם נאום ה' מחשבות שלום ולא לרעה לתת לכם אחרית ותקוה. *"I am mindful of the plans I have made concerning you, declares the Lord, plans for your welfare, not for disaster, to give you a future and a hope"* (Jeremiah 29:11).

TAKING A STAND

A. JUDAISM AND SOCIAL JUSTICE

1. Toward a Theology for Social Action

2. *Tikkun Olam* — Can We Repair the World for the Twenty-first Century?

3. Judaism in Pursuit of Economic Justice

4. Peace in Jewish Tradition

Toward a Theology for Social Action*

Were the title of this symposium *"A Theology of Social Justice,"* this assignment would be fairly simple. I would take the fundamental concepts of Judaism — God, Torah, Israel, the Covenant — and show how each of these is related inextricably to standards and goals of justice for men and society. Jewish history, values, and practices would corroborate the inherent Jewish stress on ethics. However, the title of this symposium is *"Toward a Theology for Social Action,"* and that complicates our task considerably.

The phrase *social justice* is general, abstract, and non-controversial. *"Social action"* raises both the hackles and the hecklers. *Social action* implies collective action toward specific social objectives and, to define it even more narrowly, toward political objectives such as the passage of legislation. Social action is a means for achieving the end of social justice. So long as social justice remains a generalized theological imperative or a distant goal, there is general acceptance of the term, but when social action becomes the instrumentality for achieving social justice, then both the means and the end become controversial.

The fitness of social action by religious groups

In a sense, history might be considered the process of redefining the general principles of justice. In 1776, "all men are created equal" meant that some men could live as slaves. In the 1860's it was redefined to mean that no men should live as slaves and that Negroes are entitled to the rights of citizenship. In our day, a new definition evolved which recognizes that equal rights constitute a hollow justice without equal opportunities to secure those rights. We have come to realize that, under the guise of "separate but equal," Negroes are deprived of full equality. Our increased sensitivity to racial discrimination has

---

* A symposium was convened in the Hebrew Union College — Jewish Institute of Religion in 1967 on this subject. This chapter contains excerpts from the paper presented there.

awakened our sense of justice to other fundamental social and economic inequities in society.

Collective action is necessary in order to make the structures and practices of society conform to new definitions of social justice. This collective, or social action invariably results in political conflict, but such conflict is an accepted part of the democratic process. What is not yet fully accepted as basic and proper to the political process is the fitness of social action by religious groups. Even though I am a "social action-nik," I am not unaware of fundamental philosophic and institutional problems concerning the role of religion in society — and I am not uncritical of the methods and procedures followed either by our own movement or by other religious groups — but this is not the arena to discuss those questions.

The broadening scope of religious concern and the increased pace of religious participation in social issues necessitate both the development of expertise by religious activists and the reinterpretation and reapplication of moral values by religious thinkers. This in turn requires a process of constant interchange between practitioners and theoreticians, between activists and scholars.

In the contemporary ferment in the Church, there is a close relationship between Christian thought and Christian action. The new breed of Christian leaders is very much under the influence of the "new theology." It is no coincidence that the intellectual leadership for the new movements is to be found in schools of religion and theological seminaries. The encyclicals pouring forth from Rome, the statements of the World Council of Churches and the National Council of Churches, the spate of books such as *Christian Ethics and the Sit-in; Christianity and Power Politics; Non-violence and the Christian Conscience; War, Poverty, Freedom — The Great Christian Response;* and even *God is for Real, Man* — all attest to this process of rooting the Christian response to these revolutionary times in the Christian heritage.

With one or two exceptions, our Jewish seminaries and our theologians have been quiescent. Does not Judaism have something to say to our world? What distinguishes Jewish action from Christian social action? What distinguishes a synagogue social action committee from the local chapter of the American Civil Liberties Union, whose chairman is in all probability Jewish in any case? If our social action program is not rooted in the Jewish heritage, then we act as Jews, but not in the spirit of Judaism. In the absence of scholarly creativity, one might conclude that our current social action programs are motivated more by חוקת הגוים than by חיקוי לאלוהים, more by imitation of Gentile patterns than by *imitatio Dei*. From a sociological perspective, a good case might be made for the validity of that statement. In our social endeavors, we have frequently converted מה יאמרו הגוים. "What will the Gentiles say?" into a positive force for action. There are many times when the most convincing reason given for engaging in a specific action is "The Catholics and the Protestants have already taken a position..."

I therefore welcome this colloquium as an essential first step in formulating a Jewish theology of social action. The word "Toward" in the title of the symposium is extremely useful. We are not now at the point in our development where we could, in all honesty, eliminate that qualifying word. The plain truth is that among our scholars there is still too much blatant indifference and even outright opposition to the necessity of Jewish social action, to its purposes and its methods. I would therefore like to consider these remarks of mine as preliminary in the process of working "Toward a Theology of Social Action."

I would offer three convictions prerequisite to determining the Jewish dimension in Jewish social action:

1. Tradition is relevant to contemporary social issues

Some of our critics contend that we are what I call "posuk hunters," that first we formulate a position on a current social issue, which, because of our social stance, is invariably on the liberal side of the political spectrum. Then we hunt for a substantiation of our position in traditional sources. Such an approach, say they, is at best to engage in homiletics, and at worst, to violate tradition.

Let us examine this criticism. There is a certain scholarly virtue in emphasizing that when Hillel declared אל תפרוש מן הצבור, he did not mean "Do not separate from the community at large," but because of the context of his life, he really meant "Do not separate from the Jewish community." I suppose there is also justification for maintaining that the Bible, despite its numerous passages of universalistic content and significance, is nevertheless primarily a Jewish response to Jewish problems in a specific period of Jewish history. And I suppose that there is validity in reminding the American Jew that both our status in society and the conditions of our society are radically different from the status of the Jew and the conditions of society when the *halacha* was in its flourishing developmental stages.

But since no situation today is identical with any situation in the past, does this mean that the *halacha* is of no relevance to the modern Jew? Was Samuel Holdheim correct when he said, "The Talmud speaks with the ideology of its own time, and for that time it was right. I speak from the higher ideology of my time, and for this age, I am right." Few of us today would accept the consequences of Holdheim's radical reform. Most of us would rather agree with Franz Rosenzweig, "I am opposed to the notion of 'all or nothing.' Neither 'everything' nor 'nothing' belongs to us, but rather 'something.'"

Is not the search for "something" the dilemma for Reform Judaism in regard to all the *mitzvot*, the ethical as well as the ritual? What of Jewish tradition do we accept and what do we reject, and what are the criteria for our decisions? We know that in order to retain the spirit of Judaism, we need *halacha*, but we have not yet determined how to create a *halacha* consistent with the needs of persons and the demands for historic continuity of the people Israel. There is not as yet, and because we are Reform, will probably never be, any universally acceptable path to the "something" of tradition. That is our real עול התורה, "the yoke of the Torah" which we have taken upon ourselves as a movement. But that is also our promise.

How paradoxical it is, therefore, to find some Reform rabbis, and particularly among the scholarly element within our community, who have rejected the "all or nothing" approach when it comes to theology and ritual, but who do a complete about-face when it comes to social issues. How paradoxical for those whose movement is riddled with the uncertainties and inconsistencies which are the inevitable consequences of the search for "something," to demand total certainty and consistency in the search for relevance in the social arena. How paradoxical to hear some leaders of the very movement which stresses the primacy of the ethical declare that God's revelation permeates every aspect of our lives — except the crucial issues tormenting our society. How paradoxical that those who had to reject the traditional framework of *halacha* in order to try to save the essence of *halacha,* who had to alter the *siyag laTorah* (fence around the Torah) in order to try to save the Torah itself, now suddenly turn Orthodox in one area only. They feel compelled to consider the *siyag* as an impregnable high wall, preventing action in the one dimension which Reform Judaism pioneered in reviving. Shall we, as Reform rabbis, restrict ourselves to offering guidance on matters of ritual and not on matters of conscience?

There are many streams within Judaism. One does not necessarily have to agree with what is considered to be the mainstream. But the rabbi is ordained to be a teacher of Judaism, to study tradition and teach tradition. As such, he is obligated to speak within the context of Judaism, as he sees it, whatever his interpretation may be, even if he has to invent or discover his own stream. He may select, reinterpret, disagree, or reject, but he has no right to ignore.

Whatever potential influence a rabbi has, both within his congregation and the community at large, derives from the fact that he symbolizes Jewish tradition. He is not just another person. He is not just the head of another Jewish organization speaking on behalf of a specified number of Jews. He speaks for Judaism, for a 4,000 year old tradition of morality, a tradition which has developed a unique sensitivity to issues of conscience. Therein lies his status in the eyes of both Jews and non-Jews. Therein lies his expertise. The rabbi may not have an advanced degree in the humanities, but he is supposed to have the most advanced degree in Humanity, in Humaneness. And this is supposed to come from his being a teacher of Judaism and from taking his stand within that framework. Otherwise, he has no right to call himself "rabbi."

I do not want to be a *"posuk* hunter." But I confess that in our effort to be teachers of Judaism, there are times when we have engaged in *posuk* hunting. It would be far better were our stands on current social problems to issue forth from the wellsprings of the Jewish spirit. There are times when that is impossible because, stretch as we may, the issue has no counterpart in historical Jewish experience. Does that mean that we should not concern ourselves with the issue, that we have no conscience except that of the past, that when confronted by injustice, our teeth are set on edge only when our fathers have eaten sour grapes? There are other times when Judaism does have something to say, but its message lies buried, because our scholars have not been aware of nor concerned with the relevance of the Jewish heritage for our time. What we need is a coordinated comprehensive effort to mine our treasure, to translate, collate, and apply our heritage — and this must necessarily come from נטורי קרתא, "the guardians of our city" — our scholars, and especially those who sit on the faculty of our seminaries.

2. Ethics require action and action requires risk

Ethics have meaning only when they are related to human experience. Were it not for the experience of slavery and the Exodus from Egypt, we would never have evolved the concept of freedom. Theology and life interact. Just as faith should motivate a person's actions, so actions shape a person's faith. The imperative "practice what you preach" is made more, not less, significant, by the knowledge that human beings tend to preach what they practice. That is the meaning of מצוה גוררת מצוה "one righteous deed produces another righteous deed." God's justice is an active agent in our lives. We become what we do. Social action nourishes itself, reinforcing our faith and establishing both a framework and a stimulus for further action. In Jewish tradition, salvation for the individual is inseparable from salvation for all mankind, personal ethics are inseparable from social ethics, and in our day social ethics are inseparable from social action.

Knowing when and how to engage in social action is not easy. Social issues are extremely complex. It is only בדיעבד "in retrospect" that the moral dimension becomes obvious to everyone. When we look at the social action of Reform rabbis who, after World War I, stood on picket lines to support the rights of labor to organize, to improve working conditions, and to reduce the 72-hour workweek, we can perceive the moral issue. Their critics at the time did not agree, and many of the rabbis themselves had doubts. When we look back on the August 1963 March on Washington, there would be overwhelming support for the contention that the participation of so many of our rabbis and laymen was both moral and in consonance with Jewish tradition. A month before the March we were not so sure. There was great trepidation as to the political ramifications, as to whether or not it would be good for the cause. There was fear of violence, and potentially a situation in which we would have engaged in illegal acts.

In ethics, in contrast to physics, distance, whether chronological or geographical, sharpens the vision. The closer we are, the more we know, the more do we realize that the realistic options in today's decisions are never between extremes of good and evil, but between alternatives which, by virtue of the political process, are in themselves compromises.

If one looks for guidance only to the past, and expects to find an identical situation, one will look in vain, for no two situations are ever the same. That is why I find the "new morality" of "situation ethics" to be of so little consequence. When Joseph Fletcher contends that the codes of the past no longer are sufficient in themselves to solve the demands of morality in the present, he is saying no more than what Judaism has always maintained. That is why from the *Taryag Mitzvot* (613 commandments) came the *Mishna* and *Gemara*, the *Shulchan Aruch* and the Responsa, the Reform movement and even this colloquium. Unfortunately, "situation ethics" exaggerates the demands of the "situation" and minimizes the demands of "ethics." When Fletcher, the dean of "situation ethics," posits love as the only principle, he is engaging in *Aggadah* (legend) and not *halacha*. As a matter of fact, his discussion is reminiscent of the debate in Bereshit Rabba (24:7) between Ben Azzai, Tanhuma and Akiba, concerning which is the greatest principle in the Torah.

But, if we look at the forces which have generated "situation ethics," there is a message for us. Fletcher's conclusions may be questioned, but he is well motivated. He does not want moral codes to obfuscate or prohibit the moral decisions so necessary to human welfare. The truth is that there are many who are so overwhelmed by the complexities of every situation, that the general rules of tradition become a pretext for inaction and even for lack of concern in the present.

Those who are charged with responsibility in and for the social arena cannot afford the luxury of indecision. Whenever we engage in social action in Washington, we are torn between various alternative courses, none of which is ideal. There is always a risk that our action may be mistaken. There is always a risk in going from the general to the specific. No general rule remains general the minute it is applied to a specific situation, because no two situations are alike. Every general becomes a specific, and every specific becomes a general. For example, were we today to pass a resolution, on behalf of the CCAR, endorsing the President's Civil Rights bill of 1967, that could be considered a specific application of צדק צדק תרדוף, "justice, justice shall you pursue" or some other general ethical rule. However, that specific in practice proves to be just another general. Let us say our resolution would be one page long. The bill consists of many pages. Between now and the time it is approved by the Congress, it will undergo hundreds of changes which are the result of hearings, debates, and political compromise. By the time it comes to a final vote, there will be only two options: that bill or no bill.

   Any decision we might make in regard to the final bill will be a far cry from the original resolution we passed. Action is a risk. We try to minimize the risk by acquiring knowledge. We seek information and counsel from every possible source. But after all is said and done, we must make a decision. To decide not to act is also a decision. It was Cato who said, "Never is one so active as when one does nothing." And it was our rabbis who said הלומד שלא לעשות נוח לו אלו לא נברא. "He who learns without doing something about it, it would have been better if he had not been born." The fact is that on most issues, we do not take positions. In instances when we do engage in social action, we in effect declare that the risk of no action is greater than the risk of mistaken action. If theology has its leap of faith, social justice must have its leap of action.

3. Social action should be viewed as a stimulus for the renewal of tradition

In advance of this colloquium, selected Responsa were distributed entitled "Ethical Attitudes in Medieval Jewry," dealing particularly with problems of informers, crime and punishment. The study of these Responsa is a fascinating exploration into the ethical attitudes and practices of the past. But could it not be much more? These few Responsa would be relevant to present concerns if our approach were oriented accordingly. Our nation is currently engaged in heated controversies over a number of civil liberties questions. What should be done about crime? Should our penal code and system be overhauled? What should be done with the House Un-American Activities Committee? Does government have the right to engage in wiretapping and other invasions of the privacy of the individual? These questions or *sheelot* are presently framed in legislative proposals to which the Congress is going to give its *teshuvah* (response) in the form of laws, which in turn will both reflect and shape public opinion. Are these not real *sheelot* (questions) for us and should not our study of tradition be motivated by the search for a Jewish response to them?

What I am calling for is a renewal of the traditional concept of *Talmud Torah*, from which no method is further removed than that employed in institutions which today bear the name *Talmud Torah*. *Talmud Torah* was not study for the sake of learning *lishma*, for acquiring facts about the past, but rather study for the sake of guiding human conduct in the present. *Talmud Torah* did not begin with theoretical questions such as: what was the biblical attitude toward labor, or what was the medieval attitude toward informers, but with practical questions such as: when do we recite the Shema? (significantly, the first statement in the Mishna). How should the employer treat his employee? What are the obligations of the employee to the employer? The *teshuvot* are answers to contemporary questions by teachers who have selected and interpreted the relevant sources of tradition. *Talmud Torah* is a continuous responsum, a never-ending process of renewing Judaism by reaching discriminatingly into the past to give counsel on current questions.

My criticism of our educational system, from the religious school level to our rabbinical seminaries, is that we are not asking the correct *sheelot*. Social issues are not the only *sheelot*, but they are major ones, and in our day they confront all Jews, regardless of their Jewish knowledge, because they confront all men. Why not begin the process of Jewish education with these vital issues, in recognition that אין אדם לומד תורה אלא ממקום שלבו חפץ, "No one learns Torah except through the impetus of his immediate needs"?

If social action is a fulfillment of Jewish ethics, then it is also an instrument for motivating the study of Judaism. Jewish social action must become a vehicle for creating a *Torat Hayyim* (law of life), a Torah that lives because it addresses itself to life.

At the opening of the Freies Judisches Lehrhaus in Frankfurt, Germany,

Franz Rosenzweig delivered a remarkable address which states the challenge of our day:

> A new 'learning' is about to be born — rather, it has been born. It is a learning in reverse order. A learning that no longer starts from the Torah and leads into life, but the other way round: from life, from a world that knows nothing of the Law, or pretends to know nothing, back to the Torah. That is the sign of the time ... we all know that in being Jews we must not give up anything, not renounce anything, but lead everything back to Judaism. From the periphery back to the center; from the outside, in ... It is not a matter of apologetics, but rather of finding the way back into the heart of our life. And of being confident that this heart is a Jewish heart. For we are Jews.

From the *Journal of the Central Conference of American Rabbis,* January 1968.
Also published in *Judaism and Ethics,* edited by Daniel Jeremy Silver, Ktav Publishing House Inc., 1970.

Tikkun Olam — Can We Repair the World for the Twenty-first Century?*

We convene this 27th International Convention of the World Union for Progressive Judaism in Paris, with the prescient words of the distinguished French Jew, Edmond Fleg, still reverberating in our consciousness. In his remarkable essay (1929) "Why I am a Jew," he framed the ideology which should motivate Jewish leadership, "I am a Jew, because Israel's promise is a universal promise. I am a Jew, because for Israel the world is not finished; men will complete it."

We have come to France to renew our hopes and our obligation to complete the world. We have come to identify with the promise of this Jewish community, the third largest in the world outside Israel. We salute the congregations and leaders in our liberal movement in France for your achievements, and we dedicate ourselves to a higher level of partnership in helping you propagate a vigorous, indigenous and relevant Judaism. When a terrorist bomb exploded outside the walls of this synagogue in 1980 during Sukkot, the Feast of Tabernacles, world Jewry relearned age-old lessons. When the anti-Semite seeks to attack the Jew, where does he go? To the synagogue, the sacred tabernacle of our Jewish heritage. We also should learn that if the anti-Semite cannot distinguish between Orthodox Jews and Liberal Jews, let no Jew separate Jewish hearts and Jewish destiny.

The "old world" of Europe is fast becoming a "new world." Just as the sun and stars are oblivious to geographical boundaries, so will shared values and common causes ultimately transcend vested national interests. The kaleidoscopic changes in technology are reducing the world to one small global village, intensifying the urgent call for interdependence among the human family. We are sanguine about the future of the Jews in the new Europe. Many Jewish communities have recently increased in size and vibrancy. One

---

* This was the theme of the WUPJ International Convention in Paris, France, in 1995. This chapter is based on the keynote address at the Convention.

demographic statistic is striking: the origins of most European Jews are outside the country of their current residence. This reflects contemporary European Jewish mobility in search of new economic and cultural opportunity. In this new Europe, Liberal, also known as Progressive Judaism, confronts a major challenge. Just as we are rising to the challenge in Eastern Europe with our fast developing Progressive Jewish communities in the former Soviet Union, so do we commit ourselves to nurture Jews who are in search of their spiritual roots in western and central Europe.

It is appropriate that we convene this Conference in France. Here it was, two hundred years ago, that Jews first confronted the dilemma of modernity. Here it was that we were forced to respond to the fundamental question with which we have wrestled ever since: How can we Jews take part in modern society as equal citizens, and still preserve our distinctive Jewish identity? Today it is we who pose the question, but history records that it was the leaders of the French Enlightenment who first framed the issue. To begin with, the dilemma was theirs and not ours. How could they proclaim "Liberty, Equality, Fraternity" for all men, and exclude the Jews? How could they issue their "Declaration of the Rights of Man," and not extend the benefits of citizenship to the Jews?

Paradoxically, Voltaire and other molders of the French democratic spirit could not free themselves of their virulent anti-Semitism. How did they attempt to resolve their "Jewish problem?" Citizenship was to be conditioned on the Jews affirming their loyalty to France and demonstrating their capacity to acculturate to the French milieu. The Jews were called upon to cast off the objectionable characteristics that differentiated them from all other Frenchmen. Judaism as a faith was *kosher*; the Jew as a separated people was *treife*. When the Constituent Assembly of 1789 debated the issue of rights for Jews, it was Clermont-Tonnerre, an ardent proponent of equality, who put the issue succinctly. He declared, "To the Jews as a nation — nothing; to the Jews as individuals — everything."

The Jewish collectivity

To resolve the issue of Jewish rights, Napoleon convened an Assembly of Jewish

Notables in 1806 and a Sanhedrin in 1807. He put before them the questions that would determine whether Jews could indeed be loyal citizens of the state, and whether Jewish law would in any way conflict with civil law. The leaders of French Jewry, mostly Orthodox rabbis, gave Napoleon the responses they knew he wanted. Yes, said they, we are willing to pay the price. The process of assimilation had begun. Exclusive Jewish societies were formed for Jews who don't associate with Jews. As has often been the case in other societies, some Jews went far beyond what was expected of them. A wave of conversions to Christianity followed, especially among the more established families. Even the son of the Chief Rabbi, Emanuel Deutz, converted, and his son-in-law who had begun to study for the rabbinate became a priest.

What transpired in France spread to other countries where Jews were emancipated. By the end of the nineteenth century, we Jews were forced to confront an historical paradox. The more we tried to redefine Jewish identity by contracting ourselves into a religion, the more the outside world continued to define us as a people who were different, and therefore legitimate targets for discrimination and persecution.

In 1895, a century after the emancipation, Captain Alfred Dreyfus was convicted of treason and exiled to Devil's Island. Dreyfus, an assimilated Jew, had purchased the ticket to full equality, but the entrance was closed. His trial demonstrated that the pernicious virus of anti-Semitism continued to infect democratic societies, with no relationship to what Jews did or to what they believed. Theodor Herzl, who covered the Dreyfus trial as a journalist, began to propound his ideas for "The Jewish State." The twin forces of assimilation and anti-Semitism were dooming the modern Jew to extinction. The solution proposed by the early Zionist thinkers was to seek a redefinition, to reconstitute ourselves as a people in the Jewish homeland.

The Holocaust demonstrated conclusively that we are indeed a people. Hitler did not care what Jews believed; his goal was not just to kill individual Jews. His goal was to stamp out the entire Jewish people. Conversely, the Jewish state was established not only to save individual Jews, but to preserve the collectivity called the Jewish people and the collective Jewish heritage.

Jewish survival

We have come to the end of the twentieth century. What do we discover? The dilemma first posed two hundred years ago here in France still confronts us: How do we keep the Jewish people alive and at the same time participate in the modern world?

This query must be preceded by an even more profound question. *Why* should the Jewish people be preserved? What is the purpose of Jewish survival? The *Hasidic* teacher, Rabbi Nahman of Bratzlav, once said, "Somewhere there lives a man who asks a question to which there is no answer; but he doesn't know, he cannot know, that his question is actually an answer to the first."

I contend that to pose the question *why* Jewish survival, is a partial response to the question *how* can Jews survive in the modern world.

This brings us to the theme of this conference: *tikkun olam*. In Jewish theology God is manifest not only in human life and in nature, but in the history of the Jewish people. Jewish history has a beginning and it has a goal. To be sure, God created the world, but He purposely left the world incomplete. Why has the Jewish people survived? Because God has chosen us for a sacred mission: *Tikkun olam*, to complete the universe.

This sense of mission distinguished Judaism from every other civilization. The classic civilizations of ancient times, the Egyptians, the Greeks, and the Romans, had historians who recorded historical events, but they had no sense of history. For them, history had no goal, no direction, no purpose. Christianity accepted the Jewish concept of the personal messiah, but the messiah was sent to earth in an act of God's grace in order to redeem individuals. The only choice confronting human beings is to accept or reject him. The challenge confronting Christians demands a leap of faith by individuals. The Jewish messianic era redeems all humanity. Therefore, the challenge confronting Jews demands a leap of action by the Jewish people on behalf of humanity. The entire Jewish people as a collectivity, have been mandated to become God's partner in *Tikkun olam*. The individual Jew is not permitted to escape from this world into another world of spirit or body. *Tikkun olam* is a corporate enterprise, to be achieved through the striving of the entire Jewish people here and now, to shape the future of the world and to establish peace and brotherhood among all the families of humankind.

This concept of *tikkun olam* as the collective mission of the Jewish people has permeated every movement in Jewish life. In the sixteenth century, Isaac Luria elevated *tikkun olam* to the prime component of his kabbalistic philosophy. It was an active force in the ideological development of both Reform Judaism and Zionism. Though they were diametrically opposed, both movements were neo-messianic in character. Both evolved in response to the *why* and *how* of Jewish survival. Reform Judaism proposed that in order to keep the Jewish people alive it was essential to "religionize" the Jewish experience. Zionism proposed that the Jewish experience should be "nationalized." Despite the major differences, they agreed on one objective: The Jewish people were mandated to strive for a distinctive Jewish mission. Classic Zionism for its part proclaimed a secular, messianic goal which projected renewal of the biblical spirit. In the land of Israel, the Jewish people would create a model national society, which would become an *Or lagoyim* — a light unto the nations.

Collective mission

Today we aspire to achieve a synthesis between these two neo-messianic movements. The synthesis between Reform and Zionism is best symbolized in the philosophy of Emil Fackenheim, a liberal rabbi now living in Israel. In a major philosophic thesis entitled *"To mend the world,"* Fackenheim enhanced the meaning of *tikkun olam*. He proposed that we add an additional commandment to the 613 commandments. The 614th commandment is that "Jews are forbidden to give Hitler posthumous victories." How are Jews commanded to "repair the world?" We defy and defeat the "unique and unprecedented evil" of the Holocaust. We keep the Jewish people alive.

To keep the Jewish people alive in the twenty-first century will be a far more complex and tortuous task than heretofore. Our enemies no longer demand our extinction, and our friends no longer demand our assimilation. The Jewish problem is ours, primarily ours. How paradoxical that in this most favorable context, the sense of the collective mission of the Jewish people is dissipating in both Israel and the Diaspora.

In Israel, gone is the image of the *halutz* tilling the soil with a hoe in his hands and a gun at his side, convinced that he is creating a new Jewish society which in turn will impact on all humanity. Israel is moving in the direction of other Western societies. Ambitions for personal success take precedence over group aspirations for a unique Jewish national ethic. Secular nationalism is proving inadequate to preserve the Jewish dimensions of the Jewish state. Numerous surveys demonstrate that among the 80% secular Jews in Israel, interest in Jewish studies at all levels of education, from elementary school through university, is declining at a precipitous rate. Many signs point to a diminishing kinship with world Jewry and a diminishing sense of the Jewish people's historic destiny. The coming of peace, for which we all pray, could very well increase the danger that the State of Israel will achieve "normalcy," and will become a state "like all other states," Jewish in name, but not in character, lacking a commitment to a distinctive Jewish mission.

To the credit of Reform Judaism, we have reinvigorated the social justice component of Judaism. We have demonstrated that Jews are committed to the world, not only to world Jewry. However, here too, we find ominous danger signs. Even while we are expanding our social action programs, we are losing the passion for the Jewish *collective* mission. Look what happened to the Jewish Bund, the socialist workers party organized in Eastern Europe in the beginning of the twentieth century. It proclaimed that the solution to the Jewish problem was a Marxist society. Advocating a socialist form of *tikkun olam*, the Bundists opposed Zionism and Hebrew and were prepared to have the Jewish people disappear once the Marxist Utopia had been created. Ever since emancipation, this has been the tendency of many ardent Jewish social activists who gave higher priority to perfecting their society than to preserving the Jewish people; or, even worse, who believed that striving on behalf of a better society is a substitute for keeping the Jewish people alive.

It is not enough for Reform Jews to be social activists. Social action efforts must help further the collective mission of Jewish peoplehood. When some of our leaders place the universalistic message of Judaism over the particularist concerns of Jewish peoplehood, they err tragically. They forget that the prophets preached their universalistic message to the fiercely particularistic Jewish people. Jewish universalism is rooted in and tempered by Jewish particularism, just as particularism is energized by the universalist impulse. When we fought for the rights of Soviet Jews, we were fighting for the rights of all oppressed peoples in the former Soviet Union. Jews dramatized the inequities and demonstrated the vulnerability of the communist system; thus the breakup of the Russian Empire was accelerated and rights for all other ethnic groups were advanced. When in the United States we led in the struggle for racial equality, we enhanced the rights and status of Jews. When some elements among the civil rights groups turn anti-Semitic, Jewish particularism dictates that we condemn them. The Jewish people is the barometer by which to measure humanity. Our destiny as a people is inseparable from the human condition, even as concern for all humanity is a vested Jewish interest.

Judaism and liberalism

In every society, we see evidence of the dissolution of Jewish peoplehood. We see it in Diaspora Jewry's distancing itself from Israel, a phenomenon that will likely gain momentum when an Israel at peace ceases to be the mobilizing force for Jewish unity. We see it in the diminution of the sense of Jewish community on local and national levels, a factor that has been accelerated by demographic patterns of Jewish mobility. We see it in the disintegration of the high standards of Jewish personal and family values. The turbulent waves of changing societal values are battering the age-long Jewish standards.

In society at large, the liberal religious movements seem incapable of stemming the breakdown in values. Little wonder that the religious right has stepped into the breach with an assault on pluralism, tolerance, and democracy. Within the Jewish world, right-wing Orthodox groups reject the outside world, because they are afraid of its destructive impact. They advocate a return to the ghetto mentality, discovering an anti-Semite lurking around every corner and the lures of secularism seducing every yeshiva student. In the name of God, they defame Judaism and violate the command for *tikkun olam*. Why, then, does the message of right-wing extremism strike a responsive chord? Because it points to fundamental defaults of both secularism and liberal religion.

Our religious liberalism, like liberalism in general, is under attack. Can liberal Judaism restore authenticity and fulfillment to the Jewish experience? Can we recognize the need to root ourselves deeply in the collective psyche of Jewish peoplehood? Can we renew our commitments to the land and heritage of Israel, to traditional values, to intensive Jewish education, to Hebrew as our people's living language, and to a religious lifestyle sanctifying the preservationist components of our unique civilization? Can we do all that and still retain the basic spirit of liberalism, which we declare to be the intrinsic, enduring character of Judaism?

We as a movement have a singular opportunity and obligation. Neither religious extremism nor secular nationalism offers the long-range response to the *why* and *how* of perpetuating the Jewish people. Our message is difficult to articulate and to transmit, because it is not an either/or, but a both/and approach. We cannot repair the world, if we do not repair the Jewish people. We cannot repair the Jewish people, unless we are committed to repairing the world. To what avail do we try to save the world, if we lose the Jewish people? Conversely, to what avail do we preserve the Jewish people, if the people loses its Jewish soul?

Facing tough choices

To be a liberal Jew is to know that there are no easy answers and no simplistic solutions. The extremists in religion and politics know all the answers. There is only one way — their way — to which they ascribe divine endorsement. We totally reject the position of American Orthodox rabbis sitting in the security of New York, who protest against Israel's withdrawal from any inch of occupied territory, and who are prepared to risk every drop of Israeli blood in defense of *halacha*, God's law, to which they claim exclusive rights of interpretation.

We know that to be a liberal Jew is to agonize over tough choices. The Jewish people, who take pride on being *rodfei shalom*, (pursuers of peace), will soon be forced to choose between the "pursuit of peace" and withdrawal from sections of our holy land. We liberals know that the desire to prevent war is never sufficient justification for maintaining a state of war. To save the body, sometimes we have to amputate a limb. To preserve the soul, sometimes we have to compromise pristine principles and cherished goals. We liberals have learned well how to differentiate between being moral and being moralistic, between the sober joy of triumph and the excessive mania of triumphalism.

The Talmud (*Sanhedrin* 98a) recounts a Midrash about Rabbi Joshua ben Levi, who once met the prophet Elijah. He asked him, "When will the messiah come?" Elijah replied, "He is sitting at the gate of Rome among the wretched and the sick. Go ask him yourself." So Joshua ben Levi went to find the messiah and asked him, "When will you come?" The messiah replied, "Today." When the day passed and the messiah did not come, Joshua ben Levi complained to Elijah that the messiah had lied. Elijah said, "You didn't wait until he finished the sentence. He was quoting Psalm 95:7: "Today — if you hearken to God's voice."

The messianic era will come if we but hearken to God's voice. Can we repair the world? Yes, because to be a Jew is to belong to an *Am Segula*, (a treasured people). To be a Jew is to expect more of ourselves than of others, to experience the privilege of setting extraordinary standards of conduct and responsibility for individuals, for the Jewish community, and for the Jewish State. God has given us a unique status in the world. Because He has made us the chosen people, our task is to become a choice people. Because He has given us the promised land, our task is to make it a land of promise. Can we repair the world? Yes, because the essence of the Jewish character is to "choose life." When a funeral procession comes upon a wedding procession in the street, the mourners are obliged to stand aside so that the wedding party can pass. Life conquers death. Can we repair the world? Yes, because we have learned how to transform the ashes of the holocaust into the glow of redemption. *Lamrot hakol*, despite all the tragedy, the Jew is suffused with an innate, infinite capacity for hope. Yes, we the Jewish people, *can* and *will* repair the world.

Judaism in Pursuit of Economic Justice*

> When you have eaten your fill and have built fine houses to live in, and your herds and flocks have multiplied, and your silver and gold have increased, and everything you own has prospered, beware lest your heart grow haughty and you forget the Lord your God, who freed you from the land of Egypt, the house of bondage ... and you say to yourselves, "My own power and the might of my hand have won this wealth for me." Remember that it is the Lord your God who gives you power to get wealth... (Deuteronomy 8:12-18).

Wealth can be a blessing. It can also be a curse. Wealth can be a creative influence; it can also be a destructive force. The history of nations and the biographies of men attest to both. The attitude toward material possessions and the use to which they are put determine whether wealth is good or evil. A society can be judged by the way it treats its disadvantaged. The affluent society that tolerates poverty misuses and abuses its wealth.

Judaism has something to contribute here, not in offering pat solutions to complex problems, but in projecting a system of values directing man to serve God by serving his fellow man. These values, an integral part of Jewish life through the ages, evolved under varying social, economic and political conditions. Judaism does not advocate any economic or political ideology, but it is an advocate of a specific response to life's problems. It speaks to our day in the voice of the past, but in a language which is universal in time and place.

---

* In 1964 the United States government announced a legislative program designated "The war on poverty." A coalition of major national organizations called "The Citizens' Crusade Against Poverty" was established. Walter Reuther, President of the United Automobile Workers, was elected President, and the author was elected Secretary. He was asked to present the teachings of Jewish tradition on economic issues. This chapter contains excerpts from his book "There shall be no poor," to which an introduction was written by Vice President Hubert H. Humphrey.

Wealth belongs to God; life is sacred

"The earth is the Lord's and the fulness thereof; the world and they that dwell therein" (Psalm 24:1). No man and no society are "self-made," declares Judaism. Both the resources of nature and the ingenuity of man are divinely bestowed. Every society builds upon the creativity of previous generations. The wealth of today is the fruition of the accumulated efforts of countless individuals. "Yours, O Lord, is the greatness and the power and the glory and the victory and the majesty, for all that is in the heaven and earth is Yours; ... Both riches and honor come from You" (I Chronicles 29:11, 12). Since wealth comes from God, it must be used to fulfill God's purposes. "Give unto Him what is His, for you and yours are His" (Avot 3:8).

Judaism rejects the concept of "survival of the fittest." Man is not engaged in a struggle for survival against his fellow man. Our sages formulated a philosophy which could be called "survival of the sustainers," succinctly expressed in the saying, "Not only does man sustain man, but all nature does so. The stars and the planets, and even the angels sustain each other" (Tikkun Zohar, 122 T 43). Human life is sacred, so sacred that each person is considered as important as the entire universe. When asked why God made only one man at Creation, instead of populating the earth immediately with many humans, our sages replied that God wanted to teach that, "If one destroys a single person, it is as if he had destroyed the entire world, and if one saves the life of a single person, it is as if he had preserved the entire world" (Mishna Sanhedrin 4.5).

These two emphases — all wealth comes from God; human life is sacred — became the foundation stones for Jewish treatment of the less privileged members of society. Biblical ethics are permeated with laws assuring protection of the poor. These laws relate largely to agriculture, having been developed in an agrarian society. The Bible prescribes that when a field is harvested, the corners are to be left uncut; the field is not to be gone over to pick up the produce which has been overlooked. The gleanings of orchard and vineyard are to be left untouched. All that remains is for the poor, the stranger, the fatherless, and the widow" (Leviticus 19:9 ff; Deuteronomy 24:19 ff).

Every seventh year was a Sabbatical year, during which the land was to lie fallow, and that which grew of itself belonged to all, "that the poor of your people may eat" (Exodus 23:11). All debts were to be canceled. Every fiftieth year was a Jubilee year, during which all lands were to be returned to the families to whom they were originally allocated. The law of the fiftieth year was too complex to be observed and fell into disuse early in Jewish history, but the spirit behind the law was preserved. Our forefathers realized that an unrestricted pursuit of individual economic interest would result in massive concentrations of wealth for the few, and oppressive poverty for the many. They sanctioned competition, but they rejected "rugged individualism." The intent of the law was to restore the balance, to give those who had fallen an opportunity to lift themselves up again. Land was not the permanent possession of any man. "The land shall not be sold in perpetuity; for the land is Mine; for you are strangers and settlers with Me" (Leviticus 25:23).

Jewish ethics sanction the institution of private property. "Let the property of your fellow man be as dear to you as your own" (Avot 2:17). However, Jewish tradition never asserted that property rights take precedence over human rights. Nor did Judaism accept the Puritan emphasis on the acquisition of property and worldly goods as a sign of virtue. On the contrary, for the Jew, human rights have priority over property rights. The tithe prescribed in biblical law was not a voluntary contribution, but an obligation imposed on all, in order that "the stranger and the fatherless and the widow shall come and shall eat and be satisfied" (Deuteronomy 14:19). Any man who was hungry could help himself to the produce in a field at any time, without asking permission of the owner, so long as he did not carry away food to be sold for his own profit (Deuteronomy 23:25, 26).

No man had absolute control over his own property. The person who cut down young trees in his own garden was to be punished, because he had wasted that which did not belong to him. The man who owned a well in a field had to make the water available to the inhabitants of a nearby community. Such requirements evolved out of the fundamental Jewish conviction that material possessions are gifts from God, to be used for the benefit of all men. Wealth, properly used, is a means of preserving and sanctifying life. Improperly used, it is a profanation of God and of the being created in His image.

Poverty leads to dehumanization

The poor man, as much the child of God as the rich man, has been disinherited from his Father's wealth. He has been deprived of his patrimony, of his share of the earth's bounty. Unlike some religions, Judaism does not encourage the ascetic life. Poverty is not the way to piety. Scarcity does not lead to sanctity. The search for holiness is not made easier by the insufficiency of basic necessities. Without the necessary material goods of life, man cannot attain the personal growth and satisfaction essential to human fulfillment. "All the days of the poor are evil" (Proverbs 15:15).

The common saying "Poverty is no disgrace" may offer consolation — to those who are well off. As a statement of morality, an ethical imperative, it would have much to commend it — "Poverty *should be* no disgrace." As a statement of fact, however, it is totally inaccurate. Poverty *is* a disgrace — for those who are poor. Poverty is destructive to the human personality. "The ruin of the poor is their poverty" (Proverbs 10:15).

Our sages taught that poverty was the worst catastrophe that could happen to a person. "If all afflictions in the world were assembled on one side of the scale and poverty on the other, poverty would outweigh them all" (Exodus Rabbah, Mishpatim 31:14). The poor man is the lowliest of God's creatures, not only in the eyes of others, but in his own eyes as well. "When a man needs his fellow men, his face changes color from embarrassment" (Berachot 6).

Humiliation leads to dehumanization. The poor man is not a complete man. "Even his life is not a life," said one teacher (Betzah 32). The afflictions of poverty are so severe that Jewish tradition makes the seemingly radical statement that "the poor man is considered as a dead man" (Nedarim 64b). Poverty is spiritual death. The poor man looks at life from another perspective. Like a space ship circling the moon, he sees only the dark side, while others may see only the bright side. As one sage declared, "The world is darkened for him who has to look forward to the table of others [for sustenance]" (Betzah 32). The poor man's outlook is altered. "The sufferings of poverty cause a person to disregard his own sense [of right] and that of his Maker" (Erubin 41).

The poor are different. The world asks, "Why are their values not like ours? Why are they so dirty or so sullen or so promiscuous or so indolent or so passive or so uncouth or so uneducated or so unambitious? Why are they not like the rest of us?" The Bible accurately states the consequences of difference: "All the brethren of the poor do hate him; how much more do his friends go far from him?" (Proverbs 19:7).

Why are the poor different? Because they are poor. Because material circumstances shape human values. Judaism has never drawn a dichotomy between body and soul as other religions and systems of thought have done. Those who believe that the body is the repository of all evil and the soul of all good, cannot see the dependent relationship between spirit and matter. But the Jew knows that a man's values are in great measure shaped by life experiences. "Where there is no sustenance, there is no learning," declared a teacher of the first century (Avot 3:21). Unless a person has the proper environment, learning cannot take place. To feed the mind, the body must also be fed. To nourish the spiritual life, the physical life must be nourished. A Hasidic rabbi of the nineteenth century expressed it well when he said, "Take care of your own soul and of another man's body, not of your own body and of another man's soul" (Kotzker rebbe).

Poverty does not inevitably lead to ruination, just as wealth does not inevitably lead to well-being. But for the most part, the poor man in an affluent society lives in another world. Psychologically, it is a world of humiliation, a world which fails to see that a man cannot pull himself up by his own bootstraps if he has no boots and no straps. The world which callously calls upon the poor to disregard material circumstances, asks a man to be more than a man and makes him feel less than a man.

Not charity, but justice

To aid the poor is to "rehumanize" children of God. It is to restore rights which have been denied. The elimination of poverty is not an option, a voluntary decision benevolently made by an individual and a society. It is not charity as thought of in our day. The word "charity," originally derived from the Latin *caritas*, meaning "love," has come to have the connotation of a contribution motivated by sentiment. In our day, a person gives charity not because he feels an obligation, but because he is moved by good will or social pressure. Charity is presumed to come from the goodness of the heart. In the Jewish concept of charity, the heart plays an indispensable role. But assistance to the poor is more than love. There is no word in the Hebrew vocabulary for "charity" in the modern sense. The word used is *Tzedakah*, which literally means "righteousness." *Tzedakah* is not an act of condescension from one person to another who is in a lower social and economic status. *Tzedakah* is the fulfillment of an obligation to a fellow-being with equal status before God. It is an act of justice to which the recipient is entitled by right, by virtue of being human.

Because God is a God of justice, the beings created in His image must treat each other with justice. Injustice to man is a desecration of God. "Whoso mocks the poor blasphemes his Maker" (Proverbs 17:5). On the other hand, "He that is gracious unto the poor lends unto the Lord" (Proverbs 19:17). Jewish tradition went so far as to state that "the poor man does more for the rich man than the rich man for the poor man" (Ruth Rabba 5:9; also 19). The poor give the righteous an opportunity to perform good deeds, to sanctify the name of God. Refusal to give charity is considered by Jewish tradition to be idolatry (Tosephta Pe'ah 4:19).

Only the concept of obligatory justice would have impelled Isaiah to thunder his criticism against the leaders of his time:

> It is you who have eaten up the vineyard;
> The spoil of the poor is in your houses;
> What mean you that you crush My people,
> And grind the face of the poor?
> Says the Lord, the God of Hosts.
>
> (Isaiah 3:14, 15)

Throughout the Bible, injustice is constantly identified as failure to relieve the plight of the poor:

> Seek justice, relieve the oppressed,
> Judge the fatherless, plead for the widow.
>
> (Isaiah 1: 17)

Cursed be he who perverts the justice due to the stranger,
fatherless, and widow.

(Deuteronomy 27:19)

Another frequently used Hebrew term for charity is *mitzvah*, which literally means "a divine commandment." Alleviating poverty is a *duty*, stemming not alone from a person's inner sense of love and justice. It is an obligation ordained by God. Our ancient commentators taught that Abraham was more righteous than Job. According to rabbinical tradition, when great suffering befell Job, he attempted to justify himself by saying, "Lord of the world, have I not fed the hungry and clothed the naked?" God conceded that Job had done much for the poor, but he had always waited until the poor came to him, whereas Abraham had gone out of his way to search out the poor. He not only brought them into his home and gave them better treatment than that to which they were accustomed, but he set up inns on the highway so that the poor and the wayfarer would have access to food and drink in time of need (Avot de Rabbi Nathan 7:17a, b). To fulfill a "divine commandment" is not to watch others struggle through the game of life, but to be an active participant, to take initiative, to seek out those who require assistance, even if they do not request it. True charity is to "run after the poor" (Shabbat 104c).

Self-respect — poverty's antidote

Acts of charity are the means, but not the end. The end is to restore the image of the divine to every man. The essential ingredient is human dignity. The manner in which assistance is given is even more important than the assistance itself. The sensitivities of recipients are to be safeguarded at all times. "Better no giving at all than the giving that humiliates" (Hagiga 5a). Every effort was made throughout Jewish history to dispense charity anonymously. "He who gives charity in secret is even greater than Moses" (Bava Batra 3).

In the Temple in Jerusalem, there was a "chamber of secrecy" where the pious placed their gifts and the poor drew for their needs — all in anonymity (Shekalim 5:6). The same practice was observed until modern times. In every synagogue, a charity box with a sign *Matan Beseter* (an anonymous gift) was placed.

The Talmud recounts the lengths to which great scholars went in order to protect the self-respect of the poor. A rabbi and his wife, accustomed to giving alms while recipients were asleep, were surprised when one poor man awoke (Ketuvot 67b). In order not to offend him, they jumped into a still heated oven, risking serious burns. Another rabbi would tie money in a scarf and when he was near a poor man, would fling the gift over his back, so that the poor man would not have to suffer the embarrassment of facing his benefactor (Bava Batra 10b).

Tradition stressed human dignity in declaring that even greater than *Tzedakah* was "*Gemilut hasadim*," or "acts of loving-kindness." "Loving-kindness" entails personal devotion, service, and empathy. "He who gives a coin to a poor man is rewarded with *six* blessings, but he who encourages him with kind words is rewarded with *eleven* blessings" (Bava Batra 9b). The Midrash interprets Isaiah 58:10: "If you draw out your soul to the hungry and satisfy the afflicted soul," to mean "If you have nothing to give a poor man, console him with kind words. Say to him, 'My soul goes out to you, for I have nothing to give you.'" "*Gemilut hasadim*" was considered superior to almsgiving in three ways: "No gift is needed for it but the giving of oneself; it may be done to the rich as well as to the poor; and it may be done not only to the living, but to the dead" (Sukkah 49b).

In connection with funeral practices, an early custom had evolved to bring the deceased into the house of mourning in expensive caskets of silver and gold, whereas the poor were placed in wicker baskets made of willow. The Talmud decreed that everyone should be placed in wicker baskets "in order to give honor to the poor." To this day, Jewish tradition frowns on lavish funeral practices, because "the grave levels all," and the primary emphasis of Jewish burial rituals is to ascribe equal worth to all persons.

Jewish tradition wrestled with the problem of how to preserve the dignity of recipients of charity. People vary in their needs. Some have higher standards of living or higher values than others. If human dignity is the objective of charity, then will not some persons have to be given more than others — and wherein is the justification of such preferential treatment? The rabbis based much of their discussion on the commandment, "If there be among you a needy man... you must open your hand, and lend him *sufficient for whatever he needs*" (Deuteronomy 15:7, 8). The phrase "*for whatever he needs*" was interpreted to mean that if a man did not have sufficient funds to marry, the community should assume responsibility for providing him with the means to support a wife (Sifre Deuteronomy Re'eh 116). The phrase "sufficient for his need" became the peg on which to hang the concept that a man was entitled to be sustained at a standard of living to which he had become accustomed. One Babylonian rabbi sent his son to give a contribution to a poor man on the eve of Yom Kippur. The boy returned to his father and complained that the poor man was not in need since the boy had seen him imbibing precious old wine. Over the protests of his son, the rabbi doubled his normal contribution, on the grounds that the gentleman had been used to a better life than the rabbi had originally thought (Ketuvot, 67b). The Talmud recounts how the great scholar Hillel, learning of a man of high station who had become poor, gave the man a horse to ride, and when he could not find a servant to run before him for three miles, as was the man's custom, Hillel himself ran ahead of him for three miles (*Ibid.*).

These incidents, similar to numerous others recounted in rabbinic literature, were undoubtedly exceptional, but they do serve to transmit the underlying spirit of Judaism. Throughout the Bible, the poor man is not called "poor," but "your brother," thus establishing a relationship of equality between poor and rich. The recipient of charity is a "brother" to the donor. The poor man's needs are spiritual as well as material. Because the poor man lacks material blessings, he is likely to feel inferior. Therefore, treat him like a brother. Spare his feelings. Zealously guard his dignity. Respect from others is poverty's most helpful counterbalance. Self-respect is poverty's most effective antidote.

The highest degree of charity

The verse from Deuteronomy quoted above also became the basis for a highly developed system of loans. "You shall surely open your hand ... and shall surely *lend* him." Throughout rabbinic literature, a loan is emphasized as the finest form of charity. "Greater is he who lends than he who gives, and greater still is he who lends, and with the loan, helps the poor man to help himself" (Shabbat, 63a). Almost a millennium after this was written, the medieval philosopher Maimonides defined the various types of charity and categorized them into his famous "eight degrees of charity," the highest of which is to enable a man to become self-supporting. Until modern times, every Jewish community had a "*Gemilut hesed*" society, whose primary purpose was to grant loans to the needy without interest or security.

Jewish tradition recognized that an outright gift, no matter how well-intentioned, might instill feelings of inferiority in the receiver. However, a loan is a transaction between equals. Sometimes the loan was a delicate fiction. In those instances where a poor man is too proud to accept a gift, one should offer a loan, even though one might never expect to have the money returned, and then subsequently the loan could be considered as a gift (Ketuvot, 67b).

The rabbis dealt in a direct fashion with those who in our day would be called "freeloaders," the poor who exploit the system of welfare. They looked askance at beggars who went from door to door. Instead, the rabbis favored the "silent sufferers." A person should exert every effort not to be dependent on others. "Skin the carcass of a dead beast in the market place, receive thy wages, and do not say, 'I am a great man, and it is beneath my dignity to do such work" (Bava Batra 110a). A person should esteem his independence more than his dignity, even more than his piety (Berachot 8a).

Nevertheless, even though the rabbis maintained a severely critical attitude toward imposters, they were generally liberal in offering them assistance. They realized that even those who made false claim served some purpose. "Be good to imposters. Without them our stinginess would lack its chief excuse" (Ketuvot 68a). No person is beyond human concern. No man is beyond repentance and rehabilitation. No man is so bad that the community may be absolved of responsibility. The response to those who would eliminate or diminish welfare programs because of occasional abuse is to be found in the midrashic comment on a biblical verse: "If your brother be waxen poor, you shall not suffer him to fall. He is like a load resting on a wall; one man can then hold it, and prevent it from falling, but if it has once fallen to the ground, five men cannot raise it up again. And even if you have strengthened him four or five times, you must (if he needs it) strengthen him yet again" (Sifra 109b). The task is never finished until "your brother" is raised from a condition of dependence to the state of self-reliance and self-support.

The organized Jewish community

In the Talmudic period, it became clear that the amelioration of poverty was too complex a task to be left to individuals or to privately organized charity groups. Personal charity alone was too haphazard and spasmodic. The Jewish community supplemented the obligations of private charity with an elaborate system of public welfare — the first in history. Jewish tradition has always been nurtured in and through the community. Hillel's famous "Do not separate thyself from the community" sets the pattern (Avot, 2:5). Even Jewish worship is a communal experience. Almost all the prayers, including those recited by an individual in private, are written in the plural. So it was only natural for the Jew to look upon poverty as the responsibility of the entire community. The existence of the poor was an indication of social inequity which had to be rectified by society itself. The system of social welfare became the means of restoring integrity to the community.

The practices and theories of Jewish philanthropy anticipated many of the most advanced concepts of modern social work and became the basis for the excellent programs and high standards of Jewish welfare agencies. The organization of Jewish welfare evolved through the centuries, but the principles were established during the second century.

Every Jewish community had two basic funds. The first was called *kuppah*, or "box," and served the local poor only. The indigent were given funds to supply their needs for an entire week. The second fund was called *Tamchui*, or "bowl," and consisted of a daily distribution of food to both itinerants and residents. The administrators of the funds were selected from among the leaders of the community and were expected to be persons of the highest integrity. The *kuppah* was administered by three trustees who acted as a *Bet Din*, or "court," to determine the merit of applicants and the amounts to be given.

The fund was operated under the strictest regulations. Collections were never made by one person, but always by two, in order to avoid suspicion. The collectors were authorized to tax all members of the community according to their capacity to pay, and if necessary, to seize property until the assessed amount was forthcoming. All members of the community were expected to contribute, even those who were themselves recipients of charity — testimony to the principle that no person was free of responsibility for the welfare of all. "He who does not accept his part of the sufferings of the community will not share in the comfort it will receive" (Ta'anit 11a).

Community responsibility

By the Middle Ages, community responsibility encompassed every aspect of life, as the community fulfilled obligations which its individual members were incapable of fulfilling. The Jewish community regulated market prices so that the poor could purchase food and other basic commodities at cost. Wayfarers were issued tickets, good for meals and lodging at homes of members of the community who took turns in offering hospitality. Both these practices anticipated "meal-tickets" and modern food-stamp plans. Jewish communities even established "rent control," directing that the poor be given housing at rates they could afford. In Lithuania, local trade barriers were relaxed for poor refugees. When poor young immigrants came from other places, the community would support them until they completed their education or learned a trade.

The organization of charity became so specialized that numerous societies were established in order to keep pace with all the needs. Each of the following functions was assumed by a different society on behalf of the community at large: visiting the sick, burying the dead, furnishing dowries to poor girls, providing clothing, ransoming captives, supplying maternity needs, and providing special foods and ritual objects for holidays. A host of other miscellaneous societies were formed to cover every possible area of need. In addition, there were public inns for travelers, homes for the aged, orphanages, and free medical care. As early as the eleventh century, a *Hekdesh* or "hospital" was established by the Jewish community of Cologne — primarily for the poor. Many of the activities centered in and around the synagogue, which in some communities was the only building of a public character. Caring for the poor became a matter of civic pride. Scholars were warned not to live in a community which did not have an adequate system of public welfare. A community was judged by the extent to which it became the agent for guaranteeing just treatment to all its inhabitants.

This brief review of Jewish tradition demonstrates the relevance of Jewish values to contemporary social issues. Jews developed unique forms of social welfare legislation dealing with poverty, medical care, education and the rights of labor. The Talmud states, "There is no poverty in a place of wealth" (Shabbat 102). Where a society is really wealthy, it understands its purposes and allocates its resources in a manner which eliminates human want, offering an equal opportunity to all to enjoy "the fullness of the earth."

Excerpted from *There Shall Be No Poor*, published by the Union of American Hebrew Congregations for the Commission on Social Action of Reform Judaism, 1965.

Peace in Jewish Tradition*

J ewish values are applicable to the vicissitudes of international relations. They do not offer instant solutions, nor are they to be considered pronouncements spelling out the foreign policy which a modern nation should pursue under specific circumstances. They provide moral guidelines rather than practical guideposts and comprise a framework in which both national purpose and international harmony can be charted. Central to these Jewish values is the moral imperative of seeking peace and pursuing it.

Attitudes in antiquity

The records of antiquity are mainly chronicles of war. The monuments, hieroglyphics, and epics left by ancient man recall in colorful detail glorious victories over enemies, with the gods playing a crucial role. A deity, like man, was tested by his capacity to wage war. In Homer's *Iliad*, the outcome of battles in the Trojan War was determined by the strength of the deities representing the opposing sides. Victory of a people meant prepotency for the deity, and defeat represented either the inferiority of a deity or a sign that he was angry and must be appeased.

When an ancient nation was conquered, its people generally adopted the cult of the conquerors on grounds that the conquering deity must obviously be more powerful than the conquered deity. For some ancient peoples, war was the ideal state. The heaven of the Norseman, Valhalla, was a "Hall of the Slain" from which the heroes rode out every morning to spend the day in battle. War was thus the accepted pattern of relations between nations.

---

* In the context of the Vietnam war, the author wrote a book *"Thy Most Precious Gift — Peace in Jewish Tradition,"* which presented the relevance of Jewish values to issues of international relations. Excerpts from the book are presented in this chapter.

Against the indiscriminate use of force

The Bible, being a record of the historical experience of the children of Israel in primitive times, contains many militaristic passages. War is accepted as a legitimate instrument of foreign policy. Israel was commanded by God to acquire the land of Canaan by conquest and to evict or destroy its inhabitants. The memory of the bitter enemy Amalek was to be obliterated. After the Exodus from Egypt, God is jubilantly proclaimed as a "man of war" (Exodus 15:3): "For the Lord your God is He that goeth with you, to fight for you against your enemies, to save you" (Deuteronomy 20:4). Young David challenges Goliath to fight "in the name of the Lord of hosts, the God of the armies of Israel" (I Samuel 17:45). The children of Israel carry the ark in battle as an assurance of victory (I Samuel 4, 5, 6). The books of Judges, Samuel, and Kings report incidents of armed ruthlessness and merciless destruction.

By concentrating on passages such as the above, it would be possible to portray the ancient Hebrews as a warlike people, no different from their contemporaries. However, such a reading of the Bible, made particularly by detractors of Judaism, is highly inaccurate. While there are numerous passages glorifying combat and justifying wars, the bulk of biblical writings reject militarism and the indiscriminate use of force.

Condemnation of violence

Chapter 34 of Genesis reveals a classic example of condemnation of deeds of violence. When Jacob's daughter, Dinah, is dishonored by Shechem, the son of Hamor, two of Jacob's sons, Simeon and Levi, resort to treachery. They consent to give their sister to Shechem as a wife on condition that he and all the males of the community be circumcised. Hamor and Shechem agree, and, while they are recuperating from the physical effects of the circumcision, Simeon and Levi steal into the city and slay all the males. The Bible considers this a dastardly deed. The dishonor to their sister did not justify the acts of vengeance and the indiscriminate slaughter perpetrated by Simeon and Levi. Jacob never forgives his sons and even on his dying day curses their action.

War and its instruments are condemned throughout the Bible. God himself is pictured as despising war: "And I will break the bow and the sword and the battle out of the land, and will make them to lie down safely" (Hosea 2:20).

David and the arrogance of power

There is no better illustration of the fundamental antipathy to war than the gradual reinterpretation of King David's personality. From the perspective of the military historian, David was the great hero of ancient Israel. Through the might of his armies and his military prowess, he conquered a vast territory, united the disparate tribes, and established the largest and most powerful empire of ancient Israel.

Yet the Bible focuses sharply on the transgressions and character defects which were the consequences of his use of power. The most dramatic of these transgressions is recounted in II Samuel 11, 12. David engages in illicit relations with Bathsheba, the wife of Uriah the Hittite. Then he orders Uriah to be placed in the front of the battle lines where he is killed. Following Uriah's death, David marries Bathsheba.

In a classic condemnation of the arrogance of power, the prophet Nathan denounces David for his sin and prophesies the death of the first child Bathsheba bears to David as punishment. When, as the crowning achievement of his life, David wants to erect the Temple in Jerusalem, he is prohibited from doing so: " ... God said unto me: "You shall not build a house for My name, because you are a man of war, and have shed blood" (I Chronicles 28:3).

David transformed into scholar

In the post-biblical literature, the rabbis attempted to reconstruct the character of David, muting his aggressive characteristics and stressing his creative and contemplative qualities. Tradition minimized his military feats and emphasized his literary achievements and musical talents. The entire Book of Psalms was ascribed to his authorship, even though only 73 of the psalms designate David as author. Rabbinic literature portrayed him as devoting most of his time to prayer and the study of Torah. So anxious was he for scholarship that he was satisfied with "sixty breaths of sleep," and every midnight the strings of his harp would begin to vibrate on their own and awaken him to study. The character of the great warrior of biblical times thus became transformed. By talmudic times, David was considered to be a humble man of piety (Sukkot 26b and Berachot 36).

The metamorphosis of David was true of others as well. In Genesis 14:14, Abraham leads forth 318 "trained men" to smite those who captured Lot. In the Talmud, these same men are considered to be scholars. In the Bible, Jacob refers to the portions he amassed "with my sword and with my bow" (Genesis 48:22). In the Talmud, the rabbis interpret Jacob's "sword" to be "prayer" and his "bow" to be "supplication." The "men of might, even seven thousand ... all of them strong and apt for war" of II Kings 24:16 are transformed by the rabbis into scholars of the law (Sanhedrin 38a).

Instruments of war tainted

Post-biblical interpretations reflect an abhorrence of the use of instruments of war for anything associated with sacred observances. The Torah prohibited the use of tools in the erection of sacrificial altars. "And if you make Me an altar of stone, you shall not build it of hewn stones; for if you lift up your tool (cherev — literally, "sword") upon it, you have profaned it" (Exodus 20:22).

The disapproval of war led the rabbis to interpret the verse as follows: "Iron shortens life, whilst the altar prolongs it. The sword, or weapon of iron, is the symbol of strife; whereas the altar is the symbol of reconciliation and peace between God and man, and between man and his fellow" (Mechilta Jethro 25 and Sifra Kedoshim X1, 8).

Jewish festivals demilitarized

The rabbinic emphasis on peace modified not only the biblical portrayal of personalities and the character of legislation but also the character of festivals. Most noteworthy is the evolution of Chanukah. The major historical source for Chanukah is to be found in the Books of the Maccabees which recount the story of rebellion against tyranny and the regaining of freedom through a military victory. But, as the observance of the festival evolved through the centuries, the triumph of arms and the subsequent restoration of national power were de-emphasized. The religious rather than the martial aspects were stressed.

In all of rabbinic literature, there is not one word extolling the military or political aspects of the Maccabean victory. Thus, when the Talmud describes the "miracle which was wrought," it refers to "the oil in the cruse (which) burned eight days" and not to "the might of the Hasmonean" (Shabbat 23b). The central observance of Chanukah, the kindling of lights, was a religious event, accompanied by blessings and commemorating the rededication of the Temple.

A rabbinical legend offers a reason other than the flask of oil for the kindling of lights for eight days. "When the son of the Hasmonean, the high priest, defeated the Greeks, they entered the Temple and found there eight iron spears. They stuck candles in these spears and kindled them" (Pesikta Rabati 2). This Midrash epitomizes the rabbinic determination to transform the instruments of war into instruments of peace.

Peace in post-biblical literature

The yearning for peace resounded throughout post-biblical literature. Among the many statements are the following:

> Bar Kapparah said: If the heavenly beings who are free from envy and hatred and rivalry are in need of peace, how much more are the lower beings, who are subject to hatred, rivalry, and envy, in need of peace (Deuteronomy Rabbah v. 15).

> Great is peace, because peace is to the earth what yeast is to the dough. If the Holy One, blessed be He, had not given peace to the earth, the sword and wild beasts would desolate the world (Baraita de Perek Hashalom).

> Great is peace — for at the hour the Messiah reveals Himself unto Israel, He will begin in no other way than with "Peace." As it is written: "How beautiful upon the mountains are the feet of

the messenger of good tidings, that announceth peace" (Baraita de-Perek-ha-Shalom).

Great is peace, for it is equal to everything, as it is said (Proverbs 3:17) "He makes peace and creates all" (Isaiah 45:7).

The Torah is compared only with peace, as it is said, "Her ways are ways of pleasantness, and all her paths are peace" (Proverbs 3:17).

Great is peace, for God's name is peace, as it is said (Judges 6:24). "And he called the Lord peace" (Leviticus Rabbah 1X, 9).

The rabbis believed that peace was intended as part of God's plan for mankind even before the creation of the universe.

Mankind was first created as a single individual because of the various families which have issued from him, that they should not quarrel one with the other. Since now there is so much strife although he was created one, how much more so if there had been two created! (Sanhedrin 38a).

It is not without significance that the following passage was selected as the last in the Mishnah:

See how beloved is peace; when God sought to bless Israel, He found no other vessel which could comprehend all the blessings wherewith He would bless them, save peace. How do we know it? For it is said (Psalms 29:11)"The Lord will give strength unto His people; the Lord will bless His people with peace" (Uktzin 3:12 and Deuteronomy Rabbah v.15).

Seek peace and pursue it

Judaism contends that it only takes one nation to make war but two to make peace. Therefore, though a nation should be prepared to defend itself, it should exhaust all possibilities for peacemaking before embarking on war. The twentieth chapter of Deuteronomy comprises groundrules for warfare, but it is significant that the Midrash (rabbinical commentaries on the Bible) concentrates on only one sentence of that chapter. "When you draw nigh unto a city to fight against it, then proclaim peace unto it" (Deuteronomy 20:10).

The sages considered the obligation to achieve peace more urgent than the other commandments. "Seek peace and pursue it" (Psalms 34:15), became a watchword of the faith.

Forbearance, conciliation, forgiveness

In order to "seek peace and pursue it," a person or nation has to be willing to demonstrate forbearance toward others. Forbearance leads to understanding, which in turn leads to conciliation, which in turn may lead to forgiveness.

> Samuel ibn Nagrela, a Spanish Jewish poet of the eleventh century, was vizier to the king of Granada. One day a certain man cursed Samuel in the presence of the king. The king commanded Samuel to punish the offender by cutting out his tongue. However, Samuel treated his enemy kindly, whereupon the curses became blessings. When the king next saw the offender, he was astonished to note that Samuel had not carried out his command. When asked why not, Samuel replied, "I have torn out his angry tongue and given him instead a kind one" (recounted by J.H. Hertz, the Pentateuch and Haftorahs, p.501).

A person may be an enemy but he does not cease to be a human being and as such, his person and his possessions are entitled to respect. A neighbor may violate his neighborly obligations to you but this does not free you from fulfilling your duty toward him.

> If you meet your enemy's ox or his ass going astray, you shall surely bring it back to him again. If you see the ox of your enemy prostrate under the burden and would refrain from raising it, you must nevertheless raise it with him (Exodus 23:4, 5).

A person has a significant obligation to preserve the life of one's enemy, to see that basic human needs are fulfilled: "If your enemy is hungry, give him bread to eat; if he is thirsty, give him water to drink; you will be heaping live coals on his head, and the Lord will reward you" (Proverbs 25:21, 22). The commentaries on this verse indicate that more than altruism is involved, that human consideration of an enemy leads to concrete results. The Hebrew word for "reward" is related to the word shalom, "peace." The medieval commentator Rashi says that the Hebrew vocalization could be changed from *Yeshalem*, "the Lord will reward" to *Yashlim*, "the Lord will cause peace to be established." Thus, tradition maintained that if evil was met with good, peace could be the reward.

> Who is the mightiest of heroes? He who makes the enemy his friend (Avot Rabbi Natan 23).

What is true in the relations between individuals is valid in the relations between nations. Ancient Egypt had deprived the Hebrews of their liberty and forced them to become slave laborers. That enslavement was the most traumatic experience ingrained in the psyche of the Jew. Yet both biblical and post-biblical writings go to considerable length to delineate between the Egyptian people themselves and the misdeeds of their rulers.

> When a human being suffers an injury, he remembers it for ever. But God is not thus, Israel in Egypt underwent servitude with mortars and bricks; yet after all the wrongs which the Egyptians committed, Scripture has compassion on them. It says: "You shall not abhor an Egyptian, for you were a stranger in his land" (Deuteronomy 23:8), (Deuteronomy Rabbah 5,14).

Egypt, despite all its perfidy, was part of the family of nations and included in God's plan for the redemption of all mankind. When the prophets talk about the "end of days," Egypt and Assyria, the enemies and conquerors of the Hebrews, have an honored place as equals to Israel in the scheme of international relations.

> In that day Israel shall be a third partner with Egypt and

Assyria as a blessing on earth; for The Lord of hosts will bless
them saying: "Blessed be My people, Egypt, My handiwork
Assyria and my very own Israel" (Isaiah 19:23-25).

The rabbis use as a classic instance the incident of the drowning of the
Egyptians in the Red Sea. When the ministering angels wished to sing praise to
God at the moment of Egyptian defeat, God rebuked them severely: "What? The
work of my hands (the Egyptians) *is* drowning in the sea and you would chant
hymns before M*e"!*

History's higher purpose

The Jewish attitude toward peace derives from a particular conception of the
meaning of history. God is the God of history. "I am the Lord your God, who
brought you out of the land of Egypt, out of the house of bondage" (Exodus 20:2).

The Exodus experience instilled in the Jewish people a sense of history. The
struggles of the slaves to attain justice for themselves generated in them a
passion to attain justice for all men. Mankind has a purpose. History has a goal,
the *acharit hayamim* "the end of days," or as the concept was later refined in the
prophetic period, the *yemot hamashiach*, "the days of the Messiah," when all
men and all nations and even the world of nature would be at peace and live in
harmony.

This concept of historic purpose was unknown in the ancient world. For
the Greeks, the fate of nations, as well as of individuals, was predetermined.
There was no impelling urge to eliminate war, because war was the means by
which nations regulated their relations with each other. (Plato, in his projection
of the ideal state, provides for a class of warriors whose function it would be not
only to defend their state against the attacking enemy but to attack other
nations on occasion for the sake of gain.) The Golden Age was in the past and
men looked backward toward perfection, nobility, goodness. But for the Jew,
perfection lay in the future. The goal of history was to usher in the good, "to
perfect the world under the Kingdom of God."

Swords into plowshares

> "And he shall judge between many peoples,
> And shall decide concerning mighty nations far off;
> And they shall beat their swords into plowshares,
> And their spears into pruning hooks;
> Nation shall not lift up sword against nation,
> Neither shall they learn war any more.
> But they shall sit every man under his vine and his fig tree;
> And none shall make them afraid;
> For the mouth of the Lord of hosts has spoken" (Micah 4:3-4 and,
> with some variations Isaiah 2:4).

A peace for human beings

The "end of days" envisioned by Micah and Isaiah was not to be miraculously thrust into the world through divine intervention. Nor was it to be superimposed through God's grace after men, despairing of their human fallibility, had called upon Him for redemption. It was to be ushered in by ordinary human beings who had accepted the Law of God and its implications for regulating conduct between nations. The "end of days" was envisioned as a stage in history, not an apocalyptic era. It was a consequence of man's learning to live with his fellow man.

Peace was projected as attainable for all humankind, to be realized through human efforts. War was abnormal, an aberration, an abomination, a retrogression. It was not inevitable and could be eliminated in the future. Thus, not war but peace was the higher purpose of history.

From *"Thy most precious gift: peace in Jewish tradition,"* published by the UAHC for the Commission on Social Action of Reform Judaism, 1974.

B. REFORM ZIONISM

Toward a Theology of Reform Zionism*

In recent years, a revisionist form of non-Zionism has evolved within American Jewry. The non-Zionism of this generation is unlike that of the pre-state era. Then, it was possible to reject the Zionist idea, and even to establish an organization — the American Council for Judaism — to oppose it. Contemporary non-Zionism is far from anti-Zionism. Today, no responsible American Jewish leader would oppose the existence of the Jewish state. Nor would anyone deny the contributions made by the State of Israel in preserving Jewish culture, renewing the Hebrew language, injecting Jewish pride and commitment, and providing a haven for Jewish communities threatened with discrimination, persecution and poverty.

The basic tenet of the revisionist theory is simple: the State of Israel does not fulfill the Zionist vision; the real does not match the ideal. Therefore, since the Jewish people cannot rely on the Jewish state to assure its continued survival, it must develop alternative resources and instrumentalities. The non-Zionist approach does not deny or reject, but rather de-emphasizes the State of Israel.

A non-Zionist approach

This non-Zionist approach is gaining strength within the ranks of the American Reform rabbinate. A recent expression projects the mood of some influential leaders of our movement. A distinguished professor of the Hebrew Union College-Jewish Institute of Religion, has written an article entitled, *"On the Passing of the Ethnic Era."* He writes:

> "I think I am only reporting the Emperor's nakedness when I say that Israelocentrism can no longer be the engine driving

---

* The affiliation of Reform Zionism with the Zionist movement was not only organizational, but also ideological. This article served to crystallize the need for a Think Tank in order to define Reform Zionism.

American Jewish life, keeping us ahead of the assimilation
threatening to overtake us … The trajectory of our mass
disillusionment runs from Sabra and Shatila through the
intifada and the 'Who is a Jew' controversy to the recent
huckstering to form a new Israeli administration. Only true
believers can still envision today's State of Israel as our ethnic
'Spiritual center'."

What does the Professor of Jewish Thought offer as a replacement for
Israelocentrism? Belief. "Belief is now our major priority"[1]. Why do I define the
above statement as non-Zionist in character? Because it diminishes the
importance of the Jewish state as a prerequisite instrumentality for Jewish
survival. Is Jewish peoplehood a lesser dimension of Jewishness than belief? Is
ethnicity passe and faith our primary passion? Or, as some would contend, is
Israel only a reaction to the Holocaust, only an insurance policy against anti-
Semitism? The Jerusalem Platform of the World Zionist Organization declares
as the primary aim of Zionism, "The unity of the Jewish people and the
centrality of Israel." For the professor, ethnicity is secondary to belief. He writes,
"More than ever, the key issue is religious." For him, the reality of Israel is a
source of disappointment and disunity.

On the surface, the gap between contemporary Zionists and non-Zionists
is not so wide as in the pre-state era. Both groups would agree that it is essential
to have *both* a strong Israel *and* a strong Diaspora and that it is the task of Jewish
leadership to encourage a strengthened interdependence between the two.
Similarly, the issue is not one of belief *or* peoplehood but rather of *both* belief *and*
peoplehood.

In our day, the differences between Zionism and non-Zionism are much
more subtle and are expressed in nuance and emphasis. However, these subtle
differences are crucial to determining Jewish public policy. Given limited funds,
how and where does world Jewry expend its material and human resources?
Where do we direct the energies of world Jewry? What kinds of Jewish
educational institutions do we establish and sustain? What is the emphasis of
the curriculum? What is the role of the Hebrew language? Of Jewish
observance? To what extent do we encourage learning and work experiences in

Israel? What should be the interrelationship between Israel and the Diaspora? To what extent is Diaspora Reform Jewry obligated to provide funds for the development of Progressive Judaism in Israel and around the world? What are the obligations of Reform Jews to Israel and to world Jewry?

Let us debate the differences

In the final analysis, the responses to these and other questions will be determined by individual convictions and movement commitments. In fact, within our movement there are fundamental differences of opinion on the role of Israel and the Jewish people in Reform Jewish ideology. Rather than mute or modulate the differences, it is essential to bring them to the fore and to debate them in public. As a religious movement, we cannot limit our relationship to the Jewish state to the pragmatic dimensions of moral, political and economic support. A religious movement is obligated to make the effort to incorporate the phenomenon of Zionism into the very essence of belief and observance. Unless Zionism is integral to our religious *Weltanschauung* (world view) we, as a movement, will relate to the Jewish state as a passing phenomenon only. Therefore, the ultimate difference between the Zionist and non-Zionist approach is a question of ideology. Religious non-Zionists can afford to delineate between religion and ethnicity and to place religion on a higher plane. In contrast, religious Zionists can never separate belief from ethnicity, nor religion from peoplehood, nor Judaism from Zionism. They must find a way of integrating and binding these inseparable elements even more strongly.

Reform Jews have been so consumed with the intermittent crises of the Middle East and the problems inherent in the character of Israeli society and Israel-Diaspora relations that we have not devoted our attention to formulating the meaning of Israel in theological terms. I, therefore, offer the following as one religious Zionist view.

The theological significance of Zionism

Should Progressive Judaism ascribe *theological* significance to the *State* of Israel?

In posing this question, I assume universal agreement that *Am Yisrael*, the *people* of Israel, and *Eretz Yisrael*, the *land* of Israel, comprise fundamental planks in the ideological platform of Progressive Judaism. However, can *Medinat Yisrael*, the secular *state* of Israel, be incorporated into a system of *theological* belief? Does *political* Zionism have religious import?

These questions should be raised under any circumstances and at all times. However, I suspect that some people might have formulated one response in 1948, 1967 and 1973 — dates marking Israel's miracle-like military victories against overwhelming threats of annihilation — and arrive at totally different responses during times of frustration, disappointment and disillusionment with the State of Israel. It is precisely during these latter times of stress that religious conviction is tested. Whereas Jewish theology is inextricable from classic Jewish historical experiences such as the Exodus, Jewish belief should not fluctuate in response to all the vagaries of contemporary events. We should strive for a deeply-rooted, consistent, systematic and enduring faith.

It is in this context that I frame my response: the establishment of the State of Israel and commitment to its security, development and well-being represent a fundamental and integral premise of Progressive Jewish *belief*. In making this statement, it is essential to delineate between two distinct realities, at times conflicting and at times confusing.

The first reality: the State of Israel is a state like all other states. As a modern political movement, Zionism parallels the other movements of national renaissance that sprouted in the nineteenth and twentieth centuries. To be sure, the Jewish people's political claim to national independence was reinforced by a moral appeal to the world's conscience following the Holocaust. However, to the extent that the Jewish state is one among many states, it is to be judged by the same criteria of international law and democratic values as all other states. No special religious sanctity inheres in the secular instrumentalities of any state. Indeed, the Western democratic world has been sensitized to the potential dangers prevalent in societies that merge components of religion and nationalism.

An eternal covenant

The second reality: the State of Israel represents the return to the land of Israel and the restoration of the Jewish people's sovereignty. As such, its very establishment fulfills sanctified religious aspirations, even as its continued existence attests to profound religious convictions. These aspirations and convictions are rooted in the Jewish concept of the *covenant* between God and Israel. The covenant is the central theme of the Bible, indeed of all Jewish history. God and the Jewish people have made an eternal pact that obligates the people to serve God by preserving distinctive patterns of life, worship, and morality. This eternal covenant between God and the people Israel is inseparable from the *land* of Israel. "I will maintain My *covenant* between Me and you, and your offspring to come, as an everlasting covenant throughout the ages, to be God to you and to your offspring to come. I give the land you sojourn in to you and your offspring to come, all the land of Canaan, as an everlasting possession. I will be their God" (Genesis 17:7-8).

The *land* of Israel is thus the setting for keeping the *covenant*. When Christianity evolved, it recognized the centrality of the covenant. It even used the terminology of Judaism to the point where the entire New Testament is called in Hebrew — *"ha-b'rit ha-hadashah,"* the New Covenant. But in contrast to Judaism, the Christian concept of covenant is defined as an obligation between God and every human being. The Christian covenant is not tied to any specific land or people. Every person can make a personal covenant with God.

A role model

For Judaism, the covenant is a *collective* obligation, the fulfillment of which requires *collective* action in a particular place — the land of Israel. After the destruction of the Temple and the Exile, the Jewish people was compelled to reorient itself to maintaining the covenant through the collectivity of the Jewish community. But the vision of fulfilling the covenant through return to the land of Israel was retained in prayer and study. All the classic texts of tradition are predicated on the assumption that Jews will be restored to their land. Maimonides' *Mishneh Torah* is a compilation of laws to be observed in the future, when Jews will live as a sovereign people once again in their land. Maimonides defines the responsibilities of the future Jewish government and its leaders, the rules of warfare, the obligations of citizens toward the Jewish society and of the Jewish society toward its citizens, and a host of other regulations to be observed within the Jewish sovereignty. The conviction that Jews would return to the land was so pervasive that Shabbetai Zevi and other pseudo-messiahs could inspire tens of thousands of Jews to pack their belongings overnight and start on the tortuous trek to the Holy Land.

The return to Israel was inextricable from the messianic vision. Jewish particularism was rooted in a profound universalism. How could Jews bring about the era of fellowship and peace for all humankind? By creating in the land of Israel a just society that would serve as a role model for all other societies. It is not enough for the individual to find the way to God. The individual must be part of a family, his or her own family, then the family of his or her community, then the family of his or her people, and finally the family of nations. *Tikkun olam* is to be initiated by the people Israel in the land of Israel. *"At'halta d'geulah"* (the beginning of the messianic redemption), is to start with the Jewish people keeping its covenant with God by perfecting the Jewish society in the land assigned to the Jews by God.

This amalgam of religio-nationalism, rooted in biblical and post-biblical literature, provides the foundation and the inspiration for contemporary Zionism. It makes of Zionism far more than a political ideological movement. It also helps to explain much of the current ideological confusion.

Take, for example, the status of Jews in the Western world. The fundamental premise of Western democracy is to grant equal rights and civil liberties to all individuals, irrespective of national origin, race or creed. Society should judge each person on the basis of individual merit and should be oblivious to ethnic or religious identity. In America, Jewish communal organizations expend vast funds and energies to preserve the principle of separation of religion and state. The secular, non-sectarian character of the state is credited with providing the framework of equal opportunity for Jews as individuals on a par with all other citizens. In contrast, modern Zionism was initiated not to grant equal rights to Jews as *individuals*, but to assure equal rights to the Jews as a *people*. For this reason, Herzl entitled his classic work *The Jewish State*.

Jewish life in Israel and in the Diaspora

In the Diaspora, Jewish life is voluntary. A person is free to decide on Jewish identity and the extent of participation in, and support of, the Jewish community. In Israel, Jewish identity is compulsory. By virtue of living in a Jewish state, the individual Jew is obligated to identify as a Jew, pay taxes to the Jewish state and fight in the army to defend the Jewish state.

In the Diaspora, Jewish activity is confined to what is defined as the private sector: the home, the synagogue, the Jewish community. Judaism is a private experience observed in life-cycle events, the Sabbath and holidays. Jewishness is perpetuated through the linkage of ritual observance with historical memory. When Jews take group action on general social justice issues such as civil rights, civil liberties and religious tolerance, or even on matters affecting vested Jewish interests, the action is legitimated by the democratic political process, which encourages individuals to band together to have an impact on public policy. However, the Jews *qua* Jews do not deal with the totality of society, nor are Jews *qua* Jews responsible for the total society.

In Israel, the Jews are not afforded the luxury of selecting favorite issues and noble causes. All issues are Jewish and all are denominated as Jewish, both by those who live in the state and by those who live outside it. Both the private and the public sectors are Jewish. Indeed, everything is Jewish: from economy to culture, politics, the army, and the character of society.

In the Diaspora, Jews tend to distinguish between universal and particular concerns. In Israel, every issue is both universal and particular. It is impossible to separate between humanness and Jewishness. Poverty is made much more poignant by the knowledge that Jews suffer from the deficiencies of a Jewish society. The pain is more piercing when an Arab child is killed accidentally in the *intifada* by a Jewish soldier serving in a Jewish army using weapons developed by Jews.

The Jewish state has inherited the challenge first projected in Exodus 19:5-6: "Now then, if you will obey Me faithfully and keep My covenant, you shall be My treasured possession among all the peoples. Indeed, all the earth is Mine, but you shall be to Me a kingdom of priests and a holy nation."

The State of Israel is the testing grounds for keeping the covenant between God and God's people. How do Jews as a people create a just society when they are given responsibility? How do Jews use political power? How do Jews apply Jewish values in everyday conditions of a Jewish society? How do Jews relate to issues of poverty, unemployment, health care and the aged? How does a Jewish government relate to a host of other issues that affect every society?

The minority factor

To these questions must be added the questions relating to the non-integrative, non-Jewish national and religious minorities in Israel. The minority problems of Israel presaged the minority problems in Eastern Europe today. The reawakened national consciousness that broke the shackles of Communist control of Eastern Europe has stirred up the consciousness of disparate ethnic minority groups within Czechoslovakia, Yugoslavia and the (former) Soviet Republics. Similarly, the attainments of Jewish nationalism have stimulated the rise of Arab nationalism within Israel.

The minority factor is new to the Jewish historical experience. Unlike the Jews of the Diaspora, Israeli Jews do not live as a highly successful minority in a non-Jewish world. In Israel, Jews are the majority. The test of modern Israel, therefore, is a new test. It is not only political but ideological. Can the application of Jewish values in a Jewish state serve as a model for other societies?

How does a Jewish majority relate to minorities, particularly to those minorities that are not only disadvantaged, but also challenge the very existence of the Jewish state? As Diaspora minorities, Jews have been the victims of discrimination and national chauvinism. How does a Jewish society deal with Jewish triumphalism, Jewish prejudice against non-Jews and instances of flagrant violation of civil liberties and freedom of conscience? How do Jews relate to others when they are the victors rather than the victims, considered to be the oppressors rather than the oppressed? In sum, how do Jews keep the covenant in the open, visible, volatile crucible called the State of Israel?

The establishment of an independent state is only the means to a goal and not the goal itself. The state was created not only for those who live in it, but also for the purpose of keeping the entire Jewish people and its heritage alive. To paraphrase Lincoln: the Jewish state was created *of* the entire Jewish people, *by* the entire Jewish people, and *for* the entire Jewish people. It continues to serve as a central focus of Jewish loyalty, concern, and commitment. Martin Buber epitomized Jewish identity when he wrote:

> In other respects the people of Israel may be regarded as one of the many peoples on earth and the land of Israel as one land among other lands; but in their mutual relationship and in their common task they are unique and incomparable ... The idea of Zion is rooted in deeper regions of the earth and rises into loftier regions of the air, and neither its deep roots nor its lofty heights, neither its memory of the past nor its ideal for the future, both of the selfsame texture, must be repudiated. If Israel renounces the mystery, it renounces the heart of reality itself. National forms without the eternal purpose from which they have arisen signify the end of Israel's specific fruitfulness.[2]

The State of Israel is the Jewish people's symbol of hope in its own future and in the future of all humankind. It is a state that will always be confronted by the tension between the holy and the secular, the potential and the actual, the vision and the reality.

Aliyah

The hope expressed by Jeremiah is inseparable from aliyah: "And there is hope for your future — declares the Lord; your children shall return to their country" (Jeremiah 31:17). Jewish nationalism is radically different from all other nationalisms. All other nationalisms start with the struggle of a national grouping, already living on ancestral soil and preserving an ancient heritage and language, to break the shackles of an occupying power. Starting with Abraham, Jewish nationalism called on Jews to leave the land of birth and move to the land of destiny, there to renew the national heritage, language, and culture. Not just to return to the national soil, but to revivify the nation's soul is the objective.

Israel is the only state ever created by and from a Diaspora. No other state issues a call to those who have left the national soil to return. No one expects Irish Americans, Polish Americans or German Americans to return to the land of their origin after living for generations in a foreign land. Yet, American Jews, whose origins are in Europe, receive constant appeals to immigrate to the land of Israel on the basis of ancient religious imperatives going back more than two millennia.

Every other nation imposes a quota on immigration and strict rules of eligibility for citizenship. Immigrants are selected according to their qualifications and their potential contribution to the state. The well-being of the state is the goal. Not so the Jewish state. The well-being of the Jewish people is the goal. The Jewish state has no quota on Jews, no prerequisite qualifications, no limitations because of unemployment or a weak economy. The Jewish state has an open border and an open heart. Ever since it was established, no Jew anywhere in the world is a refugee or a displaced person. The Law of Return guarantees all Jews the right of citizenship the day they enter the state they call their own.

Without Zionism there is no aliya, without aliyah there is no Zionism. The commitment to aliyah does not imply that the person who lives in Israel is in any way a "better Jew" than the Jew who lives in the Diaspora. It does imply that by living in Israel a Jew can do more than living anywhere else to sustain the collective existence of the Jewish people. The Jew who comes to help build Israeli society enhances Jewish peoplehood and reinforces the state.

To live in Israel

If Israel is to serve as the spiritual center of the Jewish people, it requires a critical mass of Jews. Given the present fertility rates of the respective Arab and Jewish populations, within several generations Jews may become a minority in the borders of *Eretz Yisrael*. Already in certain sections of Israel, such as the Galilee, Jews are a minority. Even assuming a peace settlement and a territorial compromise, the population projections are discouraging. Aliyah is, therefore, a prerequisite to sustaining a state Jewish in character as well as name.

From where will this aliyah come? Traditionally, the major waves of aliyah have come from Jews in search of refuge from persecution or distress. But the number of Jews living under conditions of danger is fast diminishing. Therefore, motivated both by pragmatism and idealism, Israel must look to the Jewish communities of the Western world as the major potential pools of aliyah. From the perspective of Jews from lands of affluence, living in Israel offers opportunities for personal fulfillment: to be a full-time, active force in securing the future of the Jewish people; to help shape the society whose character will have an impact on the character of world Jewry; and to live in an environment whose mother tongue, social patterns and cultural setting are Jewish.

Aliyah is an option for Jewish living that should be encouraged. So should stays of extended duration and study and work experiences in Israel be encouraged. Israel is both a source and a resource for Jewish living. The Rabbinic sages taught, "The very air of Israel instills wisdom" (Baba Batra 5b). To imbibe of the milieu of Israel is to rediscover the deep spiritual roots of Israel's survival, and to be inspired by participating in the search for Israel's eternal destiny.

Note

1. Sh'ma 20/397 (September 21, 199), article by Eugene B. Borowitz.
2. *Israel and Palestine* by Martin Buber, published by Farar, Strauss and Young, Great Britain, 1952, page XII.

From the *Journal of the Central Conference of American Rabbis*, Fall, 1991.

Reform Zionism: From Premise to Promise*

A merican Jews in general, and Reform Jews in particular, have tended to relate to Zionism and the State of Israel in pragmatic rather than ideological terms. Given the tenuous nature of the Jewish condition, the failure to relate to ideology is understandable. After all, world Jewry and the Jewish state have gone from crisis to crisis. Our first priority is to keep the Jewish people alive. Why encourage divisiveness when the primary obligation is to unify our ranks for the challenge of Jewish survival and continuity? Besides, the latter half of the twentieth century has often been described as a post-ideological era.

This has never been my view. To mute controversial ideological issues is to postpone the reconciliation of fundamental differences. Even worse, it is to deprive Jewish life of a potential corrective force. We proclaim that Reform Judaism is a religious movement. What is a religious movement without theology? The continued reluctance to confront theological and ideological issues precludes Reform Judaism from taking a vital leadership role in reshaping the Jewish future.

The very use of the term *Reform Zionism* raises many questions. For well over a century, the Jewish world has been influenced by a veritable stream of *religious Zionists*: Rabbi Yehuda Alkalai, Rabbi Zvi Hirsch Kalischer, Rabbi Samuel Mohilever and Rabbi Avraham Isaac Kook. Religious Zionism developed a well-formulated theological approach, which in turn led to the establishment of the religious Zionist movement. This movement became institutionalized in the form of the Mizrachi Party in the World Zionist Organization. But as a life philosophy, religious Zionism is much broader and much more significant than the Mizrachi Party.

Just as the Zionist *organization* does not begin to encompass, or even necessarily to reflect, the Zionist *movement*, so Mizrachi does not encompass or necessarily reflect religious Zionism. Religious Zionism is a dynamic

* From the author's contribution to the ARZA sponsored Think Tank on Reform Zionist ideology, 1992.

movement which has successfully blended traditional Orthodox Judaism and contemporary Jewish nationalism. Though its adherents may be a minority among Orthodox Jews to this day, the movement has impacted on the life pattern, conduct and convictions of hundreds of thousands of Orthodox Jews. These Jews are prepared to devote their lives, and even give their lives, for the cause of religious Zionism.

Today, religious Zionists are a vital factor in the political, religious and cultural landscape of Israel. They comprise a distinctive movement with distinctive characteristics. And they have created many hundreds of educational, cultural and welfare institutions which reflect their ideals and perpetuate their purposes. Though we may disagree with them on some major aspects of theology and practice, we can learn much from them.

Movement and ideology

When we employ the term *Reform Zionism,* what do we mean? Are we, too, not obliged to distinguish between a *movement* and an *organization?* Let us confront our Reform Jewish reality frankly. Can we point to a distinctive Zionist *movement* within the ranks of Reform Judaism? In all honesty, I believe the answer is in the negative.

According to our own statistics, we number today more than 1,500,000 Jews around the world. Some demographers project that we shall comprise an ever-growing proportion of world Jewry in the future. Conversely, all the Orthodox together (Zionists and non-Zionists) number less than 10% of American Jewry and only about 20% of Israeli Jewry. How many of our Reform Jews feel that Zionism is a motivating force in their lives, impacting on life commitments and behavior? To be sure, we can count a handful, but if my unscientific sample is accurate, that handful is not growing, and in proportion to the increasing numbers of those identifying with Reform Judaism, is diminishing rapidly.

Why do I ask us to confront our reality? Not to castigate or condemn, nor even to express pessimism, but to offer a challenge to our leadership which identifies as Zionists. Movements are grounded in passionate convictions which move people's lives and shape their values and deeds. Otherwise, so-called movements dissipate into organizations. If we wish to mobilize a *movement* worthy of the name *Reform Zionism*, then that *movement* must have a specific ideology. The ideology must differentiate Reform Zionism from both secular Zionism and from religious (Orthodox) Zionism. Above all, Reform Zionism must be inextricable from Reform Judaism. If there is no commitment to affect Reform Judaism, or if Reform Judaism, as we know it today, contains all the elements of Reform Zionism, then why, *ab initio*, should we formulate an ideology called Reform Zionism?

Our purpose should be not only to define Reform *Zionism* but to redefine Reform *Judaism*. Indeed, I contend that without redefining and reforming Reform *Judaism*, we cannot define Reform *Zionism*.

The Zionist components of Reform theology

Where do we find the Zionist components of Reform theology? In the writings of individuals, in the collective statements of our movement and in liturgy. We can go back to the beginning of the twentieth century to record with pride the statements of a significant number of Reform Jews who were Zionists.[1]

We can point to the Columbus Platform of 1937 as the first of many collective statements on Zionism issued within the framework of the organized structures of our movement (the Central Conference of American Rabbis, the Union of American Hebrew Congregations and the World Union for Progressive Judaism).

However, if the truth be told, at the time of its passage the Columbus Platform was not considered a major departure from the established non-Zionist positions of the Reform movement. Rabbi Howard Greenstein records in his book *Turning Point: Zionism and Reform Judaism*, that less than half of the members of the CCAR were registered for the Columbus conference. Early in the proceedings, the delegates were presented with a proposal to not adopt any platform at all. Their vote on the proposal resulted in an 81-81 tie. The CCAR president, Felix Levy, cast the deciding vote to keep the platform on the agenda. When the matter finally came to the floor, only 110 rabbis were in the room for

The author enjoyed a special relationship with Prime Minister Yitzhak Rabin, beginning from the time he served as Israel's Ambassador to the United States in Washington. Here, he introduced the Prime Minister in the Knesset to the mission of the Union of American Hebrew Congregations (1974).

The author presents a gift to Leah Rabin on the occasion of her being awarded the WUPJ's International Humanitarian Award for perpetuating the ideals of her husband. At a banquet in New York, 1998.

The author, in intimate conversation with Yitzhak Navon, President of the State of Israel, at Beit Hanasi, 1979.

The author served as Chairman of the Zionist General Council (the legislative body of the World Zionist Organization) from 1987-1992. Pictured at the opening of the June 1988 session are (left to right): Simcha Dinitz, Chairman of the WZO and Chairman of the Jewish Agency for Israel Executive; Haim Herzog (President, the State of Israel); the author; Mendel Kaplan (Chairman of the Board of Governors of the Jewish Agency).

Prime Minister Menachem Begin convened a regular Bible Study Circle at his home.
The author was asked to serve as chairman of a session. Here the two enjoy a humorous
biblical interpretation (1979).

Beit Shmuel and the ▶
Campus of the Hebrew
Union College — Jewish
Institute of Religion,
Jerusalem

◀ Model of Mercaz Shimshon
facing the Old City and the
Tower of David

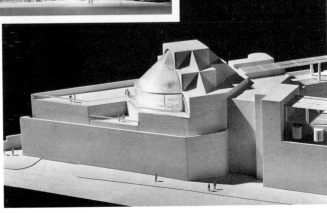

Mercaz Shimshon, model ▶

◀ Leo Baeck
Education
Center, Haifa

Beit Daniel, Tel Aviv

Or Hadash, Haifa

Kol ▶
Haneshama,
Jerusalem

The author speaks at the ceremony dedicating Kibbutz Yahel in the Arava desert, 1976.
Yahel, the first Reform Kibbutz, was followed by Kibbutz Lotan, dedicated in 1983 and Har Halutz,
a Reform settlement in the Galilee, founded in 1985.

Kibbutz Yahel

Kibbutz Lotan

the debate; many of the others were out on the golf course. The platform finally carried by one vote. Again, the deciding ballot was cast by the president of the CCAR. In other words, the now much-heralded Columbus Platform was adopted by a minority of the CCAR and definitely reflected a minority position of the movement.[2]

Nor, in fact, did the actual content of the Columbus Platform reflect a clearcut Zionist position. Its authors viewed "the rehabilitation of Palestine" as a "promise of renewed life for many of our brethren," a "haven of refuge," and "a center of Jewish culture and spiritual life." But the return to Zion is not related to the "messianic goal" of "universal brotherhood, justice, truth and peace on earth." Particularism and universalism are viewed as two separable, unrelated tendencies.

Similarly, the Centenary Perspective adopted by the CCAR in 1976 does not tie "concern for humanity" and the "Messianic hope that humanity will be redeemed" to the traditional messianic hope, the precondition of which is that the Jewish people will be redeemed. Moreover, the drafting committee unanimously refused to insert the word "aliyah" in the draft circulated before the conference convened, on the grounds that the Centenary Perspective was intended to be a consensus statement and not a new platform. The drafting committee feared that the very mention of aliyah would be divisive and would jeopardize approval of the entire document. We in Israel protested that no contemporary statement of Reform Judaism would be complete without aliyah. One moderate sentence, offered from the floor, was overwhelmingly approved: "We encourage aliyah for those who wish to find maximum personal fulfillment in the cause of Zion."[3]

To the extent that our American *Siddur, Gates of Prayer,* reflects Reform Jewish thought, the liturgy contains numerous inconsistencies. For example, the traditional prayer for *kibbutz galuyot* (ingathering of the exiles) is not included. Although some traditional prayers relating to Zion and Jewish particularism have been reinserted in the Hebrew, they are universalized in the English translation. In the *amidah* prayer תקע בשופר גדול לחירותנו — the words חירותנו (our freedom) and עשוקנו (our oppressed) are translated in English as petitions for the "liberation of [all] the oppressed" and "liberty in the four corners of the earth." In and of itself, this rendering projects a worthy aspiration, but the theme of universal freedom is authentically found elsewhere in our liturgy. To transform a petition for the freedom of the Jewish people in its land into a prayer for liberty for all humankind is to distort the meaning — and to avoid confrontation with the true Zionist dimensions of Jewish liturgy.

The Reform dilemma

I have attempted to demonstrate that we have not yet integrated Zionism into the ideology of Reform Judaism. I propose that Reform Zionists undertake to "Zionize" Reform Judaism. How can we do it? Let me concentrate on the question posed to me by the organizing committee of this Zionist think-tank: "How can an inherently universalistic religious tradition coherently embrace an intrinsically particularistic movement of national self-fulfillment?" In other words, how can Reform Judaism, "inherently universal," embrace Zionism, "intrinsically particularistic?"

I submit that the very framing of the question reflects the dilemma of Reform Judaism. The classical Reformers did indeed attempt to redefine Judaism as a "universalistic religious tradition." That is why they rejected Jewish peoplehood even before they rejected political Zionism. In terms of timing, Reform Judaism evolved 50 to 75 years before political Zionism. The opposition to Zionism was not the cause but the consequence of the fundamental premise of classical Reform. In the words of Abraham Geiger, "The people of Israel no longer lives ... It has been transformed into a community of faith." According to Kaufmann Kohler, the prime motivation of Reform Judaism was "to transform the national Jew into a religious Jew."

Once the fundamental premise had been established, everything else followed in logical sequence. The significance of the land of Israel, the people Israel and the language of Israel was minimized. The messianic era was universalized and the mission of the Jew denationalized. The prophets were transformed into universal messengers of peace and justice, thus liberating Jews from their tribal particularism. Jewish ethical imperatives were removed from their nationalistic context. Our movement stressed צדק צדק תרדוף. justice, justice shall you pursue — and forgot that the very next words were

למען תחיה וירשת את הארץ אשר הי אלוהיך נותן לך —, "that you may thrive and occupy the land that the Lord our God is giving you" (Deuteronomy 16:20).

The classical Reform attitude to *halacha* and ritual practice was also conditioned by the desire to redefine the Jews into a "community of faith." The faith called "Judaism," so they claimed, is distinguished from the faith called "Christianity" not so much by its observances as by its beliefs. It is not essential to retain practices which separate Jews from non-Jews, so long as Jews hold onto their belief in ethical monotheism. To the contrary, observances that prevent Jews from integrating into the larger society, or practices which cannot survive the test of reason, are to be discarded. Much effort was expended to ground the radical Reform departures from traditional observance in scholarly responsa and well-reasoned reinterpretation of the sources. The underlying motivation, in most instances, was to cast off all semblances of the "national Jew." Isaac Mayer Wise sincerely believed that Reform Judaism would become the predominant faith of America. In order to achieve this objective, it was necessary to universalize Judaism and to make it accessible and acceptable to all America.

Particularism and universalism

In our day, the real issue is not Zionism. Zionism is not an end in and of itself; it is a means to an end. The goal is to redefine the Jews as a people and to reinject this people into history as a collectivity. Zionism evolved as a post-Emancipation movement. Its fundamental premise was — and is — that the only way to keep the Jews alive was to restore the collective Jewish existence, and, thereby, preserve the people and its heritage.

Although the Reform movement in our day has moved quite far from the stance of classical Reform, we are still tied to its vocabulary and theological conceptualizations. We have never fully accepted the consequences of Jewish peoplehood. In a symposium sponsored by the CCAR in 1976, a Reform rabbi defined universalism as "that category of thought which tends to subordinate the distinctiveness of the Jewish people to the greater good of the general society, to minimize the distinctiveness of the Jewish people, to maximize that which it shares with other groups in society, or to put the survival of the Jewish people second to the survival of the general society."[4]

In my judgment, this definition is acceptable to the vast majority in the Reform movement and permeates the writings of our intellectual leadership to this day. For most Reform Jews, universalism connotes concerns for non-Jews, and particularism, concern for Jews. Universalism is social action on behalf of all humanity; particularism is action on behalf of the Jewish people and the Jewish state. Universalism is deemed to be selfless and altruistic; particularism is portrayed as parochial concern for self and vested interest. Universalism is internationalism; particularism is nationalism. The setting most conducive for universalism is the Diaspora; the setting for intense particularism is the State of Israel.

Contemporary Reform has restored elements of particularism and would advocate that both universalism and particularism are prerequisites to Jewish survival. Nevertheless, most Reform leaders would still contend that universalism is transcendent and quintessential, and that particularism is somehow secondary and of lesser value in the scales of eternity.

The people of Israel — a collectivity

By now it should be clear that I reject the basic premise of the question to which I was asked to respond. It demonstrates that despite everything that has transpired since the nineteenth century, Reform Judaism remains anchored to its original preconceptions. So my answer to the question is, "no." Reform Judaism can never "coherently embrace" Zionism if we continue to define Reform Judaism as "an inherently universalistic religious tradition."

Not only does this definition of Reform Judaism preclude comprehensive integration with Zionism; of even greater consequence, this Reform definition distorts the essence of Judaism. Judaism is first and foremost the faith of a people. This people encounters God not through the life experiences of an individual founder of the faith, as in the instance of Christianity and Islam, but through the experiences of the people in history. The three formative events of Jewish history all were experienced by the entire people as a collectivity. The entire people experienced the Exodus from Egypt; the entire people received the Law on Mount Sinai; and the entire people entered and possessed the land of Israel. The three events together established the triad of Jewish theology — God, Torah and Israel. God gave freedom, law and land to the Jewish people as a collectivity. The three are inseparable. הקב״ה ישראל ואורייתא חד. "God, Torah and Israel [Israel the people and Israel the land] are one."

The formative events of Jewish history are ingrained in every Jew's personal memory and destiny. Each Jew receives his or her identity through the prism of the collectivity called the Jewish *people*. The *sh'ma*, recited by the individual Jew, is addressed to the entire Jewish people — "Hear, O Israel, the Lord *our* God, the Lord is one." The covenant was made between God and God's people, but each Jew is responsible. Individual Jews cannot adopt their own standards of morality. Every Jew is responsible for the ethical standards of the entire people. Moral judgments are made by the individual Jew in relationship to the well-being of the people. No individual Jew can attain personal salvation without the salvation of the entire Jewish people. Every Jew is part of the Jewish family, the Jewish community and the Jewish people.

This relationship to the collectivity called *Am Yisrael* — the Jewish people — reveals a unique insight of Judaism. Many years ago, the distinguished Protestant theologian Reinhold Niebuhr wrote a book entitled *Moral Man and Immoral Society*. Had the book been written by a Jewish theologian, the title would have been reversed: *Immoral Man and Moral Society*. For Jews, no individual can ever be holy. We have no saints. We consider the role of the *tzaddik*, as it has evolved in *hasidic* tradition, to be a distortion. And look what happened to the one Jew who was proclaimed to be God's personification on earth! Jewish tradition has been inherently anti-personality cult.

The Exodus from Egypt was the biblical counterpart of the American Revolution. Could any account of the American Revolution have been written without countless references to its leader, George Washington? Yet the *Haggadah*, which celebrates the Exodus, does not mention Moses except in passing, in one biblical quotation.

Holiness is not abstract

God's charge is always delivered to the entire Jewish people: ואתם תהיו לי ממלכת כהנים וגוי קדוש — "you shall be to Me a kingdom of priests and a holy nation" (Exodus 19:6) Note that the collectivity, not the individual Jew, is mandated to become holy, to be a *goy kadosh*. This people is to establish a *mamlachah* (kingdom), a temporal order in its own land. The covenant mandates the Jewish people to establish a just society, a "kingdom of priests."

The "holy nation" is inseparable in God's command from the "kingdom" it is to establish. If you do not want to live in the kingdom, in human society, then (to quote Shakespeare) "Get thee to a nunnery." Holiness is not abstract. It is not a state of being, but a state of doing, a state of living in society. The land of Israel is given to the Jewish people for a purpose. The purpose is to establish a just society which keeps God's commandments.

The giving of the land is conditional. It is contingent on fulfilling the covenant, as Leviticus 18:24-28 makes specific:

> Do not defile yourselves ... for it is by such that the nations that I am casting out before you defiled themselves. Thus the land became defiled; and I called it to account for its iniquity, and the land spewed out its inhabitants. But you must keep My laws and My rules, and you must not do any of those abhorrent things, neither the citizen nor the stranger who resides among you; for all those abhorrent things were done by the people who were in the land before you and the land became defiled. So let not the land spew you out for defiling it, as it spewed out the nations that came before you.

Throughout our sacred literature a condition is attached to the return to the land and the retention of the land: ציון במשפט תיפדה ושביה בצדקה — "Zion shall be redeemed in justice and those who return to her in righteousness" (Isaiah 1:27). The Zohar declares, "When the people Israel is worthy, the land is called after them, *Eretz Yisrael*, the land of Israel. When the people is not worthy, the land is called by another name, *Eretz Canaan*, the land of Canaan" (Zohar 58, 73).

From its inception, Jewish nationalism has been unique. Other nationalisms, including the reemerging nationalisms in Central and Eastern Europe, aspire to preserve the national culture through the restoration of national independence. Some forms of nationalism aspire to greatness through conquest and aggrandizement. Only Jewish nationalism envisions national independence as a means of serving humanity. In the words of Isaiah, "This is My servant ... I have put My spirit upon him; he shall teach the true way to the nations" (Isaiah 42:1). And again, "I created you, and appointed you a covenant people, a light of nations" (Isaiah 42:6).

Messianism equals hope

I feel that it is important to make reference here to the seeming controversy that erupted during the think-tank. I say "seeming," because I believe we should be able to formulate a consensus on this fundamental premise of Judaism.

We are all united in opposing false messiahs. Historically, classical Judaism has rejected every self-proclaimed messiah. The campaign to anoint the Lubavitcher rebbe as the Messiah is an aberration of Judaism. The rebbe is doomed to join a long line of precursors, all false messiahs.

But to negate the notion of a personal messiah, which Reform Judaism — to its credit — has been doing since its inception, is not to negate the validity of messianism, the aspiration for *tikkun olam*, the "perfecting of the universe."

To be sure, messianism as such entered Judaism late, as a post-biblical phenomenon, but the vision of a better world is inherent in countless biblical passages. True messianism is hope. Without hope there is no Judaism. Without hope there is no Zionism. Without hope there is no Jewish people.

It is no coincidence that the Israeli national anthem *"Hatikvah"* is based on the biblical concept of hope. The composer took the phrase from Ezekiel 37:11 — *avdah tikvataynu* — *"our hope is lost"* — and added the words *od lo* — "not yet" — "our hope is not yet lost." Ezekiel's chapter recounting the vision of the valley of dry bones is the classic text describing the hope for national revival.

In 1949-50, I was a student at the Hebrew University in Jerusalem. It was the year after the state was established and only a short while after Israel's victory in the War of Independence. I attended a conference of Orthodox rabbis convened to discuss the implications for the traditional liturgy of the newly established state. For example, should Jews now living in Jerusalem under Jewish sovereignty for the first time since the destruction of the Temple continue to recite לשנה הבאה בירושלים. "Next year in Jerusalem?" The rabbis were unanimous in responding affirmatively: we must continue to recite it. Why? Because Jerusalem is not just a physical place; it is also a spiritual aspiration. Hope. Messianism. באין חזון ייפרע עם. "For lack of vision, a people disintegrates" (Proverbs 29:18).

Throughout Jewish tradition, the universalistic impulse of Judaism has been integral to the particularistic impulse. Never were there two separate poles. Never was there tension between two competing forces. When Jews had control of their own sovereignty in biblical times, the mandate was to establish a *mamlechet kohanim* (a kingdom of priests). In the post-biblical period and throughout the Middle Ages, the *kehillah,* the "Jewish community," served as the setting for striving to become a *goy kadosh* (a holy people). Every Jewish community was denominated as a *kehillah kedoshah* (a holy community).

Our rabbinic sages wrote: כל צרה שישראל ואומות העולם שותפים בה צרה ושל ישראל עצמן אינה צרה. "Every problem common to Israel and the nations of the world is a problem. When it is only Israel's, it is not a problem" (Deuteronomy Rabbah 2.14).

In our day, the classic example of the inseparability of issues of universalism and particularism is the successful struggle on behalf of Soviet Jewry. The struggle for Jews highlighted the inequities of Soviet society and encouraged the rebellion of other nationalities in the USSR against Russian political and cultural imperialism. Had it not been for the struggle for Soviet Jewry, the peoples of Eastern and Central Europe would not have broken the shackles of oppression so quickly and effectively.

Having rejected the artificial dichotomy between universalism and particularism, we are nevertheless left with certain realities. There is a qualitative difference between Jewish life in Israel and Jewish life in the Diaspora. This is a problem not just for Reform Jews but for all Jews. However, since Reform Judaism is the most characteristic of the religious movements in America, it is incumbent on us to wrestle with the issue. In large measure, Israel-Diaspora relations will be determined by Israel-Reform Judaism relations.

Different realities in Israel and Diaspora

What is the reality of Israel? Jews live in collective existence under Jewish sovereignty in a *mamlachah* which is denominated as Jewish. Jewishness in Israel is compulsory, public, and full-time.[5]

What is the reality of the Diaspora, and especially of the American Diaspora? In the great waves of immigration to America, Jews were identified as a nationality. Today, Jews are considered as a "faith group" on a par with Protestants and Catholics. Jewish identity has become a private, voluntary, confessional-type commitment. The synagogue is, on the whole, the counterpart of the church. Since there is no *kehillah*, in the classic sense, no Jewish community where a person's entire private and public being is identified as Jewish, the synagogue has become the *kehillah*. It is even called the *kehillah*, although today's congregation is a far cry from the traditional *kehillah*. Indeed, the synagogue today is also becoming the substitute for the *mamlachah*. The biblical concept presumed that the entire Jewish people would be a *mamlechet kohanim*, a "kingdom of priests." But in today's *mamlachah*, the only priest is the rabbi. He or she is often the only knowledgeable Jew in the community, and the only one who lives in the "kingdom" full-time. So today, instead of having a "kingdom of priests," we have only *kohen hamamlachah* — "the priest of the kingdom."

In fact, a good case can be made for saying that the synagogue in the Diaspora is for the American Jew what the land of Israel is for the Israeli Jew, the setting for living Jewishly. The basic difference is that whereas the Israeli Jew lives in the kingdom full-time, the American Jew lives in the "kingdom" at best only part-time and often not at all.

This fundamental contrast is fully developed in sociological terms in the book, *The Two Worlds of Judaism*, by Charles S. Liebman and Steven M. Cohen.[6] The authors document how the same words have different connotations in the "world" of Israel and in that of America. Words such as "galut," "land," "people," even "state" simply do not mean the same thing to each group. "To most Israelis the State of Israel does not mean a state in the western sense of the term, but rather the power and authority of the Jewish community."[7]

The danger confronting the Israeli world is that it will concentrate its energies on *mamlachtiut,* the task of nation building, and neglect the dictate to create a just and holy society. The danger confronting the Diaspora is that it will concentrate its efforts on priestly matters and neglect community, peoplehood and national culture. Because Reform Judaism is so characteristic of the Diaspora, Reform Zionism has an opportunity and an obligation to serve as a bridge between these "two worlds."

What does it mean to be a people?

The ultimate challenge confronting Reform Judaism is to define what it means to be a people. What are the ramifications of Jewish peoplehood? In his address to the first World Zionist Congress, Herzl declared: "Zionism is a return to the Jewish fold even before it becomes a return to the Jewish land." Reform Judaism has to return to Jewish peoplehood even before we can return to Zionism.

When the French left Algeria, de Gaulle declared, "The French people have gotten married to history." We Reform Jews have to marry ourselves to history, the history which has remade us into a people. When we are married to history, we will see that what our Reform precursors designated as "rituals," "customs," "ceremonies" and "observances" were in many instances symbols of Jewish peoplehood. If Judaism is only a faith predicated on belief and reason, and if our primary task is to adjust ourselves to the general society in which we live, these symbols can be eliminated. But if we are a people, the symbols of peoplehood have to be cherished and creatively renewed.

Take the example of the *kippah.* Reform Judaism's stated reason for eliminating the covering of one's head during prayer has been that it is merely "custom." Our scholars proved that head covering is not demanded anywhere in our sacred literature. However, the prime motivation for discarding the *kippah* was to cast off the symbol of Jewish distinctiveness. In retrospect, the elimination of head covering was an historic error. I was among the hundreds of Jews who marched with Martin Luther King in Selma, Alabama. It was in our own interest to show the world that Jews were active participants among the thousands of marchers struggling for civil rights. So what did we do? Every Jew put on a *kippah.* Among them were classical Reform Jews, who marched on the public streets wearing a *kippah* as their symbol of Jewish identity. When United Nations Secretary General Kurt Waldheim visited Yad Vashem and refused to don a *kippah*, he insulted every Jew, including every Reform Jew. Is the *kippah*, then, only a custom or is it a symbol of Jewish peoplehood?

What about other "observances" such as *kashrut*, Shabbat, the Festivals, fast days? Are they only "rituals," or are they symbols of Jewish peoplehood? What about study? Or the use of Hebrew not only for prayer but as a living language? Is Hebrew "only" a language, or has it become a vital symbol of a revivified Jewish people? The decision to preserve or abandon such symbols affects the individual Jew's conduct and personal lifestyle and patterns of synagogue worship. And traditional components of the Jewish community have criticized Reform Judaism for introducing changes in personal or congregational practice.

But matters of *ishut* — issues related to personal status — fall into a totally different category. Here, the stance of the Reform rabbinate has much greater significance and far-reaching implications. Positions regarding *ishut*, adopted by Reform rabbis, affect an individual's status as a Jew and therefore have a potential impact on the entire Jewish community. For that reason, this is where the potential for controversy is more intense — and where the Reform rabbinate has to become more sensitive to the demands of Jewish peoplehood.

Responding to modernity

This leads to the crucial controversy over patrilineality. The Progressive movement in Israel and around the world adamantly opposed the patrilineal resolution adopted by the Central Conference of American Rabbis. We understood the circumstances and even empathized with the motivations of our American colleagues. Nevertheless, we could not comprehend how our colleagues could sanction a person becoming a Jew without conversion. We could not agree to adopting a standard which represented such a radical departure from the standards of *K'lal Yisrael*. When Reform rabbis welcome non-Jews into the Jewish fold, we are in effect giving them a passport to the Jewish world. It is our obligation as representatives of the Jewish people to ensure that these new Jews are acceptable in as many corners of the Jewish world as possible.

Even though we know in advance that the Orthodox establishment will never consider our acts authentic, we should at least strive to be authentic in our own eyes and in the eyes of the majority of world Jewry who are secular. Our divergence from the accepted ways of entering the Jewish fold is viewed as a rejection of Jewish peoplehood by these secular Jews. The passage of the patrilineal resolution was a declaration that the Reform movement can be oblivious to the demands of *K'lal Yisrael* and insensitive to the pain our acts cause to major components of the Jewish world.

Professor Michael Meyer entitled his history of Reform Judaism *Response to Modernity.* That is an accurate description of the challenge which confronted us in the nineteenth and twentieth centuries. As we enter the twenty-first century, however, the new challenge will be how to respond to Jewish peoplehood. We have successfully demonstrated that we can live as a movement in the modern world. Now, how do we live with the Jewish people? That is the question Zionism poses to Reform Judaism.

The respective paths of Reform Judaism and Zionism can be summarized in what transpired with one biblical verse, בית יעקב לכו ונלכה באור ה'. "O House of Jacob! Come and let us walk by the light of the Lord" (Isaiah 2:5). When BILU, the first modern Zionist movement, was organized in Eastern Europe in 1881, they selected as their motto the first four Hebrew words of the verse. They took the first letter of each word בית יעקב לכו ונלכה. "O House of Jacob! Come and let us walk" (meaning, let us go on aliyah to the land of Israel), and formed the acronym BILU. They left out the last two words, באור ה' — "by the light of the Lord," because they were either indifferent or antagonistic to religion.

The Central Conference of American Rabbis was organized in the United States during the same decade. In an amazing coincidence, the CCAR selected as its motto the same verse. However, because the CCAR members were opposed to peoplehood and Zionism, they left out the first two words — בית יעקב "House of Jacob." To this day, the motto on the insignia of the CCAR is לכו ונלכה באור ה'. "Come and let us walk by the light of the Lord."

What is the task of Reform Zionism today? To complete the cycle. The Jewish people are desperately in need of wholeness. We need people, land and faith. Our prime mission should be to respond to the call in its entirety. "O House of Jacob! Come and let us walk [together] by the light of the Lord."

Notes

1. The Zionist, non-Zionist and anti-Zionist positions of individuals have been recorded in many places. See for example *Renew Our Days — The Zionist Issue in Reform Judaism*, by David Polish, published by the WZO in cooperation with the WUPJ, 1976; *Turning Point: Zionism and Reform Judaism*, by Howard Greenstein (Brown Judaic Studies, 1981); *HaHipus Achar HaZehut HaLeumit*, by Yosef Gorney (Sifrei Ofakim — Am Oved, 1990).
2. See *Turning Point: Zionism and Reform Judaism*, pp. 9-32 for a full discussion of the subject.
3. See *Reform Judaism Today, Book Three*, by Eugene B. Borowitz (Behrman House, 1979), pp. 68-73.
4. *CCAR Journal*, (Summer 1977), p.39.
5. See my earlier article for a fuller elaboration of this point.
6. Yale University Press, 1990.
7. *Ibid.*, p. 83.

Published in the *Journal of Reform Zionism*, by Association of Reform Zionists of America, Volume 1, number 1, 1993.

Liberal Judaism: Opportunities And Dangers*

The theme for this Conference is קדושת העם, קדושת הארץ. "Holiness of the people, holiness of the Land." The root connotation of קודש (holy) is to distinguish that which is related to the divine from חול (secular), that which is secular and mundane. *Kedushah,* holiness, is that which is separated, transcendent, consecrated to God.

I must confess that I have considerable difficulty with the mandate to become a holy people. ואתם תהיו לי ממלכת כוהנים וגוי קדוש. "You shall be to Me a kingdom of priests and a holy nation" (Exodus 19:6). How can we consider seriously a concept that expects an entire people to be holy, not only on the Sabbath once a week, but 365 days a year? How can the entire Jewish people be expected to be *kadosh,* when in our tradition no individual Jew has ever been *kadosh?* Our tradition must have intuitively recognized that impossibility. The imperative קדושים תהיו. "You shall be holy" (Leviticus 19:1) is not included in the 613 commandments.

Nonetheless, Judaism provides an answer to this trying question. For the Jew, holiness is not a divinely bestowed characteristic, a state of being or an emotional experience. Holiness is not a description but a prescription, not a fact, but a goal to be sought. Holiness is an aspiration, a direction, a mandate to perform *mitzvot.*

People and land

Here is where the land of Israel enters. If the people Israel is commanded to be holy, where are they to achieve holiness? God needed a setting, a specific place, in which the Jewish people could enact the divine commandments. The people needed the land assigned by God in which to aspire to holiness; the land needed the Jewish people to fructify it. From the moment God called to

---

* Excerpts from the author's keynote address at the Central Conference of American Rabbis convention, Jerusalem, 1995, on the theme: "Holiness of the People, Holiness of the Land."

Abraham, עם ישראל (the People of Israel) and ארץ ישראל (the Land of Israel) were inseparable.

לך לך מארצך וממולדתך ומבית אביך אל הארץ אשר אראך: ואעשך לגוי גדול ואברכך ואגדלה שמך והיה ברכה.

"Go forth ... to the land I will show you ... and I will make you a great nation ... and be thou a blessing" (Genesis 12:1, 2).

To this day, Judaism is distinguished by the inseparability of people and land. The twin conception of people and land distinguishes the Jew from all other peoples and faiths. The Romans were a people before they adopted Christianity. The Arab tribes had developed their cultural traditions before Mohammed. The classic religions of the Far East are not conterminous with geographic borders or demographic boundaries. Only for the Jew were faith, peoplehood and land simultaneous and interdependent. The land of Israel was the center stage for the drama that has shaped Jewish character and destiny.

The issue of centrality

In truth, many of our lay and rabbinic leadership find it difficult to accept the formulation of the World Zionist Organization's Jerusalem Program that the first aim of Zionism is "the unity of the Jewish people and the centrality of Israel in Jewish life." Why should we have such ideological turmoil over the issue of centrality? When in the 1940's the Union of American Hebrew Congregations moved from Cincinnati to New York, it did not mean that the individual Jew in New York was any better than the Jew in Cincinnati. It did mean that henceforth the headquarters of the American Reform Movement was in the center of American Jewish life.

The move represented a significant historic ideological statement which enabled Reform Judaism to become more of a major force in American Jewish life than would have been possible had it remained in Cincinnati. Similarly, when it was first proposed that the World Union for Progressive Judaism move its headquarters from New York to Jerusalem, controversy erupted. There were those who objected on grounds that our movement could not move its headquarters to a country where the Reform movement was not recognized. But the transfer was a declaration of intention that the World Reform Movement was going to participate in בנין הארץ (the upbuilding of Zion) from within as an integral part of the Jewish people. With this move, we became actors in the historical drama of the people of Israel rather than mere spectators in the audience.

We can view the theme of this Conference *Kedushat ha'am, kedushat ha'aretz* as an intellectual exercise of exploring the past, or we can consider it a mandate to secure the future. If it is to be the latter, how can the terms *holiness of the people, holiness of the land* be applied in our day? It is my contention that the conditions of Jewish life in America make it exceedingly difficult to retain the distinguishing characteristics of Judaism — the sense of covenant between God and the Jewish people and the collective and this-worldly character of Judaism. Israel provides a more embracing and emotionally supportive climate to sustain a living Judaism and a potentially holy people.

Let us compare some of the factors in America and Israel that impact on this potential.

1. *Demographic patterns: the American Jewish population is decreasing and the Israeli Jewish population is increasing. Given present population trends, early in the twenty-first century, the majority of world Jewry will live in the State of Israel.*

In terms of Jewish education, there are approximately three million school age Jewish children in the world today, 1.5 million of whom live in Israel, speak Hebrew as their mother tongue and receive an intensive Jewish education (without reference at this point to the quality or impact of the education). Another one million Jewish children live in America, the majority of whom receive no or minimal Jewish education. Little wonder that assimilation is considered the gravest threat to American Jewish survival. The 1990 National Jewish Population Study, the new revised standard Bible of American Jewry, has given birth to a new buzzword. *Jewish continuity* has replaced the old buzzword *Jewish survival*, attesting to the redefinition of the threat to American Jewry as *spiritual* rather than *physical* extinction.

2. *In America, Jewish identity is voluntary and therefore individualistic and private; in Israel, Jewish identity is compulsory and therefore collective and public.*

The openness of American society has made it possible for a Jew to forgo or forfeit Jewish identity without pain, pressure, or stigma. In this sense, not only converts, but all born Jews are "Jews by choice." In Israel, every Jew is a Jew "by no-choice." Israeli society is a reflection of the application of Jewish values in a Jewish society. Whatever happens in Israel is considered to be "Jewish" by the nations of the world.

3. *In America, Jewish identity is becoming "religionized:" in Israel, Jewish identity is becoming "nationalized."*

American Jews are identified today more as a religious group than an ethnic group. The changing identity is reinforced by demographic patterns: the dissolution of cohesive Jewish neighborhoods; the fracturing of the traditional Jewish family through divorce and changing life styles; and the rising multiculturalism which tends to categorize Americans in racial rather than ethnic groups. The synagogue has become the place "to Jew it," the accepted institutional setting for Jewish identity, Jewish life-cycle events and for occasional celebration of holidays, even though paradoxically, most American Jews are not religious in practice.

In Israel, we find the obverse. The synagogue as an institution is relatively unimportant. The rabbinate and the religious parties exercise power far beyond their proportional representation in the electorate. However, their influence is more political than religious and there is an inverse ratio between their political power and their impact on personal or public religious values.

Modern Zionism represents the renationalization of Jewish peoplehood. Zionism was driven by two competitive thrusts: the first, toward "normalization," espousing a state "like all other states;" the second, toward the creation of a state whose Jewish character will flower into a new indigenous Israeli Judaism. Until now, continuing external pressures have forced these two thrusts to coexist. Should peace come, the conflicting views could well fracture Israeli society. The controversies could be much more complex and acrimonious than the struggle for religious rights in which we have been involved to date. At stake is not only the question "Who is a Jew?" but the more profound question "What is a Jewish State?"

Let us look with a critical eye on some potentially deleterious consequences of these factors:

In America

Even among active Jewish communal leadership there has been a perceptible distancing from Israel. The trend has been reinforced by the prospects of peace and the improving Israeli economy. In many quarters there is a conviction that instead of a weak Israel desperately requiring the support of a strong Diaspora, the roles have been reversed. A new psychology may be evolving, "If Israel doesn't need us any more, then maybe we don't need Israel." Even some Israeli political leaders have been issuing pronouncements that instead of American Jews supporting Israel, "let them raise funds to save themselves."

Given the above circumstances, it is understandable that some of our colleagues have suggested changing the vocabulary to which we have become accustomed. They say that the terms *Zionism, peoplehood, ethnicity, community,* even *Israel*, do not speak to the younger generation of American Jews. Younger Jews are being attracted in significant numbers to a potpourri of cults and New Age religions. In order to reach the inquisitive, intelligent, searching American Jews, we have to approach them in terms they comprehend: terms such as *faith, spirituality, healing*. To be sure, this is a vocabulary that can be made to resound with Jewish meaning, content, and fulfillment. We may not have "The Twelve Steps of Recovery" but our tradition certainly encompasses the ten *sefirot* (spheres) of Kabbalah and other spiritual and esoteric components of mysticism.

In theory, therefore, there is no reason why the new emphases on spirituality and faith should not lead to an enhanced understanding of Jewish peoplehood, and an enriched utililization of Israel as an experiential and inspirational resource. But if my reading is accurate, the new trend may evolve as a *replacement* rather than as a *reinvigoration* of Jewish peoplehood and ethnicity. I confess trepidation when I see the direction in which our American Reform movement is moving. I am concerned about the trend toward syncretism, the inability to set definitive boundaries, and the readiness to accept the latest fads in theological experimentation. But most of all I am concerned about the growing concentration on a personalized faith that makes little effort to express itself through the prism of Jewish peoplehood. Even in the *Shema*, our affirmation of faith, the word "Israel" comes before the words "our God." God is manifest through the experiences of *Am Yisrael*, the Jewish People. Without a profound sense of Jewish peoplehood, Judaism as a faith will not survive.

The dimension of Jewish peoplehood

Look at the developments of the last two years. The United Nations rescinded the resolution on "Zionism is Racism." The Catholic Church established formal relations with the Jewish state. Even the PLO has recognized the right of the Jewish people to a state of its own. Nation after Arab nation is recognizing the Jewish state. Would it not be paradoxical, if at the very moment the entire world recognized Jewish peoplehood, an increasing number of American Jews withdrew recognition, and our movement was in danger of becoming transformed into another American "Protestantized" religious sect?

Despite all the problematics of American Jewish life, should our movement not have as our objective the strengthening of the dimension of Jewish peoplehood? If the characteristics of peoplehood are language, culture, relationship to a land and a sense of common destiny, should we not translate these priorities into programs, institutions, and budgets?

I could choose many areas of concern, but let me take the area of Jewish education as an example. If in the next century, the Hebrew language will be the mother tongue of the majority of world Jewry, surely we should project as an educational objective knowledge of Hebrew as a second language for American Jews. This objective should be implemented through a vast, interlocking network of day schools, camps, and study programs to Israel for every Reform child and young adult. By this time, we should have developed a minimum of one hundred day schools throughout America, and each year we should be bringing tens of thousands of our young people for extended study programs to Israel. If we are serious about our peoplehood, how can we permit the continuation of a situation where Reform Jews who want their children to have an extensive Jewish education are forced to enroll them in an Orthodox day school? Why are young adults who are eager to study classic Jewish texts in an intensive manner obliged to go to Orthodox *yeshivot* in America or Israel? Should *we* not create the institutions where Reform Jews can be enriched by an experience of intensive Jewish learning and living? (In this regard, I am pleased to announce that we have opened a Reform Beit Midrash/Yeshivah for Israelis and a similar program for students from abroad.)

Yes, we are becoming the largest Jewish religious movement in America, but there is little room for triumphalism in our size. If we were indeed serious about ourselves and our mission, we would ask: *What would American Jewish life be like if we were the only religious movement in America and if the future of American Jewry were exclusively dependent upon us?*

If we were to answer that question, how would we relate to our Jewish peoplehood? I submit that modernity would no longer be an excuse for minimalism; relevance would no longer be a pretext for irreverence; and autonomy would no longer be a euphemism for license. Reform Jews would be known by what we practice and not by what elements of Orthodoxy we do not practice, by our Jewish knowledge and not by our Jewish illiteracy, by our commitments and not by our disavowals, by our high standards, and not by our lack of discipline.

In Israel

Let me assure you that in the Israeli context, we are confronted with comparable dilemmas. The fundamental question is: what will be the J.Q., the Jewish Quotient of life in Israel? A recently published report commissioned by the Ministry of Education revealed a precipitous decline in interest in Jewish studies in Israel's state schools. So few secular teachers are being prepared to teach the required subjects of Bible, Talmud, Jewish Thought, and Jewish History that the Minister of Education has predicted that within another decade school principals will be forced to choose between dropping these courses altogether, or engaging Orthodox and ultra-Orthodox teachers. Similarly, at the university level there has been a steady drop in enrollment in courses of Jewish content.

There is a growing desire in Israel for "normalization." In my judgment, those who espouse normalcy may be considered to be in the assimilationist camp of Israel. Yes, it is possible to assimilate even in Israel. When I attended the Hebrew University in 1949-50, immediately after the War of Independence, an articulate, activist group of intellectuals had developed the hypothesis that with the establishment of the State it was essential to create a new form of Israeli identity. In addition to Jews, this new Israeli identity would include all the peoples living in the new state, Moslems, Christians, Druse, and other ethnic groups. The Israeli identity would differ radically from Jewish identity, because it would trace its antecedents back to the earliest biblical times. Hence this group was called the Canaanites. They advocated elimination of traditional Jewish forms of observance, and rejected any special relationship with world Jewry and the Diaspora experience. Whereas the Canaanites have been quiescent in Israel for many years, a revised form of Canaanism may well return.

Under conditions of peace, the tendency among Israeli Jewry to distance itself from world Jewry and from the traditional sources and experiences of Judaism may well intensify. This tendency could be especially strong among the so-called "secular Jews" who comprise eighty percent of the Jewish population.

The early generations of Zionist leadership, symbolized by David Ben-Gurion, called themselves secular but they were thoroughly imbued with knowledge and love of the Bible and the land of Israel. They knew that the Lord in whom they claimed not to believe was the prime mover of holy scripture and Jewish history. They considered themselves the authentic new Jews. The title of Herzl's novel *Altneuland* (Old-New Land) could have been their motto. They were ideological *halutzim* who viewed their return to the "old country" as an opportunity to create a "new land," a new society, a new Judaism.

Unfortunately, this desire to create a new Judaism is not a declared mission of this generation of secular Jews, who themselves are the products of an either/or education, either Orthodox or secular. There is nothing in between. Their lack of Jewish knowledge has bred an inferiority complex. In effect, they say, ultra-Orthodoxy is authentic Judaism, but we reject it. The militancy of establishment Orthodoxy, and the extremism of ultra-Orthodoxy, have become pretexts for the secular majority to avoid wrestling with those issues that define the Jewish character of the Jewish state. That is why they tend to be indifferent to issues of religion and state, and why the political leaders of the major parties are willing to make such outrageous compromises of *principle* to meet the demands of the religious parties.

Dream and reality

The fact that I have not stressed the subject of rights for the non-Orthodox movements in Israel is not because religious rights are unimportant. On the contrary, in recent years we have intensified our struggle and achieved considerable success. For us the very struggle itself has served as a fortifying and unifying factor. Indeed, we are indebted to the Orthodox establishment. Because of their opposition, and contrary to their intentions, we have received public recognition as an indigenous force in Israeli society. It is the Orthodox Jews, and not the secular Jews, who have given us status.

Our ultimate problem is not with Orthodoxy, but with ourselves. Our target audience has to be the majority Israeli population who have either been repelled or alienated by Orthodoxy. Some of these are searching for meaning and content that we should be able to offer. Our ultimate test will be to meet their spiritual needs, just as the ultimate test of our movement in America will lie not in how many non-Jews we can bring into the Jewish fold, but in how many Jews we can inculcate the passion to search for *kedushah* in their lives. To what avail is a successful struggle for rights without a critical mass to exercise the rights?

Can a liberal Judaism meet the spiritual needs of the twenty-first century? That is the real challenge facing us. In the camp of liberal Judaism, I include Reform, Conservative, Reconstructionist (who already are affiliated with the World Union for Progressive Judaism) and even the few remaining courageous, pluralistic, elements of modern Orthodoxy. The impulse for *kedushah* should unite us all as allies in the struggle for renewal of the search for holiness. Can we together build the educational institutions and programs, can we develop the message to impact on the lives of the secular Jews of Israel? Can we train the messengers to deliver the message in the Jewish setting of Israel? The ultimate question: if we cannot develop the message and the messengers in the Jewish environment of Israel, will world Jewry continue to authenticate our message in the non-Jewish environment of America?

I am all too painfully aware of the moral dilemmas confronting world Jewry in relation to Israeli society and politics. A movement like ours, deeply committed to social justice, is bound to experience anguish when it views

Israel critically, as we are obligated to do. How much easier was it for us in our non-Zionist days, when we were able to separate the universalistic mission from the land and people of Israel? How much easier to live with the dream than with the reality, but without the reality, would we be able to dream? בשוב ה' את שיבת ציון היינו כחולמים, which I translate as, "We have been able to become dreamers, because God returned us to Zion" (Psalm 126:1).

If we truly understand and accept our responsibility, we can perform an historic task. We have our feet planted firmly in two worlds — Israel and the Diaspora. From the depths of the Israel experience, we can imbue the Diaspora with the conviction that without Jewish peoplehood, there can be no Judaism. From the Diaspora experience, we can help to imbue Israel with the conviction that without a relevant Judaism, the Jewish people will not perpetuate its unique inheritance. Our task is to help ensure that the Jewish state is Jewish in *character*.

Rabbi Yohanan Ben-Zakkai taught: "If you have a sapling in your hand and people cry out to you, 'Behold, the Messiah is coming, let us go out to greet him.' first plant your tree and then go out to greet him" (Avot d' Rabbi Natan 2:31).

Let us seed and nurture programs and institutions in both Israel and the Diaspora that will contribute to a revitalization of our people's heritage, language, and culture. Let us lend our hands to cultivating the soul of our people. Let us participate fully in the political process of the state of Israel and of the representative bodies of world Jewry. Let us aspire for the *kedushah* that will bring the celestial Jerusalem to the terrestrial Jerusalem, and in so doing let us work for the day when we can greet the messianic era.

From an address printed in the Central Conference of American Rabbis Yearbook, 1995.

C. RELIGIOUS PLURALISM IN JEWISH LIFE

1. A Jewish State or a State of Judaism?

2. Progressive Judaism and Established Orthodoxy: Challenges of Coexistence

3. In Defense of Diversity: A Response to Mizrachi

4. Conservative and Reform Judaism in Israel: A Call for Realignment

A Jewish State or a State of Judaism?

The twentieth century witnessed radical change in every field of science, politics, the arts, public mores and personal lifestyles. Reform Judaism itself is a product of radical change. Our movement evolved in the nineteenth century out of a liberal mindset. The world was progressing toward a better tomorrow. Victor Hugo phrased it well in *Les Miserables*: "Would you realize what revolution is, call it Progress and would you realize what Progress is, call it Tomorrow." We learned the hard way in the twentieth century that not every revolution leads to progress and not all progress leads to a glorious Tomorrow. Except for Zionism, most of the political revolutions of the twentieth century — socialism, communism, fascism, and dozens of national uprisings — betrayed their pristine principles and disintegrated into petty totalitarian dictatorships. The war "to make the world safe for democracy" was followed by the worst depravity and destruction in human history. The radical changes in personal mores and life-styles threaten the sanctity of home, family, and faith.

In his book *Powershift*, Alvin Toffler predicts that in the next century "the primary ideological struggle will no longer be between capitalist democracy, and communist totalitarianism, but between twenty-first century democracy and eleventh century darkness." Until the enlightenment, the industrial era and the birth of western democracy "organized religion had a virtual monopoly on the production and distribution of abstract knowledge." However, with the coming of the industrial era and secular culture, the social, moral, and political power of organized religion was diminished. Today we are experiencing a counter-revolution, buttressed by a negative reaction to the deterioration of morality in contemporary society. This has induced a spate of religious movements which nurture the soul and enrich the spirit of the individual believer. We behold a burgeoning of mystic and eastern cults, off-brand sects and New Age movements. Many of these groups separate themselves from society. Some would even separate themselves from this planet. Witness the California sect which committed mass suicide in the belief that their souls would ascend to heaven's gates in spaceships manned by aliens.

However, another far more dangerous religious phenomenon is evolving, organized not by those who would withdraw from society, but by those who would impose their religious views and standards on society. Throughout the world we find the spread of religious fundamentalism and xenophobic nationalism: Khomeniism in Iran, Islamic fundamentalism throughout the Middle East, the Christian right and militias in the United States, Yamatoism in Japan, the skinheads in Europe, Le Pen in France, Pamyat in the former Soviet Union, and even in our beloved Israel. Occasionally, nationalist and religious movements are separate, but increasingly one finds an unholy alliance between religious fanaticism and political extremism.

Religion-State issues in Israel — impact on the Diaspora

The developments referred to above are impacting on world Jewry and on the relations between the Jewish State and the Jewish people. They have special relevance for the religion-state issue which continues to engage our attention as a movement. Therefore, I think it important to concentrate on putting this issue in perspective.

The State of Israel has become a prime focus, an inspiration, a central factor, a unifying force for world Jewry. Yet, ironically, precisely because Israel is so central, developments within the State have injected an unparalleled divisiveness in world Jewry. The closer we Jews are brought together by the wonders of instantaneous communication, the more do profound theological, ideological, and political differences threaten to rend us asunder. An outrageous statement by right-wing Orthodox rabbis in California, invalidating the Jewishness of Conservative and Reform Judaism, reflects the debate within Israel. The Chief Rabbi of Great Britain, acting in hypocritical cowardice, refuses to attend the funeral of a universally beloved Reform rabbi in London, and thereby all but buries hope of reconciliation between Orthodox and Reform Judaism in England and elsewhere.

Indeed, the premise that any Chief Rabbi can represent all Jews is invalid and un-Jewish. Chief Rabbis do not speak *for* us. They do not speak *to* us. If they do not speak *to* all Jews, they cannot speak *for* all Jews. It was the British who in the mandatory period in Palestine first appointed a Chief Ashkenazi Rabbi and a Chief Sephardi Rabbi. A Chief Rabbi appointed through a civil political process is alien to Jewish tradition. It was the erudition of Maimonides which made him the most universally respected interpreter of Jewish law. It was the scholarship of Rabbi Joseph Soloveitchik in Boston which gave him status as the foremost authority of Jewish law in our time. No political group and no government had to elect or appoint them.

We, therefore, applaud the stance of our Reform and Liberal colleagues in Great Britain who have forthrightly declared that our movement is independent of the British Chief Rabbinate. We do not ask Chief Rabbis to recognize our authenticity. We do not recognize their authority. They are not our Chiefs, and we are not their Indians.

The radicalization of the Orthodox

The institutionalization of an established political rabbinate is symptomatic of a major defect in the relationship between Judaism and the Jewish State. Theodor Herzl's book *Der Judenstadt* was translated into Hebrew as *"Medinat Hayehudim,"* literally the "State of the Jews." In effect, the Orthodox would define the State as *"Medinat Hayahadut,"* meaning "the State of Judaism." They would have the State governed by the rules of *halacha*, the body of Jewish law shaped during the last 2000 years of exile. The *halacha* evolved as a guide for how Jews should live as a minority with no political rights among a non-Jewish majority.

Today, the Jewish condition has undergone radical change. In the State of Israel Jews are a majority. Jews are sovereign in a modern, secular, democratic state. When the State was established, the secular political leadership, led by Ben Gurion, made an accommodation with the Orthodox religious parties. They thought that Orthodox Judaism in turn would accommodate itself to the new Jewish condition. The founders of the state had as their model the first Chief Rabbi, Abraham Isaac Kook, who until his death in 1935 maintained that the return to the land of Israel represented the *Athalta di'geullah*, the beginning of divine redemption. Kook believed that Zionism, which had begun as a political movement for renewal of Jewish sovereignty, would eventually lead to a spiritual revival of Jewish religion and faith.

Tragically, the aspirations of both Ben Gurion and Abraham Isaac Kook have been rejected. Neither of them could have predicted what has subsequently transpired. Instead of a reciprocal accommodation between political Zionism and Judaism, the Orthodox religious forces have become radicalized. Motivated in large part by views characteristic of Christian and Islamic fundamentalism, they demand that Israeli society be governed by *halacha*, as interpreted regressively by them, rather than by the rules of the democratic process. The ultra-Orthodox reject secular culture and secular education, immersing themselves in a ghetto-like milieu. They profess anti-Zionism openly, refusing to serve in the army, sing *Hatikva* or observe Israel Independence Day.

However, the major blow to the vision of Rabbi Kook has come not from anti-Zionist Orthodoxy, but from Zionist Orthodoxy itself. The formerly moderate Orthodox voices are being stifled. The modern, highly cultured, liberal leadership of Orthodoxy, with whom we had much in common and open lines of communication in the past, has been replaced by a narrow, militant, chauvinistic leadership. The turn to the right in religious terms has inevitably led to a turn to the right politically. Whereas the earlier generations had forged what was known as *habrit hahistorit*, "the historic covenant" with the Labor Party, this generation has allied itself with the most extreme right-wing political forces. They have become adamant opponents of the Oslo Peace Process. Those who are entrenched in an unchanging past can see no opening to a changing future. Those who would exclude fellow Jews do not hesitate to exclude Arabs and other non-Jews. It is from the ranks of the ardent Zionist Orthodox that the assassin of Prime Minister Rabin and other perpetrators of verbal and physical violence have come. In effect, the National Religious Party is becoming the Nationalization of Religion Party, or the Religionization of Nationalism Party.

Struggle for the soul of the Jewish people

In this context, we must view the move of the World Union for Progressive

Judaism to Jerusalem and the efforts to build a liberal religious movement in Israel as a development of historic proportions. Its significance goes far beyond our present numbers and far beyond our admittedly limited impact to this date. When the "Who is a Jew" controversy erupted in 1988, the amendment which we and all Diaspora Jewry successfully opposed was to ban recognition of non-Orthodox conversions performed abroad. In 1997, less than a decade later, recognition of our conversions abroad was not under serious challenge, at least for the time being. This represents a major advance. Without a movement in Israel we would never be engaged in this struggle.

Observers have noted that many, if not most, secular Israelis are indifferent to our struggle for recognition in the Jewish State. But every Orthodox Jew now knows we are in Israel. Their opposition to our obtaining full religious rights represents the highest form of recognition of our presence and of our potential. Indeed, the irony is that the Orthodox are more aware of our potential impact and strength than are we ourselves. We should put them on our public relations payroll. The Orthodox understand, even if we do not, that through our presence in Israel the issue has been joined.

Why is the very concept of pluralism anathema to them? Because pluralism contradicts the fundamental premise of *Medinat Hayahadut*, "the State of Judaism" which they would impose by coercion. Pluralism means a victory for a secular, democratic Jewish State and a resounding defeat for a sectarian, anachronistic, triumphalistic Orthodox political establishment. They know, even if others do not, that we are engaged in a struggle for the soul of the Jewish people. At heart, this controversy is not over who is a Jew or who is a rabbi, but what is the Jewish State, what is the Jewish people, and what is the character of the Jewish State and the character of the relationship between world Jewry and the Jewish State.

Conflicting Jewish identities

In the Diaspora, Jewish identity as an ethnic group is diminishing, even as Jewish identity as a religious group is increasing. The primary framework for identifying as a Jew and the primary instrumentality for preservation of the

Jewish heritage is the synagogue. In Israel, except for the Orthodox, the primary framework for Jewish identity is the State and society. In effect, Jewish identity in the Diaspora is becoming religionized, whereas Jewish identity in Israel is becoming nationalized. The evolution of conflicting identities poses a threat of schism between Israel and the Diaspora.

The potential for schism is sharpened by demographic statistics. According to the National Jewish Population study issued by the Council of Jewish Federations in 1990, only 6% of American Jewry identify themselves as Orthodox Jews. The remaining 94% identify with one of the non-Orthodox movements or have no religious orientation. Elsewhere in the world, the percentage of those who identify as Orthodox may be somewhat higher, but in essence the vast majority of world Jewry is not Orthodox, and even among the so-called Orthodox a high percentage are non-observant Orthodox.

If the Jewish State does not recognize the validity of the religious identity of over 90% of Diaspora Jewry, it casts doubt on the authenticity of their Jewishness. It sends a message which is counterproductive, repelling those whom it wants to attract, influence, and inspire, and whose moral, economic and political support is essential to its existence.

Exclusivism versus inclusivism

In adopting the Law of Return, the Jewish State declared that its gates would be open to all who choose to identify with it. World Jewry joined enthusiastically, raising vast sums over the years for immigration and absorption, and in recent years for Operation Exodus and Operation Moses to bring Soviet Jewry and Ethiopian Jewry home. Even while the State has maintained an inclusivistic policy, the rabbinate has adopted an exclusivistic one.

The rabbinate and the Orthodox parties advocate adhering to the traditional definition of Jewish identity: "a Jew is a person born of a Jewish mother." The Nuremberg laws of Hitler's regime decreed that if one grandparent was Jewish, a person was liable to be cast into a concentration camp. The State of Israel declared that a person who could have been exterminated by Hitler because of Jewish identity was entitled by right to become a citizen of the Jewish state. Therefore, in an amendment to the Law of Return enacted by the Knesset in 1970, rights of citizenship were extended to "the children and grandchildren of a Jew, to his spouse, as well as the spouse of his child or grandchild, excluding a person who was a Jew and who of his own free will has embraced another religion."

Many of these immigrants who came to Israel during the 1990's, especially those from the former Soviet Union, are non-Jews according to *halacha*. There has been increasing pressure to change the Law of Return to exclude these non-Jews. Furthermore, the rabbinate has insisted that only persons who adhere to an Orthodox way of life will be considered for conversion. Some of these immigrants have studied with Conservative and Reform rabbis and have undergone conversion, even though they were aware in advance that their conversion would not be recognized by the Chief Rabbinate. Reform and Conservative rabbis have also converted infants adopted by their Jewish parents, in instances when the Orthodox rabbinate refused to convert children whose parents did not agree to live an Orthodox life style.

Following these conversions, these converts have applied to the courts, asking that their conversion be recognized as valid by the state. This in turn created a government crisis, with the Orthodox parties demanding legislation prohibiting the recognition of non-Orthodox conversions. The present legislation is vague. The Orthodox parties are insisting that the situation in which Orthodox conversions are recognized by the state be made *de jure* rather than *de facto*. Otherwise there is a likelihood that the courts will validate Reform and Conservative conversions performed in Israel.

In order to avoid a government crisis and the injection of divisiveness within Israel and the Diaspora, the Netanyahu government appointed a Commission headed by the then Minister of Finance, Ya'akov Ne'eman, and representatives of all the streams. After extensive meetings, it was prepared to issue a report which called for the establishment of institutes of learning in which the faculty would be selected from Orthodox, Reform and Conservative representatives, whereas the conversion itself would be performed by the official Orthodox rabbinate.

Unfortunately, the report was vehemently rejected by the Chief Rabbinate and so was never signed by the non-Orthodox. The Knesset nevertheless adopted the principle of the Ne'eman Report by an overwhelming majority vote and a pilot program was initiated by the Jewish Agency in cooperation with the government of Israel. In the absence of any agreement, the Reform and Conservative movements are pushing ahead with their court cases, and with the policy of offering conversion courses to potential converts.

In agreeing to perform their conversions, the Reform and Conservative movements are not fighting for vested interests of the movements, but for the human rights of the converts and their right to be Jews. Even more important, we are fighting on behalf of the interests and the official declared policy of the Jewish State and world Jewry. It is we who are the authentic representatives of the open door policy which is both the premise and the promise of the Jewish State.

It is essential that these new immigrants be made to feel at home in their new homeland. They are the products of over seventy years of forced assimilation. Many of those involved have experienced virulent anti-semitism. It is inconceivable that those who in their countries of origin have been victimized as Jews would be considered second-class citizens on their arrival in the Jewish state. Every effort must be made to encourage these new citizens to identify as Jews and to convert to Judaism. This will require intensive Jewish and Zionist educational programs, starting in the former Soviet Union and continuing in Israel.

Religion-State issues — central to Israel-Diaspora relations

If, as we declare long and loud, Jews are one people with one destiny, then we must have one worldwide policy. The winds of pluralism cannot prevail throughout the Diaspora and suddenly stop blowing when they reach the eastern shores of the Mediterranean. Divergent expressions of Judaism, legitimate in the Diaspora, cannot forever be deligitimized in the Jewish State. Freedom of religion cannot be separated from freedom of speech. A State which cannot tolerate differing interpretations of religious views, will eventually not be tolerant of differing political views.

Therefore, the issue of religion and state is not the narrow, isolated, tangential issue which many Israelis allege. It goes to the essence of the entire Jewish enterprise. Unless the religion-state issues are met head on, the Jewish State will cease to be the State of the entire Jewish people. Diaspora Jewry will cease to identify with the State, just as Israeli Jewry will cease to identify with world Jewry.

Is there hope for some kind of reconciliation of these controversial issues? Yes! Ultimately, these issues cannot and should not be resolved by the Knesset or the government. The State, already overburdened with weighty domestic and foreign policy crises, should not be saddled with additional burdens of trying to resolve controversy among the religious groups. Given good will on all sides, it should be possible to seek compromise solutions. On conversion, we are prepared to recommend uniform standards for a curriculum of study and a conversion ceremony. We are and should be prepared for compromise. To compromise is a sign of strength, not weakness. In the words of a distinguished Orthodox scholar, Rabbi Eliezer Berkowitz, "Within *halacha* there are possibilities for an approach between the various ideological groupings of the Jewish people. The responsibility of striving for unity in the spirit of *Ahavat Yisrael*, "Love of Israel," is equally binding on all of us. *Halacha* has to be stretched to its limits in order to further Jewish unity and mutual understanding."

Progressive Judaism's commitment to Klal Yisrael

What should be the Progressive Jewish response to the situation which confronts us? Even while we continue to struggle for rights on the political front, we should maintain our commitments to *Klal Yisrael*. Unfortunately, some Diaspora Jews have declared their intention to stop or reduce their contributions to the UJA and Keren Hayesod campaigns. They are not aware that the Jewish Agency tasks — immigration and absorption, Zionist Jewish education and renewal of the land — are conducted irrespective of Israeli government foreign or domestic policies. The average person may not possess the information to distinguish between policies of the government and policies of world Jewry. However, there is no excuse for our leadership being unable to distinguish. The Reform and Conservative movements cannot declare on the one hand that we represent 90% of world Jewry and on the other hand try to undermine those institutions which represent world Jewry. If we represent the majority of world Jewry, then we must act as a responsible majority.

Whereas we should remain critical of many aspects of the Jewish Agency — World Zionist Organization operations, our criticism must be from within and not from without. It is we who have taken the lead in efforts to reorganize, restructure and renew the Jewish Agency — Zionist movement. Our task is to be constructive, not destructive, supportive, not divisive. Pluralism entails not only a fight for rights within *Klal Yisrael*, but also the assumption of obligations on behalf of *Klal Yisrael*.

Most of the leaders of the fundraising campaigns, particularly in North America, are Reform and Conservative Jews. However, many of them are only nominal members of our congregations. Some of them feel closer to the State of Israel 7,000 miles away than they do to their synagogue around the corner. In effect, Israel turns them on more than do our congregations. But, they are Jews who are turned on Jewishly. They are good Jews, so passionately committed to the survival of our people that they give generously of their material and human resources. We have defaulted in relationship to them. It is our obligation to reach out to them. They have begun to understand that it is not enough to mobilize funds in support of Israel in general. They must be concerned about the quality of life in Israel. Today's donors are becoming more sophisticated. They want their funds to be channeled to institutions and programs which will create a society reflecting their values, an Israel with which they will be proud to identify. They need the non-Orthodox movements in Israel. They need us, even as we need them. This current crisis has generated in Diaspora leadership a new receptivity to support our institutions and programs which strengthen the democratic, pluralistic components of Israel. I have every reason to believe that if we act responsibly, we shall find them responsive. We shall become true partners in a common cause.

Progressive Judaism's commitment to ourselves

Finally, we must be self-critical. Our efforts to date have been woefully inadequate. Why are we so aroused by this crisis? Because we instinctively recognize that Israel is not just another geographical region of our international movement. Israel is the pulsating heart of the Jewish people. We need a strong heart to pump the life-sustaining blood to other parts of the Jewish body. If we are only a Diaspora movement, we shall be diagnosed by other Jews as an unhealthy, not fully authentic limb of the Jewish people, even as our own members will experience a debilitating relationship to the Jewish heartland.

Ours is the ultimate responsibility for invigorating Progressive Judaism in Israel. We need an injection of synagogues, schools, youth movements, *yeshivot* and centers of learning, educational and cultural programs. Resolutions from New York and Johannesburg are important, but resolute action in Israel is essential. Faxes from London and Melbourne are desirable, but facts in Israel are prerequisite. Special delivery messages from abroad are helpful, but the message of Progressive Judaism must be delivered in Israel by Israeli messengers.

The Bible recounts how the prophet Jeremiah, imprisoned because of his outspoken views, is visited by his cousin who advises him to buy a field in his native village of Anatot. כי לך משפט הירושה ולך הגאולה קנה לך ואדע כי דבר ה' הוא. "The right of inheritance is yours, and you have the duty of redemption. Buy it. Then I knew that this was indeed the word of the Lord" (Jeremiah 32:8). Jeremiah, though languishing in jail, buys the field to demonstrate his confidence in the future.

We in our movement are like the prophet Jeremiah. We work under severe disabilities in Israel. Nevertheless, we are committed to the future of Israel and to our role as an integral part of that future. Ours is the duty to participate in the redemption of *Am Yisrael*, the People of Israel, through the redemption of *Eretz Yisrael*, the Land of Israel. We have been given an historic role, a splendid opportunity. Let us buy into it. Ours is the field. Ours is the obligation. Ours is the challenge. Together with our fellow Jews, we shall reap the harvest. In participating fully in the act of redemption, we as a movement shall be redeemed.

From a keynote address to the 28th International Conference of the WUPJ, Johannesburg, South Africa, 1997.

Progressive Judaism and Established Orthodoxy: Challenges of Coexistence*

The program theme for the 23rd International Conference of the World Union for Progressive Judaism was *Progressive Judaism and Established Orthodoxy: The Realities and Challenges of Co-existence.* Initially, a sub-title asked the question: *Confrontation or Cooperation?* My response to the question is not either/or, but both/and.

Confrontation? Yes. When? When a leading American Orthodox rabbi issues an *halachic* ruling that the marriages of Reform rabbis are invalid. When the community day school in Perth, Australia, welcomes gentile children, but refuses to register the children of women converted by Reform rabbis. When ultra-Orthodox fanatics put a *mechitzah* around the fresh grave of a distinguished Reform Rabbi, because they do not want the remains of a Reform rabbi to contaminate the graves of the pious righteous ones buried on the Mount of Olives.

Confrontation? Yes. Where? Wherever Jews live. But we as a movement have yet to come to terms with the new fact in contemporary Jewish life. The front lines of the struggle are in Israel. Why in Israel? Because Israel is where the dark forces of reaction have drawn the battle-lines and learned the uses of political power and of physical and verbal violence. Because what happens in and to Israel impacts on the character, reputation and fate of world Jewry. Because Israel is the setting for testing the applicability and integrity of Jewish values.

If we, potentially the largest and strongest movement in religious Jewry, are to play our role, then we will have to accept the reality that Israel today is the center stage of the Jewish drama. If Israel is Broadway, we cannot afford to act only off-Broadway. If we have so far successfully thwarted the campaign to

---

* The ongoing controversies between Orthodox Judaism and Liberal Judaism inject divisiveness into the body politic of world Jewry. This chapter, based on an address to an international conference of the World Union, discusses the dilemmas involved in seeking a balance between the principles of pluralism and the need for unity.

amend the "Who is a Jew" legislation, it is not only because we conducted a lobbying effort in the Diaspora, but because we engage the forces of neo-messianic zealotry from within Israel. In Israel, we speak not as spectators, but as "builders of Zion," in Zion, with our congregations, our schools, our settlements, our rabbis, and our world center. Yet, despite all our efforts, we have hardly begun to mobilize our energies and resources to wage the battle effectively and to confront the forces of retrogression on the field selected by them. Until we build spiritual ramparts of Progressive Judaism through people, institutions, and programs in Israel, we shall not exploit to the fullest our capacity to make a distinctive contribution to Jewish destiny.

Cooperation? Yes. We have many allies in the effort to advance the Jewish people as an enlightened force among the nations. Many groups, religious and communal, ideological and political, public and private, are at work in both Israel and the Diaspora. In the instance of the Law of Return we have taken initiative to forge these groups into a broad coalition, both in Israel and abroad. It is now becoming clearer to the Jewish public that "Who is a Jew" is symbolic of larger questions: who is a rabbi, and what is Judaism, and who can belong to the Jewish people, and what should be the relationship between Judaism and the Jewish state, and between the Jewish state and world Jewry? We shall continue to expand our cooperative endeavors with all with whom we share a common vision of a humane, liberal, and pluralistic Jewish people.

Modern Orthodoxy — sharing and differing

Within the groups of allies, or more accurately, potential allies, I include those who denominate themselves as "modern Orthodox." Unlike the anti-Zionist ultra-Orthodox, who in Israel discourage their adherents from serving in the army or observing Independence Day, the modern Orthodox remain steadfastly Zionist. In the United States, they cooperate with the Conservative and Reform movements on a host of Jewish public concerns. We respect and applaud them for their efforts to maintain institutions of intensive Jewish learning and for their steadfast observance of Jewish tradition. We share much in common with them, especially the conviction that without a vibrant Judaism there will be no continuity for the Jewish people. Whereas we may differ with each other on the emphasis we attach to the Jewish imperatives of ethical conduct and ritual observance, they recognize that the strictest adherence to ritual commandments does not necessarily assure moral behavior, just as we understand that strict adherence to a moral code does not in and of itself assure the preservation of Judaism.

We shall continue to be separated from them by our respective attitudes towards *halacha*. They hold to the *halacha* as the supreme, divinely bestowed standard, subject to varying interpretations, but unchangeable. We consider *halacha* as a venerated guide, but subject to modification, and even rejection, if it does not conform to our ultimate values and purposes. Thus, even though divergent views of *halacha* will continue to separate us, it is to be hoped that our mutual respect for *halacha* and our concern for the unity of the Jewish people will provide a basis for dialogue and accommodation.

A willingness for compromise

The alternative is horrendous to contemplate. Consider just the following two facts:

1. Reform conversions are not recognized by the Orthodox who, therefore, do not accept the progeny of women converts as Jews.

2. A Jewish woman receives a civil divorce, but not a Get (a Jewish religious divorce), remarries and has a child with the second husband. In the eyes of the Orthodox that child is a *mamzer* (an illegitimate child), and a *mamzer* can only marry another *mamzer* and their progeny can only marry *mamzerim* for ten generations.

Projecting backward one generation and forward one generation, a significant percentage of persons who are considered full Jews in every sense by our movement, will not be considered Jews by the Orthodox, or even by some Conservatives. It has been estimated that, given the high rates of conversion and divorce without a Get, one fifth of the American Jewish population will not be considered by the Orthodox as eligible for marriage with other Jews by the end of this century.

Most Jews are unaware of the problem, and even most rabbis will conclude that nothing is to be done. There appear to be no partners for dialogue. We are headed on a collision course and a spirit of triumphalism and self-righteousness prevails in all the groups, including our own. After all, we are the majority in North America. But what a tragedy if we were to create two separate Judaisms: in America, a Judaism where *Ishut*, personal status, is defined unilaterally by a Reform Judaism oblivious to the stance of the rest of world Jewry; and elsewhere, a Judaism defined and imposed by the Orthodox, indifferent to the special needs and problems of Jews living in an open society. Each side lobbying in the Knesset with the identical slogan: Preserve the unity of the Jewish people! But unable to sit down around a table outside the Knesset to translate the slogan into reality.

We have every right and obligation to advocate pluralism to others. But does not the very exercise of the right entail an obligation to look in the mirror of self-criticism? I would plead with the leaders of our movement, to keep our minds and hearts open; I would plead with them not only to call for understanding and compromise on the part of Orthodoxy but to articulate willingness for compromise on *our* part. This would involve a long and difficult process of negotiation, trying to formulate agreed upon standards and practices, or modifying long-held principles, but few principles are of higher priority than to seek the unity of *Klal Yisrael*.

Learning to live together

I know full well that a call for coexistence with Orthodoxy and potential merger with Conservative Judaism in Israel and Latin America will in all probability not receive a positive response from official quarters. Then why issue the call? Because a liberal movement committed to *Klal Yisrael* must be committed to changing the current deteriorating direction of intra-Jewish relations. Because just as we have a right to expect of the modern Orthodox that they speak out forthrightly against ultra-Orthodox violence and fanaticism, so they have a right to expect our responsible leadership to modulate the strident voices of those in our movement who are insensitive to the needs of the Orthodox community. Because the task of a liberal movement is to keep the door open in hope and prayer that our brothers will one day want to enter.

The Sassover Rebbe described the true meaning of brotherhood when he recounted the conversation of two simple peasants. The first said, "Tell me, Ivan, do you love me?" "Of course," responded the second. "I love you deeply." The first: "Do you know, my friend, what gives me pain?" The second: "How can I know what gives you pain?" The first: "If you do not know what gives me pain, then how can you say that you truly love me?" The Sassover Rebbe concluded, "to truly love means to know what brings pain to your brother." If we, indeed, believe in the brotherhood of *Am Yisrael*, then we must know that certain decisions of our movement and practices of individual rabbis deeply pain other Jews. However, the reality is that liberal Judaism is here to stay, just as Orthodoxy is here to stay. The challenge is to coexist, to learn to live together, despite our differences.

I am well aware that what I have said about our relationships to the Orthodox and Conservative movements may not represent the views of the majority in our movement. Is my message unrealistic? Naive? Premature? Perhaps. However, knowing the radical changes in our movement during the last sixty years, I am convinced that we need to position ourselves for kaleidoscopic changes during the next sixty years. If in the past our challenge was to respond to modernity, in the future our challenge will be to respond to Jewish peoplehood. How do we as a movement vivify *Am Yisrael*, our people, our land, our language, our heritage, our faith? We shall have to engage in long-range policy planning. We shall have to create new institutions and new programs. We who have embarked on an Outreach Program to Jews of choice and non-Jewish spouses need an outreach program to our fellow Jews. We shall have to relate to the fact that we are only one part of the Jewish people. If we as a part do not act as integral to the whole, then we shall not be considered authentic, not in the eyes of others, and eventually, not even in our own eyes. It is for that reason that I suggest an extended process of negotiation, if not among organizations, then among individuals, with the modern Orthodox on the one hand, and the Conservative on the other hand, both separately and together. We need serious dialogue, away from the glare of acrimonious public disputations and heated Knesset debates, among those of us who are committed to Judaism as the life-enriching source of the Jewish people's existence.

To reason is not treason, to seek reconciliation is not appeasement, to strive for moderation is not political expediency, and to express a willingness to compromise is a sign of strength, not weakness.

When Leo Baeck gave his first address to the World Union after his return to freedom in 1946, he declared: "We are Progressive, Liberal Jews not for the sake of Progressive, Liberal Judaism, but for the sake of Judaism, of Judaism as a whole ... Progressive Judaism can have its significance only in the midst of the whole of Judaism, of all Jewish life, only with a strong feeling for the common tasks, for the whole that is before and above all the parts, for *Klal Yisrael*. We do not want to be a mere party, great or small, but a movement; not a sect, but an energy in Judaism. An egoist Liberal Judaism which would only think of itself, which would forget that it has its task for the sake of the greater whole, such a Liberal, Progressive Judaism would be a contradiction in terms, it would be neither Liberal nor Progressive, nor would it be Jewish."

As we embark on the next stage in the history of *Am Olam*, our people's journey to eternity, let us be liberal, progressive and Jewish, in spirit as well as in name. Let us approach our fellow Jews motivated by the words of the prophet Malachi:

אז נדברו יראי ה' איש אל רעהו ויקשב ה' וישמע. "Let those who serve the Lord speak one to another, and then God will hearken and heed" (Malachi 3:16).

Based on an address to the 23rd International Conference of WUPJ, Toronto, Canada, 1986.

In Defense of Diversity: A Response to Mizrachi

Forum, *a publication of the World Zionist Organization (WZO), sponsored a panel on the subject of "Religion and Democracy" in its Spring 1982 issue. The first article, entitled "Do not change the ground rules" was written by Rabbi Louis Bernstein, Professor of History at Yeshiva University, member of the WZO Executive, and veteran leader of the Mizrachi religious Zionist party. It argued forcefully against the introduction in the WZO of resolutions by the Reform and Conservative movements on religious pluralism in Israel. Rabbi Hirsch replied on behalf of the Reform movement.*

Rabbi Louis Bernstein of Mizrachi is a person of profound knowledge and deep commitment to both Zionism and Judaism. Since the views he expresses are representative of many Orthodox Jews, I will endeavor to respond to his legitimate concerns, without entering into side issues. But first, let me restate, objectively, Rabbi Bernstein's major arguments:

- The 29th World Zionist Congress resolution on religious pluralism threatens the historic partnership and on-going working relationship between secular Zionism and religious (Orthodox) Zionism.

- Orthodox Zionism is thus being forced to reappraise its role within the Zionist framework and, by implication, may withdraw from it.

- The resolution "calls upon the State of Israel, the homeland of the Jewish people, to put into practice the principle of assuring full rights, including equal recognition, for all rabbis, and equal assistance to all the trends in Judaism."

- This threatens to establish a dangerous precedent whereby Diaspora Jews will interfere in internal Israeli policies.

- For Orthodox Zionism, "the unity of the Jewish people is a paramount consideration."

- The differences in practice and ideology, among the Conservative and Reform "cause havoc in Israel and chaos in the Diaspora."

- The non-Orthodox claims to represent the majority of American and world Jewry cannot be demonstrated by any competent demographer.

- "The personal tragedies that will result from pluralism defy numbers." An "endless evil ... will be released if this grotesque Pandora's Box is ever opened."

Endangering the Orthodox monopoly

My response: Orthodoxy has opposed the growth of non-Orthodox movements since the era of Emancipation. What new factor has now caused Rabbi Bernstein to be the harbinger of evil tidings for the Zionist movement? So long as Zionist participation was limited to Reform and Conservative Jews *as individuals,* no objection was ever raised. What would American Zionism have been without Reform rabbis Abba Hillel Silver and Stephen S. Wise, and Conservative rabbis Solomon Goldman and Israel Goldstein? But now that Reform and Conservative Judaism have formally committed their movements, organizational structures, personnel, and programs to Zionism, and are developing frameworks in Israel, the Orthodox are filled with trepidation.

The Western democratic governments stress civil liberties and freedom of worship, and unlike the Prussian government of the nineteenth century, will not permit themselves to become instruments in the hands of Orthodoxy to suppress Reform. But in Israel, the Orthodox have become accustomed to the lush fruits of government-sanctioned monopoly. The activation of Conservative and Reform movements in the Zionist framework endangers the monopoly. No wonder Rabbi Bernstein hankers for "the good ol' days" when deals could be struck and accommodations made so easily with irreligious or anti-religious secularists. It is only when these trusty secular partners support resolutions on religious pluralism that they suddenly become transformed into "strange political bedfellows, dogmatic Marxist Zionists and American capitalists," as if Rabbi Bernstein and his Mizrachi associates were not themselves American capitalists!

What twisted reasoning induces the Orthodox to seek partnership with secular Jews, while declaring as an "endless evil" those committed to preserving the basic components of the religious heritage? In a conversation with a Chief Rabbi of Israel, I asked, "What would you prefer that the Jews of Tel Aviv do on *Rosh Hashanah* — spend the day on the beach, or pray to the God of Israel in a Reform or Conservative synagogue?" The response: "Let them be on the beaches. Perhaps some day they will see the light and return to the true faith, and if not they, then their children. But once they enter a Reform or Conservative synagogue, they are on the road to assimilation and conversion." A similar attitude motivates the Jerusalem Chief Rabbinate to declare that in attending services of the Conservative or Reform movements, one cannot fulfill the *mitzvah* of hearing the *Shofar* on *Rosh Hashanah*. What a betrayal of the rabbinic mandate — to prefer the vacuum of indifference, to the fulfillment of the *mitzvot* of worship, study, and observance!

Broadening the Zionist base

Rabbi Bernstein hints that Mizrachi may withdraw from the World Zionist Organization. Have no fear! They "are at ease in Zion" — and in Zionism. They have chalked up so many constructive achievements, have introduced so many creative programs in the various WZO departments over which they have control or influence, and have reaped so many benefits in budgets, programs, and positions, that neither a WZO resolution nor increased participation by Conservative and Reform Zionists will budge them from active participation in the Zionist organization. Nor is there any reason for them to depart the scene. Their success is a model for the Conservative and Reform to follow.

Had the Conservative and Reform movements entered the Zionist movement in full force, as did the Mizrachi, before the establishment of the state, both the Zionist movement and Conservative and Reform Judaism would have been inestimably strengthened. Instead of penalizing Reform Judaism for its past anti-Zionism, Rabbi Bernstein should view Reform participation in the WZO as a great victory for Mizrachi, and a vindication of its definition of Zionism.

If anything, Reform and Conservative Zionists are in greater ideological harmony with the Mizrachi than with any of the secular Zionist groups. For unlike the secularists, the Reform and Conservative movements uphold the synthesis of Judaism and Zionism. Only the Orthodox, Reform and Conservative Zionists are committed to an intensive Jewish education rooted in observance of religious tradition.

The affiliation of the Reform and Conservative movements offers Zionism new vistas of creative opportunity and identification. Their participation is a threat only to those who perceive the Zionist movement as a closed, politicized, small band of aging, irrelevant, and inconsequential functionaries. If Rabbi Bernstein believes in expanding the representative character, influence, and impact of Zionism, he should do everything in his power to develop an inclusive policy. Let him welcome the broadening of the Zionist base, and seek a voice and full participation for the Reform and Conservative Zionists. Pluralism is not an enemy of Orthodoxy, but an ally, bringing millions of Jews closer to the religious heritage of our people.

The potential for Reform in the USA

Rabbi Bernstein on the one hand decries the "numbers game," but then on the other hand he commends the high fertility rate and aliyah rate among Orthodox Jews. Obviously numbers are important, for through numbers we gauge our success in preserving the Jewish people. Professor Bernard Lazerwitz, foremost expert on American Jewish population statistics, professor of sociology at Bar-Ilan University, is a traditional Jew identified with an Orthodox-sponsored institution. I list these credentials in order to remove any accusation of his being biased in favor of Reform. Basing his findings on the National Jewish Population Survey of 1980 sponsored and financed by the Council of Jewish Federations, Lazerwitz states that "among U.S. Jewish adults...11% identified with the Orthodox denomination, of whom 7% claimed synagogue membership; 42% identified with the Conservative denomination, of whom 24% claimed synagogue membership; and 33% identified with the Reform denomination, of whom 17% claimed synagogue membership." Thus, of all American Jews, 48%

are synagogue affiliated; 7% actually belong to an Orthodox synagogue and 41% to Conservative and Reform synagogues. Lazerwitz states: "the trends are clear and dramatic...the Orthodox denomination of the future will be but a few percentage points of the United States Jewish population. Apparently, this denomination has derived much of its membership and support from foreign-born Jews. Unless the number of aging foreign-born Jews is augmented by substantial numbers from abroad, Orthodoxy will gradually decline from its present 11% toward a level akin to the 3% Orthodox among those Jews both of whose parents are U.S. born. Orthodox Judaism in the United States has yet to develop an attraction for the native-born Jewish masses. U.S. Jewry of the near future will be more inclined toward Reform Judaism than Conservative Judaism. While the official members of both denominations will be about equal, Reform will appeal to more of the "identified with a denomination, but not joining a synagogue" type of Jew. This gives the Reform denomination more potential members than the Conservative denomination. (41% Reform and 30% Conservative among persons both of whose parents are American born.)[1]

Various population studies have projected that given the low Jewish fertility rate (below zero population growth), the high incidence of intermarriage, and assimilation, the world Jewish population will have suffered a precipitous drop by the turn of the century.

In North America, the vast majority of religious ceremonies (marriages, burials, conversions, etc.) are performed by non-Orthodox rabbis. In many countries (Argentina is an example) it is impossible to obtain an Orthodox conversion. Only an infinitesimal percentage of divorcing couples abroad obtain an Orthodox *get*. Most divorcing couples file only civil divorce proceedings. Given the high rate of divorce and second marriages, the Orthodox rabbinate's preoccupation with genealogical purity, its rigid interpretations in regard to *ishut* (personal status), and its failure to recognize religious acts performed by the rabbis who serve the majority of world Jewry — the number of persons recognized by the Orthodox as *halachic* Jews will be further reduced.

An anachronistic approach

These figures are recounted in sadness. I and other Reform Jewish leaders view Orthodoxy as a vital preservative force in Jewish life. But Orthodox Jews will have to face reality. The reality is that Orthodox Judaism has appealed only to a small percentage of world Jewry — and according to all sociological projections, will appeal to an even smaller percentage in the future. No movement in Jewish life has discovered the miracle drug that can immunize the modern Jew against intermarriage, assimilation, and indifference.

Enough of self-righteousness and hypocrisy! Enough of Orthodoxy's making a *kapparah* (vicarious atonement) out of Reform and Conservative Judaism! Where did all the secular, Conservative, and Reform Jews come from, if not from the ranks of Orthodoxy? In countries like France, should the two liberal congregations numbering only 5,000 individuals be blamed for the rampant assimilation, intermarriage, and paucity of Jewish education among the 600,000 Jews who ostensibly are served by an established *Consistoire* and Chief Rabbinate? Let the truth be told! Orthodoxy has defaulted by failing to respond to the needs of modernity. Israeli Orthodoxy especially is still operating with an eighteenth century ghetto mentality, and not as a spiritual and moral guide to a twentieth century society where Jews are a majority. Israeli Jews have left the *galut*, but Israeli Judaism remains in *galut* (exile). The Israeli Orthodox establishment's addiction to the smoke-filled rooms of politics has drugged Judaism and drained it of integrity. Orthodoxy's political strength is the source of its moral weakness. Israeli Orthodoxy is identified as a retrogressive and anachronistic force.

Historically, Reform and Conservative Judaism evolved in order to prevent the disappearance of Jews who had been alienated by Orthodoxy. In the free societies of the Western world, it is comparatively easy to cease identifying as a Jew. No one joins a liberal movement and pays dues to a congregation in order to destroy Judaism and the Jewish people. The Reform and Conservative movements are a positive salutary force in the on-going struggle to keep the Jewish people alive, and are so considered by all those who identify with them.

What is true abroad is also true in Israel. There is no possibility that the majority of the Israeli population will become Orthodox. In their increasingly successful development in Israel, the Reform and Conservative movements are responding to the need of Israeli Jews to find religious meaning in a relevant, purposeful observance of the Jewish tradition. Competition with Orthodoxy is neither inherent, necessary, nor desired. The potential adherents are not those who are already committed to Orthodoxy, but those who have for one reason or another rejected Orthodoxy. No effort whatsoever is made to wean Jews from Orthodoxy, but every effort is made to win Jews for Judaism. In developing congregations, schools, kibbutzim, youth movements, and educational programs, the Liberal Israeli movements demand equal rights — but also affirm an equal obligation to fulfill the Zionist objective.

Against second-class status

Rabbi Bernstein and his Orthodox colleagues call for "unity of the Jewish people." But their "unity" has a price tag marked "uniformity." The unity they demand is on their terms. The Orthodox rabbinate has legitimate concerns that are shared by the responsible rabbinate of the other movements. Conservative and Reform rabbis have repeatedly expressed a willingness to sit with their Orthodox counterparts and negotiate differences within the framework of religion separated from Israeli politics. But these offers have been consistently rebuffed by the Orthodox in a Khartoum-like formula: "no negotiation, no recognition, no peace."

The "chaos" and "havoc" of which Rabbi Bernstein warns is not in the future, but is already a reality. In great measure it is caused by Orthodoxy's obstinacy in refusing to recognize and come to terms with the existence and viability of the other religious groups. Instead, it has exerted the political power of the religious parties in Israel's Knesset and has abused the secular instrumentality of the Knesset, composed in the main of secular Jews as well as non-Jewish legislators, to impose *halachic* standards on the Israeli public, as well as on the Jews of the Diaspora.

Should the world movements of Conservative and Reform Judaism remain passive when world Orthodoxy pressures the Knesset to invalidate conversions, marriages, divorces, and other religious ceremonies performed by non-Orthodox rabbis? If any interference is involved, it is by the Knesset in the internal affairs of Diaspora Jewry. The Reform and Conservative movements care so deeply about Israel that they refuse to accept second-class status. The alternative is disinterest and a weakening of the bonds of identity with Israel. If Israel is only for Orthodox Jews and secular Jews, then vast numbers of Jews will be read out of the Zionist cause.

Pluralism for a modern world

We loudly and proudly proclaim that Israel is the spiritual center for all Jews. If so, then all Jews must accept full responsibility and enjoy full participation in the upbuilding of Zion. The struggle for equal recognition is not a struggle by and for the non-Orthodox alone. It is a struggle to establish a democratic, pluralistic society that will inspire the love and loyalty of world Jewry. This is a cause which all Jews should support and which many enlightened Orthodox Jews do support.

It is indeed ludicrous to find Rabbi Bernstein warning of the dangers inherent in Diaspora Jewry's interference in Israel's internal affairs. Has he never heard of Rabbi Soloveitchik whose *halachic* pronouncements issued from Boston have at times appeared to elevate him to the status of Chief Rabbi? Has he never heard of the Lubavitcher and Satmer rebbes' repeated incursions into Israeli politics? Has he not seen the Orthodox-sponsored advertisements in the *New York Times* and Israeli press, calling on Israel to adopt specific policies concerning religious and foreign policy issues, including demands that Israel not evacuate one inch of territory? Has he not felt the reverberations of the Satmer's *Rav Tov* Vienna operation, designed to entice and cajole Soviet Jews to go any place but Israel? Where were the protests of Mizrachi when more than 10,000 Hasidim demonstrated in New York against the archeological excavations in Jerusalem and distributed leaflets calling Prime Minister Begin "a Nazi murderer?"

Apparently, some Diaspora Orthodox Jews believe they have an inalienable right to address any issue in Israel with impunity, whereas statements of the non-Orthodox are considered to be dangerous interference in Israel's internal affairs. Indeed, the article opposing pluralism in Israel by Rabbi Bernstein, himself a Diaspora rabbi, is a classic example of the very interference he himself decries.

Why has the Mizrachi leadership donned earmuffs and blinkers in the face of intervention by Orthodox Jews, some of it anti-Israeli and even anti-Semitic? The so-called moderate Orthodox leadership represented by the Mizrachi is afraid of the "Orthodox right, a strong and expanding community." The moderate Orthodox are being pulled to the right by the ultra-Orthodox, and are themselves adopting more extreme militant positions, of which Rabbi Bernstein's article is an example. In consonance with the rightward turn of Orthodoxy in both the Diaspora and Israel, the only unity encouraged is the unity of the moderate Orthodox with the right-wing Orthodox. This has produced more intolerant, isolationist, radical and chauvinistic Orthodoxy — to the detriment of Israel, the Jewish people, and Orthodox Judaism itself.

As to the "grotesque Pandora's Box" of pluralism — it was opened long ago, not by Reform and Conservative Judaism, but as a consequence of the Emancipation and the pressures on Jews to adjust to a modern world. Students of mythology know that one blessing remained in Pandora's Box — the blessing of hope. Hope is the very essence of Judaism, even as it is the theme song of Zionism — *Hatikva*. The activation of Conservative and Reform Judaism in the Zionist cause represents the hope of Zionism. Instead of fanning the embers of prejudice and discrimination, let Rabbi Bernstein and his colleagues nurture the blessing of hope to its fruition.

Rabbi Bernstein points with pride to Rabbi Samuel Mohilever, who played a formative role in seeking the blending of Orthodox Judaism and Zionism. Rabbi Mohilever sent this message to the First Zionist Congress: "It is essential that the Congress unite all 'sons of Zion' who are true to our cause to work in complete harmony and fraternity, *even if there be among them differences of opinion regarding religion.*"

Let Mohilever's words become the motto for Rabbi Bernstein and his Mizrachi colleagues. Orthodox, Conservative, Reform and secular Zionists share a common goal and a common vision: a united Jewish people restored to its own land, rooted in respect for an observance of tradition. The differences regarding religion are minor compared to the major crises of physical and spiritual survival, and to the challenge of forging a society Jewish in character as well as name.

Note

(1) Bernard Lazerwitz, "Past and future trends in the life of American Jewish denominations," Journal of Reform Judaism, Summer 1979, pp. 77-82.

Reprinted from *Forum*, published by the World Zionist Organization, no. 44, Spring 1982.

Conservative and Reform Judaism in Israel: A Call for Realignment*

In the post Six Day War period, the Conservative and Reform movements were presented with an historic opportunity. Whereas until that time, neither movement had expended great effort in establishing an indigenous movement in Israel, the Six Day War had motivated both movements to take new initiatives. How wasteful if the institutional and ideological competitiveness which pertained in the States would be transferred to Israel. How symbolic if the two movements together were to work for the creation of one united movement of liberal Judaism for Israel.

This was the propitious moment for the Conservative and Reform movements to band together. Israeli society was in a continual process of defining its Jewish character. It was essential to create a force of liberal Judaism to inculcate Jewish values through education and moral suasion rather than through religious coercion. We would declare to the State of Israel and world Jewry that our shared commitment to shape a worthy Jewish society took precedence over theological differences and institutional interests. A commitment to pool the human and material resources of the two movements would dramatize the significance of the merger for the Jews of Israel and accelerate the mobilization of support in the Diaspora.

Over the years, numerous overtures to leaders of Conservative Judaism yielded no results. Even though some persons agreed in theory, no one in a key leadership role was willing to take the lead to discuss the issue seriously. When asked how the Reform movement would respond, I replied frankly that the proposal would generate intense debate. However, there was good reason to believe that we could eventually win the support of the majority of the leaders of Progressive Judaism both in Israel and the world.

An important step in the direction of collaboration was taken in 1990. After

---

* In the Fall of 1967, the author proposed that the Conservative and Reform movements collaborate to establish one liberal alternative to Orthodoxy in Israel. In this chapter, the author advances the proposal anew.

years of negotiation, the Federation of Reconstructionist Congregations and *Havurot* (today called the Jewish Reconstructionist Federation) affiliated with the World Union for Progressive Judaism. The two organizations agreed to build one joint movement in Israel and have been cooperating to achieve this objective ever since.

I renew the call for realignment of the Conservative and Reform movements in Israel. What are the considerations justifying the proposal?

The approach to Halacha in Israel

Both the *Masorati* (Conservative) and *Yahadut Mitkademit* (Progressive, Liberal Reform) movements tend to be more traditional than in North America. This is natural, because both are evolving in the Israeli environment where the peoplehood experience is more intense than in the Diaspora.

Conservative Judaism defines itself as an *halachic* movement, yet the Orthodox rabbinate rejects the claim of the Conservative movement to legitimacy. The Orthodox contend that the Conservative interpretation of the *halacha* is not authentic. The Conservative movement has had difficulty in formulating a clear ideological stance. The general perception by outside observers is that Conservative Judaism stands somewhere between Orthodox and Reform Judaism. For example, it claims to adhere to the Orthodox position on questions of *Ishut*, "personal status." However, it has endorsed the Reform practice of ordaining women rabbis and assuring women an equal role in ritual observance. A major problem for the Conservative movement has been that a high percentage of the congregants do not adhere to the life patterns set by the rabbinical leaders. Therefore, the average Israeli has difficulty in comprehending the distinctions between Reform and Conservative Judaism.

For its part, Progressive Judaism in Israel is considerably to the right of Reform Judaism in North America. It considers *halacha* a guide rather than a guard. It has respect for the *halachic* process, even while it does not accept full adherence to the *halacha*. For example, unlike the Central Conference of American Rabbis, the Israeli rabbinic group rejects the patrilineal resolution and prohibits any rabbi from participation in a marriage ceremony between a

Jew and a non-Jew. All institutions of the movement observe *Kashrut* (Jewish dietary laws). In the creative liturgy of the Israeli Progressive movement, the passages referring to the return to Zion have been reinstated. Indeed, visitors from abroad frequently observe that Israeli Progressive Judaism is to the right of American Conservative Judaism. In effect, Israeli Progressive Judaism has accepted most of the historical agenda of Conservative Judaism.

Ideology is not the only factor

In the instance of Reform and Conservative Judaism, demography, ethnicity, socio-economic conditions, the timing and nature of waves of Jewish immigration to America, all were important factors. The character of nineteenth century American Reform Judaism was shaped by the German Jewish wave of immigration to the United States in the middle of the nineteenth century. The rise of Conservative Judaism was a consequence of Eastern European Jewish immigration in the latter part of the nineteenth century. In fact, it was the German Jews identifying with the Reform movement who supported the effort to bring Solomon Schechter to the Jewish Theological Seminary, to train spiritual leadership for Jews of Eastern European origin.

There was nothing inevitable about the development side by side of two separate American liberal religious movements. In every step along the way, the role of individual leaders was crucial. Decisions made by these leaders were motivated not only by ideology, but by complex personality factors, inter-personal relations and vested institutional interests. The reality is that almost all the differences *between* the two movements were reflected in differences *within* each movement. Reform Judaism had its Zionists, and Conservative Judaism had its non-Zionists; Reform had its traditionalists, moderates and classical Reformers, and Conservative Judaism had what Moshe Davis has called "the traditionalists, the developmentalists, and the progressives." At every stage, individuals in each movement found more in common with persons in the other movement than they did with many in their own movement.

In North America, leaders of the two movements collaborated in the establishment of the Jewish Publication Society, the Hillel Foundations, the

Jewish Community Center and YMHA movements and immigrant aid associations. Together they took joint action on issues of religious freedom and civil rights. In Israel, there has been the closest collaboration on religion-state issues, such as the struggle for the right to convert, to marry and to receive equitable government funding for educational and religious institutions. The two movements have engaged in joint public relations campaigns and in developing the Tali educational system, integrating a liberal religious education program with secular studies.

Consolidation or competition?

A case can be made for the proposition that American Jewry is a richer, more variegated community, because of the existence of two non-Orthodox movements, with their multiplicity of institutions and programs. The existence of two seminaries, two rabbinic bodies and two congregational bodies has given strength and direction to the respective movements. A case can also be made that the sum total of involved members and leaders is larger than if there had been one movement only. However, even though acknowledging that competitiveness can often be a spur to creativity, there have been numerous instances where the failure of cooperation has led to duplication, wasted funds, lack of direction and inadequate exploitation of opportunities. The congregational bodies have engaged in competitive development of non-Orthodox Judaism throughout the world. Latin America is a prime example where, had the two movements actively supported the establishment of one non-Orthodox movement, Latin American Jewry and the international movements themselves would have been reinforced.

In Israel, the two movements have developed separate training programs for rabbis, cantors and educators. Yet, surely the preparation required for these leaders of liberal religious institutions should be identical. Does an Israeli Conservative rabbi require different training from an Israeli Reform rabbi? Why should there not be one joint program? What applies to rabbinical education applies to all the activities of both movements.

The reality is that in Israel and throughout the world, graduates of Reform rabbinical training programs are serving in Conservative congregations and graduates of Conservative training programs are serving in Reform congregations. In a number of instances, congregations have merged, due to circumstances such as diminishing memberships or inability to engage adequate rabbinical and professional leadership. Also, lay members of congregations have often transferred loyalties, leaving a congregation affiliated with one movement to join a congregation affiliated with the other movement.

The need for an indigenous liberal religious movement

Initially, both the Conservative and Reform movements were led by persons trained and reared in the United States. To their credit, these early leaders have recognized that an Israeli religious movement must eventually develop its own indigenous character. The spiritual leaders of the future will be Israeli-reared and Israeli-trained. Both movements are grounded in a commitment to make Judaism relevant to their adherents' needs. Accordingly, it is to be anticipated that eventually differences will develop between religious movements rooted in the Israeli experience and those rooted in the Diaspora experience. Because of their liberal character, the world movements understand that it is essential for the Israeli movements to develop their own Israeli oriented life patterns.

The stage has been set for peace between Israel and her neighbors. If and when the international tensions are lessened, it is likely that the domestic tensions will be exacerbated. Israeli society will turn to long-postponed internal matters, among them the simmering religion-state issues. It is essential that an effective liberal religious force evolves as a counter-balance to the fundamentalist right-wing Orthodox components, which have been gaining in numerical strength and political influence.

Given the nature of the religious crisis, there is no justification for two separate liberal religious movements. I understand full well the difficulties inherent in the proposal. I appreciate the complex ramifications for relationships between the movements in Israel and their institutional counterparts in North America. However, we are challenged by a major objective: to establish a just and Jewish democratic society in Israel. Just as peace will be conducive to a realignment of the political forces in Israel, so do I believe the new conditions call for a realignment of the religious forces.

Recognizing that it may be premature to address the goal of full merger at this time, the two movements should initiate joint programs, such as nursery schools, camps, publication of educational materials and development of new synagogue centers. A process of shared initiatives will be conducive to creating a framework of interdependence. The two movements should have already discovered that the achievement of one is an advance for the other, just as the failure of one is a setback for the other.

Competitiveness and duplication impede the maximum fulfillment of the potential inherent in liberal Judaism. Judaism in Israel is in danger of spiritual stultification. The new partnership would help induce a creative and innovative regeneration of the religious heritage.

טובים השניים מן האחד אשר יש להם שכר טוב בעמלם. "Two are better than one, in that they have good reward for their labor" (Ecclesiastes 4:9).

D. PROGRESSIVE JUDAISM IN ISRAEL

The Rationale for Progressive Judaism in Israel*

I would put before you three theses: 1. Reform Judaism needs the State of Israel (2) The State of Israel needs Reform Judaism (3) Non-orthodox American Judaism needs a dynamic non-orthodox Israeli Judaism.

1. Why does Reform Judaism need the State of Israel?

Reform Judaism is a product of the emancipation. With the advent of the French revolution and modern democracy, there arose in Western Europe a fundamental question: Who are the Jews, and what should be done with them? If they are a "church," a group of persons distinguished from all others only by religious beliefs and practices, then in a new social order marked by respect for differences of opinion, the Jews are to be accepted as equals with full rights. But if the Jews are a "nation," a "separate" or "separated people" who intend to return to their own land, then the Rights of Man do not apply to them, and they can be legitimately excluded from citizenship in a democracy.

It is now an ironic twist of history to note that the first modern Zionists were anti-Semites in France. They advocated that, instead of being given French citizenship, the Jews be given a sparsely populated section of France, Austria-Hungary or Southern Russia; some radical persons even suggested they be given Palestine. Conversely, it was the philo-semites who stressed that Jews differed from gentiles only in their religious beliefs.

Napoleon was the first to ask the question, "Who are the Jews?" in a formal manner. In 1806 he convened an Assembly of Jewish Notables to whom he put a series of questions. The answers would determine whether the Jews of France and its conquered countries were to be given full citizenship.

Confronted by the choice of individual enfranchisement as adherents of a faith, or collective exclusion as a nation, it was only natural that Jews began to

---

* The proposal to transfer the International Headquarters of the World Union for Progressive Judaism to Jerusalem generated controversy within the movement. This article, written in 1972, presented the reasons for the move.

dilute the nationalistic, folk, ethnic, cultural dimensions of Jewishness. The way to integration was paved by a conscious deculturation.

Reform Judaism did not begin to develop until at least a generation later. Reform Judaism did not initiate deculturation, but was its product. Almost all American Jews, Orthodox, Conservative and Reform, have been affected by the process in one way or another. For in the American environment ethnic differences have tended to disappear. When my grandfather arrived on these shores and he was asked by the official on Ellis Island, "What are you?" he responded "Jew," meaning that he was on a par with other new Americans — Greeks, Frenchmen, Germans and Irishmen. When my son, his great grandson, is asked, "What are you?" and he responds, "Jew," he believes that the questioner is asking him to which religion does he subscribe — Protestantism, Catholicism or Judaism.

It is now almost two hundred years since the emancipation. We are equal citizens with full rights in western democracies. But in every generation the supposedly quiescent volcano of anti-Semitism has erupted and the lava of discrimination has come pouring out, wreaking havoc on us and on the societies in which we live. We discovered that the discrimination against Jews was not directly related to theological beliefs, to Judaism as a religion. On the contrary, the world theoretically accepted Jewish beliefs. It spoke with pride about the "Judeo-Christian heritage" and "biblical values." Like the man who said, "I love mankind, it's just people I can't stand," the anti-Semite said, "We love Judaism, it's just Jews we can't stand." And we began to realize that no matter how much we tried to reshape ourselves to conform to the new definition of religion, we were rejected because of the old definition of Jewish peoplehood. We had paid the full price of admission to the box seats, and then were either not admitted or were given seats in the bleachers.

Then came the Holocaust, and then came the State of Israel rising out of the smoldering ashes of six million Jews. And in 1967 came the Six-Day War, when the brands plucked from the fire were once again threatened with extinction. The trauma experienced by American Jews in the last two generations has reinforced the lesson of history: the Jews are a people. A threat to the State of Israel is a threat to the Jewish people, and therefore, the State of Israel is inseparable from the Jewish people. So the State of Israel has restored,

In 1984 in London, the Reform Synagogues of Great Britain dedicated its religious, educational and cultural center, housing also the Leo Baeck College, academic center for rabbinical training. Originally called the Manor House, it has been renamed the Sternberg Center, in honor of Sir Sigmund and Lady Hazel Sternberg. The honored guest was Prime Minister Margaret Thatcher, shown here with the author.

Prime Minister Yitzhak Shamir and the author enjoy a laugh at the WUPJ 24th International Convention in Jerusalem in 1988.

The opening session of a World Union for Progressive Judaism convention in Israel, 1993.
Left to right: The author; Shimon Peres, Foreign Minister (subsequently Prime Minister);
Teddy Kollek, Mayor of Jerusalem.

On October 26, 1994, Israel and Jordan signed a peace agreement at a moving ceremony on the Jordanian-Israeli border. The author met with clergymen of other faiths.

The author with Natan Sharansky (Minister of Industry and Commerce, and former Prisoner of Zion), at the cornerstone laying ceremony for Mercaz Shimshon, 1998.

The author presents the World Union's International Humanitarian Award to Senator Frank R. Lautenberg (New Jersey) accompanied by Senator Joseph Lieberman (Connecticut). September, 1996

The World Union for Progressive Judaism convened its 28th International Convention in South Africa in 1997. During the convention, the International Humanitarian Award was bestowed on Nelson Mandela, President of South Africa, and on Archbishop Desmond Tutu, Chairman of the South African Commission on Truth and Reconciliation.
From left to right: The author; Archbishop Desmond Tutu; Austin Beutel, President of the WUPJ.

In March, 1999, the author was awarded the degree of Doctor of Humane Letters, Honoris Causa, by his colleagues and friends, Professor Alfred Gottschalk, Chancellor; and Rabbi Sheldon Zimmerman, President, Hebrew Union College -Jewish Institute of Religion.

Bella and Richard Hirsch in the Galilee on the day the site
for the Har Halutz settlement was selected (1984).

The Hirsch family, August 2000.

and is continuing to restore, the dimension of Jewish peoplehood to all Jews. The manifestations of peoplehood are evident throughout the Jewish world in the renewal of Jewish culture, the revival of the Hebrew language and the reawakened consciousness of Jewish identity. However, nowhere is the impact of peoplehood stronger than in Reform Judaism, which of all the religious movements in Jewish life had strayed farthest from its traditional moorings. The future of Reform Judaism is dependent on strengthening its bonds with the land and people of Israel. Israel today has become a prime instrumentality for living and learning Judaism, an educational tool for experiencing, not just studying about, Jewish life. The State of Israel has given body to the soul, breath to the spirit as we have come to recognize that a Judaism bereft of Jewish nationalism is a diluted distortion.

2. Why does the State of Israel need Reform Judaism?

There is much divisiveness within Israeli life, but by far the sharpest cleavage is between so-called religious and non-religious Jews. I stress the word so-called. Because when the Israeli says he is *dati* (the Hebrew word for "religious") he really mans that he adheres strictly to the Orthodox pattern of Jewish observance. And when he says he is *lo-dati* (non-religious) he means simply that he is not observant. The *lo-dati* or non-observant Israelis represent the majority of the population and a growing number of the young people.

The Eastern European Jews, those who set the cultural tone, came from a society which never experienced any liberalization of religion in general or of Judaism in particular. The "founding fathers" of modern Zionism came to Israel in part as a rebellion against the inflexible authoritarianism of the East European rabbinate and organized Jewish life. They adopted the anti-religious stance of the Eastern European forces of social progress, which is still manifest in the lives of their children and grandchildren. This anti-religious mentality has been reinforced in reaction to the extreme public positions taken by the official rabbinate and the Orthodox religious parties.

In Israel today are to be found many Orthodox Jews whose life pattern reflects the nobility of traditional Jewish observance, enriched by the fertility of the Israeli soil, and uncontaminated by intolerance and fanaticism. But the image projected by the Orthodox establishment alienates the non-Orthodox and only serves to justify their stereotype of Judaism as irrelevant.

The rabbinate of Israel is by and large insulated from contact with the westernized secular milieu of Israel. Few of the rabbis are university graduates. Most have received their education exclusively within the closed society of the *yeshivot*. Though living in the twentieth century, they are reared in an environment which resembles the eighteenth century shtetl. With rare exceptions their Jewish orientation is legalistic and their social orientation, reactionary. For the most part, the rabbi is a *mashgiach* (supervisor) rather than a *madrich* (counselor), a ritual overseer rather than a spiritual leader, a guard rather than a guide. The rabbinate tends to view the secular society with supercilious disdain. Yet, paradoxically, even while the rabbis reject participation in Israeli society, they seek to impose their narrow views on that society. In the name of Judaism, they pervert Judaism.

The Chief Rabbinate — an alien concept

The very concept of a Chief Rabbinate is alien to Judaism. During the Second Commonwealth, the Sanhedrin had functioned as the governing body on matters of Jewish law. After the destruction of the Jewish state by the Romans 2000 years ago, decisions were rendered by the heads of *yeshivot* or outstanding rabbinic scholars, whose judgments were accepted by virtue of their learning and not by virtue of appointment by a secular government. The Chief Rabbinate is, therefore, a foreign concept, derived from Christianity and introduced into Jewish life by non-Jewish civil authorities who wanted one central religious figure to whom they could relate.

The tragedy of contemporary Israel is that both the Orthodox establishment and a large percentage of the non-observant Jews share the identical narrow, distorted perception of Judaism. Both the *datiim* and *lo-datiim* confine their definition of "religious Judaism" to full compliance with Jewish ritual. For the Orthodox, compliance becomes the end-all and be-all, whereas the non-Orthodox reject the demand for compliance. But both agree that full compliance with Orthodoxy is the criterion by which to gauge religiousness. Confronted by only two alternatives — "all or nothing" — it is little wonder that so many Israelis have chosen the latter rather than the former.

The consequences of this "all or nothing" environment are already manifest in a series of studies conducted by Professor Simon Herman, social psychologist of the Hebrew University, and published in a book entitled *Israelis and Jews*. Professor Herman attempted to probe what Jewishness means to the new generations born in Israel, and how strong are the bonds between the younger Israelis and Jews in the Diaspora. He posed a number of questions to a representative country-wide sample of youth born the year the State was declared:

1. "If you were to be born all over again, would you wish to be born a Jew?" 94% of students who were religious responded "yes," whereas only 54% of the non-religious students responded in the affirmative.

2. "If you were to live abroad, would you wish to be born a Jew?" Of the religious students, 84% responded "yes." Of the non-religious students only 37% responded "yes," 34% "it makes no difference," and 29% "no." Yet when these same non-religious students were asked, "If you were to be born again, would you wish to be born an Israeli?" 83% of them responded "yes."

These responses lead to the conclusion that for students with a religious orientation, Jewishness is a prime factor in their lives, wherever they may reside. But for a high percentage of the non-religious, commitment to Jewishness is predicated on their living in Israel. A characteristic response is quoted: "Jewish religion has no meaning for me. In Israel where all are Jews, I don't mind also being a Jew. But outside of Israel — why be a Jew?"

Professor Herman, who is himself non-religious, significantly concludes, "The religious decline poses the question as to what can be the strength and durability of a secular Jewish identity. Religion and ethnicity are so closely interwoven in the Jewish identity that any tendency toward their separation raises serious problems."

Within the framework of Jewish tradition

Some years ago the leaders of Israel tried to counteract these "serious problems" by introducing courses of "Jewish consciousness" in the schools. Especially since the Six-Day War, when the solidarity of world Jewry was so manifest, Israelis have been in search of their Jewish identity. They are asking themselves a good Jewish question, "Why is this state different from all other states?" Was not the aim of Zionism to save the Jewish soul, as well as the Jewish body, and if so, how can the religious dimension be expunged from the Jewish soul?

The Six-Day War has created moral problems totally alien to Jews. The Jewish people has always found meaning in the role of oppressed minority. But to find a rationale for being the victor rather than the victim, the occupier rather than the occupied, the caretaker rather than the refugee, is much more difficult. Those for whom socialism was a prime force are discovering that socialist ideals must be compromised as they wrestle with the problems of balancing the needs of the group with the rights of the individual, the needs of labor with the nation's needs for capital investment and development.

Neither Zionism nor socialism provides the answers to some of the major public questions, and certainly not to the personal questions of life. What do Zionism and socialism have to contribute to an understanding of tragedy, of sickness and death? How can Zionism or socialism sanctify the profound moments of an individual's life, of birth and marriage, or the great events in the life of the Jewish people?

The holidays of Chanukah and Passover can be nationalized easily into the idiom of contemporary Israel. The Maccabees are the forerunners of the state's victorious army and the Exodus from Egypt can be considered the symbol of redemption in our day. But wherein lies the significance of the two most sacred events in the Jewish calendar, Rosh Hashanah and Yom Kippur, which celebrate no historical or national event, but rather focus on the individual and one's relationship to God?

The most sensitive non-religious Israelis are beginning to realize that Jewishness cannot be compressed into the boundaries of Israeli citizenship, that even the most well-formulated political and social philosophy cannot submerge the human aspiration to search for eternal verities, and that in Israel this search must be conducted within the framework of Jewish tradition. Many popular songs, written by so-called secular Jews, are permeated with religious connotations. Israelis are drawn to the *Kotel* in Jerusalem, the Western Wall of the Temple, by a fervent mystical impulse which cannot be explained in nationalistic terms alone. Indeed, it is becoming clear that the very attachment to *Eretz Yisrael*, the land of Israel, reflects an inner passion of the Jewish people that can be rooted only in a profound faith.

So today, non-religious Israelis are in search for Jewish meaning. This search is not being conducted within a theological framework. The starting point of the search is not God, but the Jewish people and Jewish tradition. In 1950 I attended a Seder in a kibbutz which had prepared its own *Haggadah*. It contained some skeletal references to the traditional *Haggadah*, but for the most part it read like an annual productivity report, giving the number of children and cows born during the course of the year, the amount of produce raised, the number of buildings erected and the economic growth of the kibbutz. In the intervening years, the various kibbutz movements have begun to publish *Haggadot* for their member kibbutzim. And what did they discover? That the one common denominator which unified all the kibbutzim and which gave meaning to the Seder service was the tradition. Today the *Haggadah* used by the non-religious kibbutz, though still containing contemporary selections, has a prominent traditional emphasis.

The various kibbutz movements have published magnificent guides to the observance of the Shabbat. Whereas when I worked on a kibbutz, the Sabbath was not marked by any special observances, today one enters a kibbutz on Sabbath and sees white tablecloths, flowers, and other festive decorations. In a number of kibbutzim there is a Kabbalat Shabbat service, and candles are lit. Bar Mitzvah has become a common feature of kibbutz life. The kibbutznik who, a generation ago, would have scoffed at having his son participate in any ceremony of religious affirmation, is now proudly attending his grandson's Bar Mitzvah.

The intellectual and spiritual ferment in the kibbutzim is characteristic of Israeli society as a whole. If the founders of the kibbutz would not have had their perception of Judaism distorted by their contact with the rabbinic authoritarianism of Eastern Europe, they might well have considered their socialist Zionism not as a rebellion against Judaism, but as a "reform" of Judaism. The previous generations rejected Judaism ideologically. The present generation is not in rebellion against Judaism. To the contrary, "Hansen's law" is operative here — what the son tries to forget, the grandson tries to remember. The Israeli experience teaches us to beware of facile delineations between religious and secular. Much of what transpires in a secular framework in Israel could be defined as religious — just as many activities in an American synagogue can be considered secular, even if preceded by an opening prayer.

The contribution of Progressive Judaism

Reform Judaism, or Progressive Judaism, as it is called in Israel, is confronted by one basic question. Do we have something to contribute to the *lo-datiim*, the so-called non-religious Israelis who are in search of Jewish meaning? I submit that Progressive Judaism has much in common with the *lo-datiim* and much to offer. We do not demand obeisance to the concept that God transmitted the *halacha* to Moses on Mt. Sinai, and that, consequently, its fulfillment as interpreted by the Orthodox rabbinate is binding upon all Jews henceforth. Instead, we advocate a concept of progressive revelation, obliging each generation to interpret *halacha* in the light of its needs. For Reform, Jewish law is not a wall to block out the influences of a secular world, but rather a guide for retaining the beauty and integrity of Jewish tradition in the world. We are not blinded by the light of secular society shining in on us, but rather welcome and participate in the secular society, its political process and its culture, even while we would illumine secular life with the light of Jewish tradition. As a movement, we share with the non-religious Israelis the same humanist orientation, with its emphasis on the responsibility of human beings to perfect the universe. We share with them a love of the Bible, with full respect for the Talmudic rabbinic tradition, but without the emphasis of Orthodox Judaism on the primacy of the Talmud. We share with them a concept of the role of the Jewish people in history, which is dependent not only upon God's providence, but upon the kind of society Jews create. We do not wait and pray for the Messiah to bring peace to Israel and to the world, but we call upon the Jews and all humanity to strive to achieve their own destiny. We encourage innovative use of new forms of worship and ritual, rooted in tradition, but relevant to the demands of the present.

We do not limit the role of the rabbi to an ecclesiastical functionary, a "marrying Sam" or a "burying Bennie." We do not limit the synagogue to a *Bet Ha-Tefilah*, (a house of prayer), but insist that it must also be a *Bet Ha-Midrash* and a *Bet Ha-Knesset*, (a place of study and of communal concern). We do not confine a Jewish religious movement to a narrow, compartmentalized ghetto of life, but maintain that Jewish moral and religious values must permeate life.

A liberal alternative to Orthodoxy

Will this approach to Judaism appeal to Israelis who have rejected the approach of Orthodoxy? That is the question. Are we trying to import something to Israel? In a way, yes, but what in modern Israel is not imported? Orthodoxy, too, is an importation from the East European shtetl. We have no intention of transplanting American Reform Judaism with all its forms and practices to Israel.

There is no question that eventually a liberal alternative to Orthodoxy will appear on the Israeli scene. It may be that the alternative will arise as a revolution from within Orthodoxy. But sooner or later a liberal alternative will be found. I believe that the Reform and Conservative movements together can help to shape the alternative. There is no valid reason why on the Israeli scene these two movements should not be united. Hopefully, efforts will be initiated to achieve that objective.

3. Why does non-orthodox American Judaism need a dynamic non-orthodox Israeli Judaism?

A realistic, sober analysis of the situation reveals that neither the opposition of the Orthodox nor the indifference of the government is responsible for the failure to develop a non-Orthodox movement of size and significance in Israel. If the Jews of Israel should discover that a non-Orthodox approach to Judaism has something to contribute to their lives, then the movement will flourish and become integrated into the panorama of Israel as an indigenous expression of Judaism. However, if Progressive Judaism should fail to take root in Israel, the consequences will deleteriously affect the liberal movements of Judaism in America.

I believe that the State of Israel, and not America, provides the ultimate testing ground for Reform Judaism. We have always maintained that our differences with Orthodoxy were over fundamental theological tenets. We could not accept the traditional concepts of revelation, divine origin of *halacha*, the personal Messiah, the resurrection of the dead, and what we held to be other theological anachronisms. We claimed that moral values were primary and stressed the prophets, the mission of Israel, and social justice. We presented our movement as the means to reconcile the sacred and the secular, the past and the present.

Today Reform Judaism is a major movement in American Jewish life, with a growing percentage of the synagogue-oriented Jews identifying with us. If we were to probe beneath the surface and ask ourselves why, we might be shocked. Do our members belong to Reform synagogues because they are firmly committed to our theology as opposed to Orthodox theology? Have we won Jews to our cause because of the power of our ideas, the inspiration of our worship services, the passion for social justice? In some instances, we may respond affirmatively. But I suspect that many members belong to Reform synagogues because the church-oriented American environment obliges Jews to identify with some religious institution. They belong to *our* synagogues because we offer the mot palatable, the most aesthetic, and the easiest way to be a Jew. In other words, I suspect that the most influential factor in building American Reform Judaism has been not theology, but sociology. Our claim to being a universal Jewish faith has not been demonstrated. Reform Judaism's failure to be a significant factor in every major Jewish community in the world casts doubt on the universal applicability, the vitality, the validity, the intrinsic commitment of our movement.

Israel: the test of authenticity

Israel offers a real test of our authenticity. For in Israel, there is no societal pressure or inner compulsion to join a synagogue in order to identify as a Jew. No Israeli Jew is subconsciously moved by the question, "What will the gentiles say?"; and since when are Jews moved by, "What will the Jews say?" For Israelis, the question is not "with which synagogue shall we affiliate?" but "why do we even need a synagogue at all?" The question is not "how shall we change the prayer which petitions for the restoration of the sacrifices?" but "why should we have prayer at all?"

If a man is a vegetarian, you won't get very far putting a platter of a new kind of meat before him. The plain fact is that for most Israelis, the synagogue is not their meat. The challenge which confronts us is to help the non-religious Israeli search for a new kind of spiritual nourishment. What they eventually select may not be our brand, or it may be our brand with an Israeli flavor added. At least we can help them acquire a taste for food which nourished their ancestors, but which is strange to this generation. So Israel needs our Progressive Movement. And we, the Reform Jews of America, need our Progressive Movement in Israel.

The liberal Jews in America will never have a full and proper relationship with Israel until there is a liberal movement in Israel. Until then we shall always be considered as outsiders and therefore shall consider ourselves outsiders, creations of the Diaspora, fish who can only live out of water, an American sect practicing a way of life which can flourish only in a gentile soil, aliens and oddities foreign to the authentic Judaism of *Eretz Yisrael*.

On Simchat Torah in 1969, I was in the synagogue in Moscow. There I met an old man, physically deformed as a consequence of his ten years spent in a Soviet prison camp. The old man told me that he is a regular listener of *"Kol Zion Lagolah,"* (The Voice of Israel) the Israel short-wave broadcasts. "Every night I lie in bed listening to the 10:30 to 11:00 p.m. broadcast, and the last words I hear are the singing of *Hatikvah* (the Israeli national anthem, the English meaning of which is "hope"). When I hear *Hatikvah*, I forget my own problems, my fears for the future of Soviet Jewry are dissipated, and I fall asleep with the words and melody of 'hope' in my heart. For some reason, they have stopped broadcasting *Hatikvah* at 11:00 p.m. and now broadcast it only at the conclusion of the day's programs — at 2:00 a.m. When you leave the Soviet Union, please contact the *Kol Zion Lagolah* and ask them to do a favor for one old Jew — ask them to play *Hatikvah* again."

Our ability to revitalize the Jewish people will be determined by our capacity to sustain the melody in Israel and throughout the world.

Printed by "Commission on Israel," 1972.

"To Build and To Be Built" by Eretz Yisrael — A Declaration of Interdependence*

The year 1972 marks the 1900th anniversary of the beginning of the Roman siege of Masada. Two years earlier we observed the 1900th anniversary of the establishment of Yavneh after the destruction of the Temple in Jerusalem.

Jewish life has tended to fluctuate between two polarities which may be symbolized by these two historic sites. Masada represents the national propensity of Judaism — for there a handful of Zealots led by Eleazar ben Yair held out against the invincible Roman legions until, when all hope was lost, they chose death at their own hands rather than surrender. Their heroism continues to inspire the restoration of national independence. Who has not been moved by the scene of recruits in the Israeli army standing on the heights of Masada and vowing allegiance in the words of the poet Yitzhak Lamdan: — "Masada shall not fall again?"

Yavneh, on the other hand, represents the propensity of Judaism for the pursuit of religious study and practice. Rabbi Yochanan ben Zakkai, sensing that armed rebellion was futile after the destruction of the Temple, became reconciled to the loss of national independence. Who is not moved by the tale of the rabbi being carried through the lines of the besiegers in a coffin, to appeal to the Roman commander for permission to establish a school for the perpetuation of the Jewish heritage?

The spirit of Masada and the spirit of Yavneh have often appeared to be in conflict. The classical founders of Reform Judaism, in their rejection of a return to *Eretz Yisrael*, posed Yavneh and Masada as mutually exclusive alternatives. But the same nineteenth century emancipation era which stimulated the evolution of Reform also provoked the rise of political Zionism; and the events of the twentieth century have brought about a synthesis. Today, Reform Judaism

---

* This address was delivered in June 1972 in Geneva, Switzerland, on the occasion of the installation of the author as the Executive Director of the World Union for Progressive Judaism. A year later, the Headquarters of the WUPJ were moved from New York to Jerusalem.

bears a revolutionary message — a Declaration of Interdependence — of people and faith; of Jewish tradition and contemporary needs; of the universal and the particular, of Israel and the Diaspora, of each Jew with all Jews. Without the heritage of Masada, the Holocaust would not have been followed by redemption. But without the heritage of Yavneh, why do we persist with our struggle for survival? Without the Jewish people, there is no Judaism; but without Judaism, what is the Jewish people?

Interdependence

The World Union for Progressive Judaism reaffirms this Declaration of Interdependence through the forthcoming transfer of the international headquarters to Jerusalem. Until recently, Progressive Judaism related to Israel through individuals. But while we were speaking with pride of the contribution to Zionism of the incomparable Abba Hillel Silver and Stephen Wise, the Orthodox, some of whom were and still are opposed to the establishment of the State, were creating *yeshivot* and other academies of learning. Today, the heart of Orthodox Judaism in Israel is a vast network of religious, educational, health and social welfare institutions, kibbutzim and collective settlements, which play a vital and integral role in the Israeli milieu and are sustained in part by contributions of world Jewry, including the not insubstantial funds of Progressive Jews.

In the last decade, we have begun to realize that for us to enter into an organic relationship with Israel, we must participate not only as individuals, but as a movement. The establishment of the Jerusalem campus of the Hebrew Union College and its expansion in fields of rabbinic training and Jewish study, the development of our synagogues and the engaging of rabbis to serve them, the incorporation of the Leo Baeck School in Haifa into the World Union structure, the establishment of youth programs and the appointment of rabbis to lead them, the erection by the Sisterhoods of a cultural center-chapel at Ben Shemen — all represent institutional rather than individual contributions. And now, symbolic of the new era is the projected establishment of our World Educational Center for Progressive Judaism, a coordinated venture of the

College, the Union of American Hebrew Congregations, the Central Conference of American Rabbis, and the World Union.

We hereby affirm that Progressive Judaism, as a movement, commits its energies and resources to the *mitzvah* of upbuilding *Eretz Yisrael*.

Two battles of destiny are currently being waged in the Middle East — one is the battle for the right of the Jewish state to exist in peace with its Arab neighbors. The other, ultimately the more important, is a battle for the character of the Jewish soul. What will be the quality of Jewish life in Israel? What will be the role of Jewish learning and living? How will the Jews in Israel relate to the moral imperatives and the social ideals of our Jewish heritage? How will the Jewish state deal with the problems of poverty, unemployment, education, and welfare? Will it assure fundamental civil liberties to all its citizens? How will it relate to the Arab and other minorities within its boundaries? Will Israel succumb to the pressures of becoming "a nation like all other nations," or will it be propelled by the classic vision of serving as a "nation for all other nations," an *or lagoyim* (a light to the peoples of the world)?

Due to the centrality of Israel, Jewish life in the Diaspora will inevitably be affected by the quality of Jewish life in Israel, even as the image of the Jew in the eyes of non-Jews will in part be a reflection of the social and ethical standards of Israeli Jewry. Therefore, Jewish life, values, and fate will be determined in considerable measure by the outcome of the ongoing struggle to define the Jewishness of the Jewish state.

We believe that Progressive Judaism has a contribution to make to that struggle, even as we have much to receive. We want to shape and to be shaped by the struggle, *livnot u'lehibanot* (to build and to be built by *Eretz Yisrael*).

Rights and obligations for all Jews

We have no quarrel with Orthodox Judaism as such. We cannot accept the ideological stance and many of the practices of Orthodoxy; but we respect Orthodox Judaism as our tradition, and we consider it an essential preservative force in Jewish life. We have no ambitions to break down the *siyag laTorah*, (the fence around the Torah), nor do we appeal to Orthodox Jews to modify their beliefs or observances. From our perspective, both in the Diaspora and in Israel, we are not in competition with Orthodoxy, nor is conflict inherent or inevitable. We are not foreign missionaries embarked on a campaign to woo traditional Jews from their faith.

We are religious Jews inspired by *netzach yisrael*, (the eternity of the people Israel decreed by the Eternal One of Israel). We want to enrich the lives of those Jews who, whether attracted by the lures of secular ideologies or repelled by the rigidities of an authoritarian Orthodoxy, have dissociated themselves from Jewish religious tradition. We view with trepidation the alienation of large segments of Jewry from their religious roots, and note that the separation of Jew from Judaism breeds assimilation, whether in the Diaspora or in Israel. We want those Jews who have no religious orientation to experience the sanctity of the Sabbath and Holy Days, to praise God at the sacred moments in the life cycle, and to be motivated by traditional Jewish values in their daily lives. We proudly take as our objective the motto of the beloved Chief Rabbi of Israel, HaRav Abraham Isaac Kook: הישן יתחדש החדש יתקדש (The old should be renewed, the new should be made holy.)

We would assume that the Orthodox rabbinate would share this objective of their respected leader. What rabbi committed to preserving Judaism would prefer that Jews attend no synagogue at all rather than a Reform synagogue? Where is the integrity of those American Orthodox rabbis who function within a framework of cooperation with, and often dependency on, non-Orthodox colleagues in the United States, but embark on campaigns for Israel to invalidate the legitimacy of Conservative and Reform rabbis? Since when does a vibrant Judaism require the power of the state to impose its will and maintain its institutions; and since when does a democratic state permit a minority religious view to dictate to the majority?

We Progressive Jews take our stance as Jews in every respect. We assume the obligations of all Jews, but we also demand the rights of all Jews. Neither an intransigent rabbinate nor an indifferent government will read us out of full participation in the unfolding drama of Israel. Our participation is essential to the well-being of the Jewish people.

Masada and Yavneh

On the horizon there are disturbing signs that the unity of purpose characterizing the first generation since the establishment of the state will not necessarily prevail through the second generation. Clear differences in style and policy are beginning to emerge in Jewish life, and, given conditions of peace or non-war, in the Middle East, are bound to be exacerbated. Some Diaspora leaders accuse Israelis of interfering with their autonomy and failure to understand the conditions of Diaspora Jewish life. Some Israelis, in turn, accuse Diaspora leadership of lip-service to the Zionist cause, failure to accept the consequences of recent history, and insensitivity to the needs of Israel. As one who literally has one foot in both camps, I sense much over-generalization, as well as some truth, on both sides.

It would be a mistake to interpret the differences as merely conflicts between personalities. Fundamental philosophic stances are involved. One could delineate these philosophies as a Masada vs. Yavneh conflict, or as a *shelilat hagalut* vs. a *hiyuv hagolah* conflict — the conflict between those who negate the possibility of Jewish survival in the Diaspora and those who affirm the viability of the Diaspora.

What is needed is a continuing process of refining Israel-Diaspora relations. When Jewish life is interdependent, complete autonomy of national communities is neither attainable nor desirable. The Jews of Israel and of the Diaspora have an obligation to speak to each other. We need to hear, even if we do not always heed, each other. The very presence of the World Union in Israel and the kinds of programs to be conducted at the World Educational Center will facilitate the process of dialogue for the interdependent.

We are a worldwide movement. As such we must extend our concern to the Jews of the world. An analysis of the growth of Progressive Judaism would reveal that we have succeeded in the development of strong movements only in Anglo-Saxon or western-oriented countries. Why have we not made similar progress in Latin America or in Eastern Europe, or in Israel? My hypothesis is that in its formative stages, Progressive Judaism provided a welcome rationale for Jews living under conditions of cultural dualism in which retention of Jewish identity was consistent with full citizenship rights and opportunities.

Progressive Judaism's de-emphasis of nationalist elements, and its reforms of traditional thought and practice, moderated the differences between Jew and non-Jew and between religion and other disciplines, enabling Progressive Jews to accept their Judaism and to be acceptable at the same time. But the characteristics which attracted Jews to our ranks in politically enlightened nations have no impact in environments where Jews retain a strong ethnic identity and/or in which Jewish affirmation might potentially be an impediment to individual advancement.

In a society where a Jew is identified as a member of a nationality and not as a member of a religious group, a Jewish religious movement is of less significance, particularly when that movement denies or diminishes the ethnic dimension. How much less significant is such a religious movement in a communist society where religion in general is deprecated and Judaism in specific condemned.

Now we find ourselves in a new era. Progressive Judaism itself has restored the component of ethnicity in response to the European cataclysm and the redemption in Israel and in consonance with the deep felt needs of its adherents. Conversely, the quarter century since World War II has demonstrated that Jewish ethnicity without Judaism is in itself no guarantee against assimilation and intermarriage.

Seeds for Jewish revival

In Latin America, assimilation is rampant among three-quarters of a million Jews. Living in societies characterized by unstable governments, galloping inflation and recurrent cycles of anti-Semitism, the future is bleak for Latin American Jewry. The most potent force for Jewish affirmation is Zionism. But Zionism alone is not enough to balance the inadequacies of Jewish educational institutions and the vapidity of Jewish home life. Orthodox Judaism, plagued by inflexibility, has made no attempt to modify its services or programs in keeping with the environment. In Buenos Aires, fewer than 10% of the Jews attend synagogue on the High Holy Days. Only a small percentage of youth in Latin America is affiliated with any Jewish institution or organization. If we indeed believe that our movement contains the seeds for Jewish renaissance, do we not have a responsibility to expand and intensify our Latin American program, to transmit the Torah of Yavneh together with the inspiration of Masada?

What is true for Latin America is true for other communities, especially Soviet Jewry. In connection with Soviet Jewry, the Masada vs. Yavneh debate has been heated.

Although aliyah will continue to be a prime focus among Soviet Jews, and Zionism will continue to inspire the study of Hebrew and Jewish history in the Soviet Union, over an extended period of time Zionism alone is not sufficient to satisfy the Jewish needs of Soviet Jewry. An authoritarian Orthodox Judaism cannot appeal to those who resist an authoritarian society. Do we not have a special obligation and special opportunity to initiate a program for Soviet Jews, to satisfy their yearnings for spiritual as well as national regeneration?

When archeologists began to excavate Masada, they knew that rainfall was infrequent and meager, and they found no natural spring. They were intrigued by the question of how the besieged Jews were able to obtain the water to sustain life. They discovered that Herod had engineered an ingenious system. Two small wadis pass to the north and south of Masada. Dams were constructed, and from the dams aqueducts were built leading to huge cisterns carved out of the rock. The water from the occasional flash rainstorms, which otherwise would have been wasted, was in this manner collected and stored for future use, assuring an ample water supply. Today only remnants of the system remain.

The rabbis, disciples of Yavneh, would frequently allude to water as the symbol of Torah. Jewish wisdom was aware that Torah was a life-sustaining stream, but that it had to be channeled, stored, and used creatively. Besieged by enemies, battered by hostile climes, seduced by dominant cultures, many Jews have permitted the dams sustaining the Jewish way of life to crumble, the cisterns of Jewish knowledge to be emptied and the flashes of Jewish inspiration to dissipate.

As we commence a new era in the history of Progressive Judaism, let us resolve to repair the remnants, to keep the waters of salvation flowing, to renew our covenant, to replenish our heritage, to elevate ourselves from an organization to a movement, to reinvigorate our worldwide cause for the perpetuation of Jew and Judaism. Then may the vision of the prophet Zechariah be fulfilled:

> "And it shall come to pass in that day that living waters shall go forth from Jerusalem; half of them toward the eastern sea and half of them toward the western sea...and the Lord shall be king over all the earth; in that day shall the Lord be One and His name One."
>
> (Zechariah 14:8, 9)

The World Union In Israel — Six Lessons*

For us Jews, religion and nationality have been inextricable. The Temple was not only the center of religion, but the symbol of national independence, just as the return to the Western Wall of the Temple Mount in 1967 became the symbol of renewed sovereignty. By our very presence here today, in a reunited Jerusalem, we the religious movement of Progressive Judaism, affirm the rebirth of the Jewish people. Catastrophe has been superceded by restoration, destruction by reconstruction, desperation by aspiration.

We convene to celebrate the tenth anniversary of the transfer of the international headquarters of the World Union to Jerusalem. According to Pirke Avot, when a child reaches *ben eser shanim l'mishnah* (the age of ten), he is ready to study Mishnah. The word "Mishnah" means study, teaching, lesson. The Mishnah is divided into six sections. I would like to review with you six of the lessons learned or reaffirmed during this last decade:

Lesson One: We have learned the validity of three simple interrelated premises: There can be no Judaism without the Jewish people. There will be no Jewish people without the Jewish state. There will be no Jewish state without Judaism. The circle is complete. Without the synthesis of all three components, Jewish life in the twentieth century is neither comprehensive nor comprehensible, neither endurable nor enduring.

Lesson Two: A movement, like an individual, is judged not by ideological formulation, but by life commitments; not by resolutions, but by resolute actions; not by promises, but by performances reflected in the achievements of its adherents and institutions.

Just as the Union of American Hebrew Congregations moved its headquarters from Cincinnati to New York, the center of American Jewish life, and the

---

* This chapter is based on an address to the International Convention of the World Union for Progressive Judaism in Jerusalem in 1983, celebrating the tenth anniversary of the transfer of the International Headquarters of the WUPJ to Jerusalem.

Hebrew Union College — Jewish Institute of Religion established campuses in the eastern and western centers of American Jewish population, so was it an historic imperative for our world Jewish movement to have its center in Jerusalem, the spiritual and cultural heart of the Jewish people.

To move to Israel required a comparatively easy decision; it was only a cross-ocean leap of faith. To create a vital world movement is far more complex; this requires a leap of action. And to have an impact on Israeli society demands a rocket-like propulsion of energy, personnel, and funds that our movement has as yet been unwilling or unable to commit.

The fundamental issue is not now nor has it ever been one of religious rights. To be sure, the public media and some of our own members have focused on the lack of rights, and on the numerous odious acts of outright prejudice and discrimination. So far we have waged successful political efforts against the amendment to the Law of Return, and even now have a case before Israel's High Court of Justice, demanding that two of our rabbis be allowed to serve as marriage registrars. We shall continue to plead, pressure, persuade, cajole and lobby in the pursuit of our rights. But in the final analysis, as we Jews have learned from our historic experience, rights for minority groups are never bestowed willingly by any majority. Rights have to be carved out in social conflict over generations. Although Israeli and world Jewry are truly pluralistic, given the current context of Israeli society, it is seen not to be in the interest of the major political groupings nor the religious establishment to encourage that pluralism in religion. On the contrary, the trend toward political extremism and religious fanaticism blocks the development for the non-Orthodox movements in Israel.

A movement which came a long way

The ultimate test confronting our world movement in regard to Israel is not what we say, but what we do; not what we protest, but what we create; not what we proclaim ourselves to be, but what we in fact are.

Without rabbis to perform religious acts, to what avail is the demand for rabbinical rights? Without institutions to be the recipients of government subsidies given to all other religious groups, to what avail is the insistence on government support? Without a movement to exercise religious rights in Israel, to what avail are pronouncements outside the Land of Israel?

Judged by what we would like to be, we have fallen far short of our objectives. Judged by what we were, we have come a long way. It was only twenty-five years ago that Har-El, the first Progressive congregation, was organized, and only twenty years ago that the first building of the Hebrew Union College in Jerusalem was dedicated. We have developed fifteen congregations and are planning synagogue-community center building programs in Tel Aviv, Haifa, Nahariya and Ramat Aviv. We have expanded the Leo Baeck School into an impressive institution of learning and communal activity. We are ordaining Israeli rabbis at the Hebrew Union College — Jewish Institute of Religion. We have established a flourishing Israeli youth movement with camp programs for our own youth as well as for Arab, Jewish, and disadvantaged children. Together with the United Kibbutz Movement, the Jewish Agency, and the government, we have established the first Reform kibbutz — Yahel — and during this conference we shall formally dedicate our second kibbutz, Lotan. We are now beginning work on Har Halutz, a *Mitzpeh* settlement for families in the Galilee.

We have joined the World Zionist Organization both as a World Union and through the organization ARZENU — the international movement of Reform Zionists. We are sending *shlichim* to the United States, Great Britain, South Africa, and Australia. We have created a new international Zionist youth movement, NETZER OLAMI. We have mobilized campaigns for aliyah. We have increased the number of youth and adults who participate in educational experiences in Israel. At the culmination of this conference, in full cooperation with HUC-JIR, we shall begin construction of the World Education Center for Progressive Judaism, a magnificent campus of Jewish learning and living in Jerusalem. It comprises a youth center-hostel, a world headquarters-tourist reception center and synagogue to be erected by the World Union, and an archeology museum, classroom center, and library to be erected by the College-Institute.

Lesson Three: In the process of moving to Israel and establishing a Progressive movement, the World Union itself has been transformed.

Prior to the development of our Israel Program, the world movement was an organization whose primary task was to send rabbis to far-flung Jewish communities such as Latin America, South Africa, and Australia. The World Union provided seed money for rabbis and new congregations. Once they were able to establish themselves and attain a condition of financial independence, the World Union's task was to provide a framework for sharing common concerns and encouraging cooperative ventures among the constituencies. We shall continue, and indeed strengthen, our endeavors to stimulate the expansion of those vital purposes. With the move to Israel, however, the World Union assumed a new dimension. We have evolved from a service agency, primarily, into an operating agency as well. Every new program we have initiated has attracted new support and new supporters. The more creative the programs we develop, the more funds we mobilize, and the more people we involve. The stronger we become in Israel, the stronger we become as a world movement. The greater our participation in the Zionist venture, the greater is the sense of Jewish adventure for our members outside Zion.

Lesson Four: The move to Israel has sharpened the ideological conflicts within the family of Progressive Judaism.

Reform Judaism evolved as a religious movement to offer a creative response to modernity. We have successfully demonstrated that we can construct a framework of Jewish living in the Diaspora wherein a positive Jewish identity will be retained alongside integrated participation in society at large.

But in the Diaspora, Jewish identity is a private matter, and the extent of religious observance is determined by personal choice. The principle of separation of church and state precludes the injection of the state into the religious domain, and vice versa. In Israel, in contrast, Jewish identity is a public issue. Indeed, the major *raison d'être* of the state is to forge a public Jewish identity. The numerous religion-state controversies reflect strongly held and diverse interpretations of how to define the Jewish dimensions of the Jewish state. For a Jew in the United States the question: "Should I drive a car on *Yom Kippur?*" is a personal, religious question. The same question in Israel becomes a public, national issue, since in Israel even irreligious persons do not think of driving on *Yom Kippur*. How much more serious are public controversies over major issues relating to *ishut* — "personal status" (marriage, divorce, conversion, who is a Jew, and similar issues)? These public policy questions reflect the ongoing role of the State in the process of redefining the Jews as a people.

Since the Progressive Jews of Israel live in an environment where Jewishness is an issue in the public domain, their responses to questions of religious practice are of national as well as religious import. Little wonder that significant differences of opinion have arisen between the Progressive movement in Israel and some of our Diaspora constituencies over religious practices and life-cycle rites. The Israeli movement is not motivated by political expediency, as some of our Diaspora members have charged, but by a perception of Jewishness rooted in an intense peoplehood experience.

Each of our constituent frameworks is the product not only of basic tenets of Progressive Judaism, but in keeping with the spirit of Reform, is motivated by the distinctive conditions of the milieu in which it functions. The very existence of the Progressive movement in Israel has forced the rest of the world movement to be more sensitive to the issues of *Klal Yisrael*. I predict that the overwhelming presence of the Jewish state in the Diaspora Jewish consciousness will continue to test Jewish identity. Whereas previous generations of Progressive Jews were challenged by the confrontation with modernity, future generations will be no less challenged by the confrontation with Jewish peoplehood. The internal controversies that will be generated as a consequence will help keep our movement dynamic. A movement that lacks ideological ferment eventually stagnates. We who advocate pluralism among world Jewry, should welcome and encourage pluralistic expression within our own movement.

Lesson Five: We have earned the right to take stands on the major issues confronting Israeli society.

Those who attended our conference in 1980 will recall that at the time funds for expansion of Kibbutz Yahel and for construction of the facilities at Kibbutz Lotan had not been authorized or appropriated. The issue bears a direct relationship to the availability of Israel government resources for settlements within the Green Line. When we lobbied for support of our kibbutzim, in effect we were participating in the debate over settlement policy that has riven Israeli politics. No one questioned our right to lobby and protest in Israel and abroad. Why? Because manifestly we have a stake in the issue. We address it as insiders and not as foreigners. We are here by right and not by privilege. We have literally implanted ourselves in the soil and therefore in the soul of Israel.

Similarly, when it comes to an issue such as the proposed amendment to the Law of Return which would invalidate conversions performed by non-Orthodox rabbis abroad, our right to oppose the legislation both here and abroad is unquestioned. If anything, it is we who question the right of the Knesset, a civic body comprising a majority of secular Jews and non-Jews, to pass judgment on religious acts performed by Jews abroad.

But, we have been told that foreign policy, or issues affecting Judea and Samaria, are internal Israeli matters. Jews abroad, whose sons do not serve in the Israel Defense Forces have no right to pass judgment. There have been vitriolic debates in the Diaspora over the so-called issue of the right to dissent. I say "so-called" because in my judgment both those who advocate the right to dissent and those who oppose the right are trailing a red herring.

In all my years dealing with social action issues, I have discovered that when a person agrees with you, you will not object to his right to speak, no matter on which shore or platform he stands. But if someone disagrees with you, it is easy to find fault by impugning his motives, or disapproving his tactics or his right to speak.

Needed — a sense of responsibility

The real issue, therefore, is not the right of dissent, but responsible participation in the political process, and that is dependent on the circumstances. If I had been in Israel following the tragedy at the Sabra and

Shatilla refugee camps, I would have been one of the 400,000 demonstrators in Tel Aviv, along with many members of our movement, and I would have lent my name to an ad in the Israeli press, as did the Israel movement. But had I been in Los Angeles, I would not have been among those Jews demonstrating against Mr. Begin, nor would I have demonstrated in front of Israel's embassy in Washington, nor would I have lent my name to an ad in the *New York Times*. What is the difference? I am the same person, I hold the same views whether in Jerusalem or in Washington; but the commitment to participate *responsibly* in the political process dictates different reactions under varying conditions.

In a way, it is far easier to be an Israeli than a Diaspora Jew. The Diaspora Jew not only has to judge what is right, but has to exercise right judgment. If he is circumspect, it is not because someone from Israel has told him what to do, but because he imposes on himself a sense of responsibility and discipline. He has to be more concerned about the public consequences of expressing the truth as he sees it, than does the Jew who lives in a Jewish state. The question: "Is it good or bad for the Jews?" is rarely raised in Israel. But "Is it good or bad for the Jews?" is a legitimate question for the Diaspora.

The above is not to be construed as in any way limiting the freedom of expression of Diaspora Jews. Quite the contrary. The bonds binding Jewish communities to Israel and to each other are inextricable. Neither oceans nor boundaries nor citizenship can negate the interdependence of Jewish destiny. The character and policies of Israeli society invariably affect Diaspora Jewry.

Nowhere is this more evident than in the major controversy now raging in Israel over Judea and Samaria. Fundamentally at issue is a debate between two diametrically opposed schools of Zionism. The school represented by the Herut Party and some religiously oriented political groupings, believes in *Eretz Yisrael Hashlemah*, (Greater Israel). For them, control over the territory overrides all other considerations. The second school, led by the Labor alignment and minority parties, acknowledges the historic right to *Eretz Yisrael*, but believes that human considerations, such as the demographic composition and the democratic character of the Jewish state, take precedence over retention of all territories now under Israeli control.

The right to participate

Do Diaspora Jews have a right to participate in this debate? Do we as a worldwide religious movement have a right to take sides in this conflict between two schools of Zionist thought? I submit that we not only have a right, but an obligation, both as individuals and as a movement. If Diaspora Jews have the right to speak out on internal policies affecting the fate of Argentinian Jews and Soviet Jews, do they not have the right to speak on issues affecting the Jews of the Jewish state? We have been careful not to identify our movement with any political party, and this should continue to be our policy. There are among us persons holding radically divergent political views. All of them should feel at home in our movement. But within the framework of the political process, there is a profound religious issue, to which we must respond as a movement if we would be true to our heritage.

We have before us two conflicting concepts of holiness. There are some religious Jews who, professing love of the Holy Land and obedience to God, fan the flames of religious fanaticism, violate the civil liberties of minority groups, advocate rule by force, and prevent the evolution of conditions leading toward peaceful compromise. We call their version of Judaism a perversion. Their love is blind, their Messianism false, and their zealotry dangerous. Their deeds defame the holy faith, desecrate the Holy One, and defile the Holy Land.

As religious Jews we declare that the concept of *Am Hakodesh* (Holy People) takes precedence over *Eretz Hakodesh* (Holy Land). The holy people has priority over the Holy Land. We repudiate those forces which, by silence or inaction, condone religious and political intolerance, verbal and physical violence, and anti-gentile as well as anti-Jewish acts of racism. The alliance between political radicalism and religious extremism is unholy and un-Jewish. Unless these foreboding trends are reversed, the Diaspora will be alienated, the democratic fabric of Israeli society will be rent asunder, and the Zionist vision of national and spiritual renewal will be dissipated.

The prophet Isaiah understood that holiness was dependent first on redemption of the people: "they shall call them the Holy People, the redeemed of the Lord" (Isaiah 62:12). There can be no redemption of the land without redemption of the people, and no redemption of the people without the creation of a just society.

Lesson Six: The more intense our relationship to Israel, the more acute appear the moral dilemmas within Israel and the more essential it is for Progressive Judaism to confront them.

Our movement, with its social justice emphasis, has been galvanized by the Zionist vision of integrating the renewal of the Jewish people with the renewal of a Jewish society grounded in social and economic justice. However, our active participation in Israeli society and in the framework of the Jewish Agency-World Zionist Organization has made us aware of severe deficiencies in Israel's work ethic, and in public and personal standards of morality. Is this the Chosen People? Is this the Promised Land? Is this the Jewish state for which our forefathers prayed over two millennia? How can we reconcile the dream with the reality? How do we reconcile the restoration of power with the difficulty of differentiating between the acceptable use and the unacceptable abuse of that power? How do we reconcile the plea for aliyah from lands of freedom with the reality that far more Israelis have "gone down" to the Western world than Jews from the West have "gone up" to Israel? How do we maintain our zeal on behalf of the "Let my people go" campaign for Soviet Jewry, with the reality that in recent years most Soviet Jews have preferred to "go" to every country but Israel? How do we continue to swim in the mainstream of the World Zionist Organization without being choked by moral pollution and contaminated by crass politicization? In sum, how do we till the soil of our Zionist dream without sullying our souls in the Zionist reality?

There are no facile answers to these and other profound moral dilemmas. There are those within our movement who would prefer that we distance ourselves from Israel and its institutional forums, lest, as one of our leaders has recently written, we "put national-political objectives above universal-ethical principles."

They do not understand that here in Israel, Jewish values are not tested in theory, in the abstract. Here, there is no artificial dichotomy between the political-historical-particularist dimension and the religious-spiritual-universalist dimension of existence. Here, Jewishness and humanness, particularism and universalism, body and soul are inseparable. This is the source of both our anguish and our rapture, our frustration and our exhilaration. This is the essence of Zionism.

Let those who wish to do so, withdraw from the fray. Let them preach pristine platitudes from the rarified heights of a moralistic universalism. Let them be uninvolved spectators and "objective" commentators. But for the rest of us, let us do battle with the world as it is, refusing to accept it wholly or reject it completely. And let the confrontation with the rough reality be its own reward.

The choosing people

There is a familiar Midrash of how God offered the Torah to all the nations of the world, each of whom rejected it. Finally, when offered to the Jews, they accepted the Torah with the words, *"Naaseh v'nishma,"* "We shall do and we shall listen." It is a favorite Midrash because it puts our ancestors in such a positive light. It also solves a theological problem for some Jews. After all, we were not the chosen people, only the choosing people. There is another Midrash, not so well known or so often recounted, but much more characteristic of the behavior pattern of our people. The beginning is the same. God offers the Torah to all the nations. When He comes to the Jews they give the same answer as all the pagans: God, how can we accept such high standards? We shall never be able to live by them. What does God do? He lifts Mount Sinai high over the heads of the 600,000 Jews assembled there, and he threatens them: "If you accept my Torah, it shall be good; but if not, here shall lie your graves." Only then did our forefathers say, *"Naase v'nishma,"* "We shall do and we shall listen" (Shabbat 88a).

Evidently, we Jews require grave threats to our survival before we accept the Torah and its dictates for Jewish living. Today the threat to Jewish survival hangs heavy over our heads in all places of our sojourning as well as in *Eretz Yisrael.* We have no choice. We hereby dedicate ourselves to the only alternative available. Let us persevere in our common enterprise: the preservation of the

Jewish people, the perpetuation of the Jewish heritage, and the creation of a Jewish society in this land of sanctity and eternity. Let us accept the Torah and it will be good.

Reprinted from *Forum*, published by the World Zionist Organization, no. 50, Winter 1984.

E. ISRAEL AMONG THE NATIONS

1. New Perspectives for Israel-Diaspora Relations

2. From Holocaust to Redemption: Confronting the Dilemmas of Jewish Existence

New Perspectives for Israel-Diaspora Relations

" Israel among the nations is like the heart amidst the organs of the body; it is at one and the same time the most sick and the most healthy of them" (Kuzari II: 36). This description of the Jewish people first uttered by Yehuda Halevi almost nine centuries ago retains its aptness.

We are the most sick of the nations. What other people takes its own daily cardiogram, constantly posing the question: "Will we live?" To the outside world we must appear hypochondriacal, as we incessantly seek new prescriptions for survival. In this modern age, many individuals are wracked by an identity crisis, but ours is a people with a group identity crisis. Everybody else knows who we are, but as for us, we engage in vitriolic debates over the issue "Who is a Jew."

Yet, from another perspective, we are "the healthiest" of them all. What other people could have transformed the ruin of destruction into the glow of redemption? Even as the exodus from Egypt remains the symbol of freedom for all eternity, the upbuilding of Zion in our day serves as a model of initiative, independence and national self-respect for most of the new nations dotting the globe.

The presence of the World Union for Progressive Judaism in Israel symbolizes the radical changes which have occurred in the Jewish world and in the Reform movement. The State of Israel has become the single most important factor in determining the way others relate to Jews and the way Jews relate to each other. The establishment of the state transformed the Jewish world, and in response the Reform movement has been reforming itself, struggling to come to terms institutionally and ideologically with the new reality. It is no secret that within our movement there are divisions of opinion concerning the nature and emphasis of our relationship to Israel and the theological and programmatic ramifications that should flow from this relationship. The transfer of the World Union's international headquarters to Jerusalem and the affiliation with the World Zionist Organization have not and should not submerge these differences. On the contrary, the intensified contact and involvement with Israel should stimulate a more intense debate. I believe that most of these issues can be subsumed into three broad categories — (1) **the Jew and the world** (2) **the Jew and his tradition** (3) **the Jew and the Jewish world**. The Israel factor is crucial in each of these areas. In each category we ourselves are divided on some of the specific issues. And yet I submit that as a movement we have evolved a broad consensus characteristic of liberal Judaism.

(1) The Jew and the world

Reform Judaism and Zionism were both children of the emancipation. The motto of the emancipation was simple: "To the Jew as an individual, everything; to the Jews as a people, nothing." Reform Judaism willingly paid the price, because the founders of our movement sincerely believed that the essence of Judaism was the religious component. The synagogue, faith and theology provided the framework for Jewish survival and at the same time enabled the Jew to become fully integrated into the culture of society at large. Zionism, on the other hand, maintained that the framework for preserving the Jew must be the re-establishment of collective Jewish existence, by reestablishing a Jewish state wherein Jews would pursue their destiny, not alone as individuals, but as a people.

By incorporating Zionism into Reform Judaism, our movement, in effect, has declared that if the outside world does not recognize the right of the Jewish people to exist as a collectivity, then doubt is cast on the world's acceptance of the Jew as an individual. The world has to relate to us as *we* see ourselves and not as *they* would like to see us. A Jewish state is not merely a consequence of negative forces, not merely a haven of refuge for individual Jews, but the determination to rejuvenate the Jewish people as a whole. The emancipating society had demanded the right to define the Jew in terms acceptable to the outside world. The Zionist movement restored to the Jew the right to define the character of the Jewish people on Jewish terms. Zionism returned the initiative to the Jew, enabling him to act in history as a subject rather than an object.

That is why when it comes to Christian-Jewish relations today, the place of the State of Israel in Jewish ideology, and not the Jewish rejection of Jesus, is the key issue. The differences between the Jew and other faith groups are to be found not only in divergent beliefs, but in the fact that the Jew sees the arena of history as the testing ground for religious beliefs. For the most part, the Christian world has accepted Judaism as an authentic faith and can talk with equanimity about "our common Judeo-Christian heritage." However, for us the ultimate question is not what Christians think of Judaism but how Christians relate to Jews. In that sense, the Vatican's position on Jerusalem and its failure to recognize the State of Israel are more consequential than its recent reinterpretation absolving contemporary Jews of responsibility for the crucifixion. The Christian world will never relate to the Jew properly until it can relate to the entity of the Jewish people as a force in history.

What is true of Christianity is also true for Islam. When the representatives of Islam declare that they have nothing against Jews as individuals and merely advocate the replacement of the Jewish state by a secular democratic state in Palestine, they reject the fundamental right of the Jewish people to exist.

As for the United Nations, why was the vote against Zionism immoral? Because it denied the integrity of the Jewish people. Who can imagine the United Nations even discussing a proposal advocating the condemning of Christianity, Islam, communism, capitalism or any other of the religious, political or economic "isms" represented by UN members? The right of a people or a social system to exist is not subject to an international ballot box. Truth is not determined by majority vote. We Jews refuse to recognize any distinction between anti-Zionism and anti-Semitism, because those who reject a Jewish state reject Jewish peoplehood and those who reject Jewish peoplehood would deny to Jews their very essence.

After discussing how we expect the world to relate to the Jewish people, there remains the issue of how Jews should relate to the world. In the early years of its development, the Reform movement stressed the universalistic dimension of Judaism. We modified the concept of the "Mission of Israel" by excising its particularistic connotations. Instead of recognizing the destruction of Jewish sovereignty and the subsequent exile as an historic tragedy, we declared the exile a blessing bestowed on us by God as a means of spreading the divine message to all the peoples of the world. Even our early emphasis on social justice was altruistic, minimizing the intrinsic needs and interests of the Jewish people. Subsequently, the imbalance between the poles of universalism and particularism was corrected. This generation is confronted by a new dilemma. Many of us see a danger that the pendulum is swinging too far toward the other direction. A popular song in Israel has the refrain, "The whole world's against us. It's a very old story." The words reflect much of current Jewish thinking in Israel and the Diaspora. Still under the impact of the Holocaust, reinforced by the trauma of those dark days of May 1967 and the Yom Kippur War, battered by the application of a double standard against the State of Israel in the United Nations and in world capitals, frustrated by the continuing silence or hostility of major organized Christian groups, there is a tendency among us to turn inward and to find sustenance in the biblical forecast, that we are a people destined to dwell alone.

Because of our unique emphasis, Progressive Judaism can help to maintain a vital sense of balance between isolation imposed by others and isolation that is self-imposed. As a people we have never been objective or neutral about the Jewish role in history. We have insisted that we not be measured by strength of numbers. When we proclaim ourselves in Yehuda Halevi's words to be like the heart, it is not out of a feeling of superiority, but out of the superiority of feeling. Jews feel the world and its pain, declared our sages, "Every misfortune which Jews and the nations of the world share is a misfortune; what is a misfortune for Jews alone is not a misfortune" (Deuteronomy Rabbah, 2:22). It is no coincidence that Jews enter the professions of medicine and communal services in such preponderance. We suffer whenever there is suffering. And we assume responsibility to alleviate the pain of disease and the ravages of poverty. We see the world's condition as affecting the condition of the Jews, and we see the condition of Jews as having impact on the state of the world. Long ago the Midrash announced: "When trouble comes to the world, Jacob feels it first. When joy comes, Jacob feels it first" (Midrash Lamentations, 2:9)

Throughout the centuries of dispersion, Jewish destiny has been inextricable from that of the societies among whom we have lived. The open, developing, expanding society welcomed us. The closing, deteriorating, contracting society oppressed us. No evil perpetrated against us by man can destroy our faith in the ultimate redemption of mankind. Our concern for humanity is reinforced by our concern for the Jewish people. Our passion for preserving the Jew reflects our passionate commitment for the perfection of the universe.

(2) The Jew and his tradition

The Israel factor also impinges on the relationship of Progressive Judaism to Jewish tradition. Many of our lay leaders who come in contact for the first time with Progressive Judaism in Israel are astounded by its character — *talit, kippah,* Hebrew, a more traditional liturgy and more traditional personal and congregational practices. The observances and standards of Progressive Judaism in Israel will have an increasing impact on the relation to tradition within the Progressive movement abroad and may well stir up ideological conflict. It is therefore essential that we try to comprehend the forces at work.

Rabbi David Polish, in his book *Renew Our Days: The Zionist Issue in Reform Judaism,* points to the direct relationship between the founders' early objective of denationalizing Judaism and the subsequent elimination and/or alteration of ritual observances. Abraham Geiger, the most influential of the German Reform liturgists, provided the intellectual rationale for radical change in observance: "The *people* of Israel lives no longer, not even in the hearts and desires of the present. It is resurrected as a congregation of *faith* and only what touches it has an undisputed right to our concern." The nineteenth century molders of our movement expunged or modified those rituals and laws that were manifestations of peoplehood. But now that Reform Judaism has restored the peoplehood component, the rationale for Reform practice can no longer be limited to "only what touches... the congregation of faith."

Take, for example, the question of conversion. The Progressive rabbis in Israel have established a religious court, a Beit Din that requires immersion and acceptance of *mitzvot* for all converts and circumcision for males. Furthermore, they have been urging all Progressive rabbis throughout the world to adopt similar standards and indeed some have done so on their own initiative. Some critics of this stand accuse the rabbis in Israel of betraying the principles of Reform. Others accuse them of political expediency, of seeking to compromise with the Orthodox rabbinate in order to attain recognition — which, claim the critics, will never be granted in any case. The Progressive rabbis of Israel counter that unity of *Klal Yisrael* is in itself a religious principle and that when a Progressive rabbi performs a conversion, he, as the servant of *Klal Yisrael*, in effect gives the convert a visa to the Jewish world. Is the Progressive rabbi therefore not obligated to make sure that the convert will be eligible to enter as many corners of the Jewish world as possible?

I do not intend to enter further into the merits or demerits of the respective positions, but I do refer to this issue as an illustration of the influence of the environment. The very existence of the Jewish state changes the context and content of the issue. The more a religious movement is rooted in the experience of peoplehood, the more its adherents have need for observing traditions that express the distinguishing characteristics of peoplehood. In Israel one finds the most profound merger of the religious and national elements of Jewishness. No wonder that Conservative Jews in Israel are far more conservative than their counterparts in the United States. No wonder that our young kibbutznikim, the first group of Progressive Jews ever to commit themselves to a communal existence, are in search of a more intensive pattern of Jewish living for which there is no model anywhere within the Reform movement.

Jew and human being

The motto of the enlightenment period was, in Y.L. Gordon's phrase, "Be a Jew in your tent and a human being on the outside." Some critics have contended that contemporary Diaspora Jewry's motto can be described as "Be a Jew on the outside," i.e. identify proudly with all Jewish causes, but "be a human being in your tent," i.e. adopt minimal Jewish experiences and personal commitments in your daily life. I contend that the motto of the new peoplehood orientation must declare: "Be a Jew in your own tent and a Jew outside."

In the Diaspora, the impact of that dictum will manifest itself differently than in Israel. But because of the expanding influence of Israel on world Jewry, the peoplehood dimension will continue to provoke controversy within Progressive Judaism. The so-called return to tradition is as much a factor of ethnicity as of theology. Inevitably we shall be forced to confront the primary ideological issue of how Progressive Judaism relates to *halacha*, traditional Jewish religious law, for it is the *halacha* which is the framework for determining the distinctive way of Jewish peoplehood. Ultimately, the State of Israel and all Jews are confronted by a similar wrestling. Orthodox Judaism has learned to live with a *halacha* oriented to a non-Jewish environment where Jews existed as a minority. Now the test is, whether the *halacha* can be made viable and dynamic in a Jewish society where Jews live as a majority?

The limitations of Halacha

Within the Reform movement we may differ on the extent to which we should attempt to relate to *halacha* or to make *halacha* relevant to our needs, but we have evolved a consensus concerning the limitations of *halacha*. No amount of reinterpretation will enable a complex, modern, democratic society to be governed exclusively by the dictates of traditional Jewish religious law. In this stance we differ from those Orthodox Jews who continue to insist that the laws of Israel must be determined solely or primarily by *halacha*.

We differ also from those Orthodox Jews who believe that Jewish tradition offers the sole criteria by which to formulate foreign policy, and here I refer to the development of movements such as Gush Emunim. This extremist settler movement is motivated by the conviction that we are at the *athalta di'geula*, (the initial stages of messianic redemption), and that therefore "the (present) borders, these kilometers, are sacred and cannot be relinquished by those who consider themselves representatives and guardians of the entire Jewish people" (Rabbi Z.Y. Kook, *Hatzofeh*, December 22, 1975). Inspired by messianic fervor, they categorically oppose negotiations which might lead to withdrawal from areas occupied by Israel in the Six Day War, call for Jewish settlement in all areas under Israeli military control and are insensitive to the claims and rights of their Arab residents. They have consistently violated decisions of the government and the military on grounds that the religious commandment, the *mitzva*, of preserving intact the Land of Israel is equivalent to fulfilling all other commandments and takes precedence over any other moral, political or security considerations.

Misusing Judaism

This is not the place to enter into a discussion concerning the policy of establishing Israel's borders, and I am fully aware that within the Reform movement are those who advocate retaining and those who advocate returning all the administered territories. But I do believe that this is the place and this is the time to take a stand on the misuse and abuse of Jewish tradition by Gush Emunim.

Certainly, the biblical promise to "give this land" to the seed of Abraham is of profound theological significance. It is the basis of the binding attachment of the Jewish people to *Eretz Yisrael* over the millennia. But the biblical promise of 4000 years ago cannot be invoked as the exclusive basis for drawing maps in our day. Neither Abraham nor Moses were cartographers engaged for eternity by the Jewish people. No biblical text can justify the shedding of blood to keep intact the post Six Day War borders. No tradition in Judaism will condone, let alone sanction, the declaration that it is a religious duty to oppose negotiation with enemies. To use religion as the pretext for disregarding the rights of others is to distort Judaism. To make a battleground out of the Temple Mount or the Tombs of the Patriarchs in the name of Judaism is to defame Judaism. To violate the decisions of the government of a Jewish State and of its law enforcement officials is to undermine both the democratic process and Jewish morality.

Fortunately, we are not so weak that we have to rely on blind passion to justify our rights. We do have many foundations for our claim to *Eretz Yisrael*: the continued Jewish settlement in the land; the fact that since the dissolution of Jewish sovereignty 2000 years ago no other group ever claimed independent sovereignty over this area; the League of Nations' confirmation of the Balfour Declaration and the establishment of the Mandate; the resolution of the United Nations establishing a Jewish State; the repopulation and restoration of barren areas. These claims have political validity. When the time comes, may it be *bimhera b'yamenu* (speedily in our days), for Arab and Israeli leaders to sit around the table to draw the map of peace, these claims and counter-claims will be subject to the process of negotiation and compromise. Misguided religious zealotry will impede our efforts to achieve peace and our aspirations to create a society Jewish in spirit as well as name.

(3) The Jew and the Jewish world

When the Greek philosopher Heraclitus proclaimed that the basic reality in the universe is change, he could have been describing the universe of world Jewry. The character and interrelationship of world Jewry is in great measure dependent upon demographic factors. When the major institutions of American Reform Judaism were established the last century, less than 3% of the world Jewish population lived in the United States; today over 40% live in the United States. One hundred years ago less than 0.2% of world Jewry lived in *Eretz Yisrael*; today the Jews in Israel number some five million and by the year 2010 the largest Jewish population in the world will be living in Israel.

Those statistics alone help to tell the story of Jewish history in our time. Various demographic studies project the history of our grandchildren's era. Throughout the Western world there is a precipitous drop in Jewish fertility, to the point where it is more than 35% below that of the general population, which already displays a significant downward trend. Jews have half as many children and twice as many aged as the general population. In almost every Jewish community in the world, the number of Jewish deaths exceeds the number of Jewish births. When these statistics are compounded by the high intermarriage rates, the capacity of Jewry to reproduce itself appears bleak. The only place in the world where Jewish fertility is increasing is Israel (though here too the birth rate is much lower than that of the Arab population), and large-scale immigration from the Diaspora also continues. The largest number of Jewish children in the world is today in Israel. Projecting population trends is at best hazardous and I offer the statistics with no interpretation, merely as a *possible* projection of which we should take cognizance. History may well decree otherwise.

It is essential for us to make projections not only of population statistics, but of the kind of Jewish world we would like to see, because our acts and decisions in the present reflect and determine our vision for the future. That vision is now obfuscated by the complexities of present crises, the burden of frazzled ideologies, and the obstacle course of anachronistic institutional structures.

A predictable scenario

Take, for example, the constant replay of the long-playing record of Israel-Diaspora relations. I personally have participated in dozens of these discussions on both sides of the ocean and ostensibly representing both sides of the fence. I can write the script blindfolded. The opening session starts with the American participants affirming their loyalty to Israel and Zionism. This is followed by proclaiming the right to dissent from Israel policy and the obligation of Israel to consult on matters affecting world Jewry, since in any case Diaspora Jews have discovered that Israeli leadership is neither omniscient nor untarnished and Israeli society has not fulfilled the expectations of its early pioneers. The peroration is a moving statement on the need for a dynamic American Jewish life, for where would Israel be without American Jewish support and, besides, Jewish history being what it is, we cannot put all our eggs into one basket.

Then the scenario calls for the Israeli side to take up the cudgels. First, it proclaims the continuing validity of Zionist ideology. Then it admits that America is different, but perhaps not forever — what about assimilation and intermarriage? Then it demands that American Jews acknowledge the centrality of Israel. Inject a quick expression of gratitude for Diaspora moral, economic and political support. This then prepares the way for the *piece de resistance*, a rapier thrust to the conscience calling for aliya, since without more Jews in Israel, what good are open Jewish pocketbooks in America?

After the opening rounds, the stereotyped positions begin to blur and the divisions cut across geographical lines. The major differences are not determined by place of residence, but by varying perceptions of the Jewish condition and its remedies. There is not a position of any Diaspora leader that is not articulated with at least equal force by a citizen of Israel. Every one of the statements made by both "sides" is cogent, and when explored specifically in depth as separate issues, most Jews will recognize at least some degree of validity in the respective positions. The misunderstandings arise when the issues are discussed in a psychological framework of "we" and "they." The consequence of recent developments is that the "they" is fast dissolving. The force of events is producing only a "we" framework. Those who identify affirmatively with the destiny of the Jewish people are in the process of being forged into an integrated entity that no boundaries of geography, law, or sociology can rend asunder.

Weakness of leadership

Just as the failure of many generals is that they plan for future wars using the strategy and weaponry of the previous war, so the weakness of our Jewish leadership is that they are waging the ideological controversies of earlier generations. They have not updated their intellectual arsenal to meet the strategic requirements of future generations. One major reason for this time lag is the absence of appropriate organized structures within which to relate to current needs of the Jewish people and to formulate future plans, programs and policies. A panoramic photograph of organized Jewry taken today would portray the same basic list of national and international organizations, and in some instances even the same leadership as before the State of Israel was established. The purpose, function and needs have changed drastically, but the structure and personnel are perpetuated.

At the conference of the World Union for Progressive Judaism held in London in 1974, we voted to affiliate with the two worldwide bodies of Jewish life, the World Jewish Congress and the World Zionist Organization, which includes participation in the Jewish Agency. We now sit around the tables of international Jewry. We participate, share in the responsibility and make our voice heard in constructive criticism. The best criticism we can offer is reconstructive, to recommend a restructuring of the Jewish world, to eliminate outmoded politics and to rectify the imbalances which give inadequate voice to the intellectual and spiritual leadership of world Jewry. We must strive toward the establishment of a democratic, pluralistic, comprehensive instrumentality (or instrumentalities) that will enable Israel and the Diaspora to relate to each other, to expand the number and caliber of those who participate in the decision-making process and to shoulder mutual responsibilities in a better organized, more effective fashion.

The physical and the spiritual

We Jews are affected by two worlds: *olam hazeh* (this world); and *olam habah* (the world to come). When other peoples of antiquity spoke about a Golden Age, it was always set in the past. We alone were always future-oriented. For us the Golden Age is yet to come. For us the vision of what the world should be is an activating force in the world that is. "Where there is no vision, the people cast off restraint" (Proverbs 29:18). The Jewish vision represents an exquisite blend of the universal and the particular. The political-spiritual concept of national restoration of the Jew is the harbinger of international peace for all humanity.

There are two Jerusalems: *Yerushalayim shel matah* (the terrestrial Jerusalem), and *Yerushalayim shel maalah* (the celestial Jerusalem), which will descend and be established on earth with the fulfillment of the messianic vision. Jerusalem the physical place is inseparable from Jerusalem the spiritual ideal. The destiny of *Am Yisrael* is inseparable from the destiny of all humankind. *Eretz Yisrael* is the sacred setting for man's persistent search for eternity. *Medinat Yisrael* (the State of Israel) is the conviction that the life of every nation is potential as well as existential. That is the aspiration of Judaism which makes Jerusalem the center of the universe and the Jewish people the pulsating heart of the human family.

Excerpts from the keynote address on the fiftieth anniversary of the founding of the World Union for Progressive Judaism, from the WZO Quarterly *Forum* — Number 1 (26), 1977.

From Holocaust to Redemption: Confronting the Dilemmas of Jewish Existence*

"In spite of everything I still believe that people are really good at heart." These words, penned by fifteen-year-old Anne Frank in July 1944 would be a fitting epitaph on her unknown grave and on the graves of the six million Jews for whom she has become a poignant symbol.

This Jewish child, without even being cognizant of the fact, instinctively used the words sanctified by tradition, that Maimonides formulated in the Thirteen Articles of Faith, the twelfth of which was: "I believe with perfect faith in the coming of the Messiah, and even though he may tarry, I will wait daily for his coming." אַף עַל פִּי כֵן אֲנִי מַאֲמִין. "In spite of everything I still believe." These words, set to music, became the leitmotif of the Holocaust. Innocent Anne Frank and the great Maimonides — united by the classic vision of a world of goodness and peace.

Our people is rooted in history. We remember the past, its agony and ecstasy. But we aspire toward the future. We are like the ladder in Jacob's dream: "Behold the ladder is set up on the earth, but its top reaches toward heaven" (Genesis 28:12). Our task is to create a ladder. Let us plant ourselves firmly on the ground. Let us confront our problems openly, unfettered by anachronistic perceptions, and let us reach toward our hopes. For in the words of Robert Browning, "Ah, but a man's reach should exceed his grasp, or what's a heaven for?"

Three historical moods

I believe the Jewish people is about to enter a new historical mood. I use the term "mood" rather than "period," because a period is associated with clear-cut dates, events, and economic and sociological developments, whereas a mood

---

* Excerpts from a keynote address at the World Union for Progressive Judaism International Conference, held in Amsterdam, Netherlands, 1978.

stresses psychological phenomena. I also wish to indicate that whereas an historical period has a generally recognized beginning and ending, an historical mood, which is a state of mind, can overlap various historical periods. For the sake of my analysis, I propose that in modern times, the Jewish people can be characterized by two historical moods.

The integration mood

The first is the *integration mood*. This is the easier to define, because its onset coincides with the period of emancipation. The essential characteristic of the integration mood is the desire of Jews to become integrated into the general society. The tearing down of the ghetto walls enabled Jews to be judged as individuals without reference to their being identified as members of the Jewish people. Nineteenth century liberalism evolved the precepts of meritocracy, and Jews were among the greatest beneficiaries. A Jew could enter business, a profession, play a role in secular culture and politics, establish a place in the larger society, *despite* belonging to the Jewish people.

The survival mood

The second is the *survival mood*. This became manifest in the nineteenth century with the evolution of political Zionism. It reached its zenith with the discovery of the full extent of the Holocaust, and it persists today as Jewish unity in the face of threats to the State of Israel. This mood reflects in part a disillusionment with the failure of the Western world to implement its declared principles as they apply to individual Jews, and in part the sense of being "a people which dwells alone" and whose destiny is in a perpetual state of suspension. But its predominant element is an affirmative commitment to preserve the Jewish people.

The integration mood and the survival mood exist side by side. Each has positive and negative implications. Each complements and contradicts the other. The moods interact, depending on events and environmental circumstances. The Jew is constantly confronted by conflicting values reflecting the ongoing tension between universalism and particularism. The Jew wants to be a part of the world and yet apart from the world. He demands integration, but he fears the consequences of an open society, highlighted by intermarriage and assimilation. As Western society strives to resolve its complex problems, the Jew is coming to realize that what is good for society is not necessarily good for the Jew. Jews *qua* Jews have vested interests in domestic and foreign policy, and these may conflict with other groups, the interests of other groups and even the society at large.

What is true for the individual is true for the people. The Jewish people has demanded the same right as every other people to have a state of its own, and yet it wants that state to be different from all other states. Martin Buber once wrote of the Jewish people that it is not *another* example of the species "nation"; it is the *only* example of the species "Israel."

But this unique people which has established a unique state is confronted by the dilemma common to all states. It was first posed by Macchiavelli. A Christian prince has to choose between being a Christian or a prince. This crisis is compounded in the Jewish state that is confronted by the dilemma of colliding values — between the objective of applying Jewish values and the objective of preserving the Jewish people.

Despite the continuing inconsistencies and perpetual dilemmas, each of the two moods has penetrated the psyche of the Jewish people. The integration mood — the Jew as an individual can advance in and partake of the modern world and still retain his Jewish identity and loyalties. The survival mood — the Jewish people as a collective force, epitomized by the State of Israel, has been restored to the active history of nations.

Though there may still be significant pockets of resistance among both Jews and non-Jews, most positively oriented Jews accept the above two propositions as givens in their lives. Which brings me to the hypothesis I should like to propound.

The perpetuation mood

We are on the threshold of developing a third mood, which I call the *perpetuation mood.* Despite the present impasse in negotiations between Israel and her Arab neighbors, I firmly believe that sooner or later peace will be established. Peace may come in stages, and it may take a generation or more. However, the dramatic option opened by Sadat's initiative has projected a vision of Israeli-Arab peace that cannot be completely ignored. When that blessed time arrives, "may it be soon in our day," it will set into motion forces that will ultimately prove to be as consequential as those that tore down the ghetto walls. The distinguishing elements of the new mood will be that the State's physical security will be guaranteed and that in the countries of major Jewish dispersion, the rights of Jews will be assured. The external pressures which today serve to unify Jews in self-defense will be eased. The outside world will have given full recognition to the individual Jew, the Jewish people and the Jewish State. The emphasis will then shift to a search for a distinctive pattern of Jewish living, where Jews will find purpose in perpetuating their Jewishness for its own sake. In the new *perpetuation mood*, the outside world will neither help us nor hinder us. We will have to fortify ourselves through our own inner resources, impelled by our own ultimate purposes. We have to break the chains that have bound us to rigid ideologies as we seek new responses to new conditions.

There will be those who will reject my hypothesis as being overly sanguine or simplistic. Others might agree with it, but look with foreboding on the possibility. They would contend that anti-Semitism and its more recent manifestation as anti-Zionism, is a permanent phenomenon that serves as an essential preservative to Jewish survival. Nevertheless, I present these thoughts to you because, in the minds of many affirmative Jews, we have long been in the perpetuation mood, and because the very discussion forces us to think in terms of ultimate goals. So let us explore together some ramifications of the perpetuation mood from three perspectives: the State of Israel, the Diaspora, and Progressive Judaism.

The State of Israel

The on-going Arab-Israeli conflict and the conviction that Israel is an outpost of Western democracy have contributed to Israel's sense of alienation from its

Semitic, Middle-Eastern roots. With the advent of peace, a change in direction is bound to occur. Israel will of its own initiative, and under the influence of the new political and psychological climate, be impelled to seek economic, social, and cultural integration into the Middle East. The arts, music, cuisine — all the elements of culture, will be affected. Not only will knowledge and use of Arabic assume prime importance, but even the Hebrew language, which has tended to mute the verbal characteristics of the *Eydot Hamizrah* (the Jews from Arab lands) may well return to its more oriental pronunciation. Reciprocal Arab-Israeli programs of tourism, investments, and university student exchanges may lead to radical shifts in demographic patterns, as a new kind of culture gap develops. Future generations of Israelis may worry about assimilation to Near Eastern culture. Intermarriage between Arabs and Jews which until now has been a limited phenomenon may take a sharp upturn. Jewish colonies in Arab lands, such as that which once flourished in Alexandria, may be reestablished, and a new kind of Arab Diaspora could evolve.

Preliminary studies have already been made by the Israeli government and the Jewish Agency to prepare for the expected influx of Jews who have wanted to come to Israel, but have been deterred by the fear of war. The gates of Soviet Jewish emigration may open more widely. However, a reverse phenomenon may also set in: Jews who have not wanted to desert in the face of danger may leave Israel as the psychological barriers of group self-defense are lowered and the corresponding attraction of new individual opportunities beckon, leading to a significant *yerida* (exodus from Israel). There may even be Jews who take an Arthur Koestler-like approach: once the state has been firmly established, then a Jew should choose between one of two possibilities — live in Israel, or cease being Jewish.

Realignments

The coming of peace will force the Israeli society to alter its ghetto mentality. For too many Israelis, government — even the Jewish government — is the enemy, the *paritz* — the landlord who must be outwitted. "Be guarded in your relation to the governing power:" "don't get too close to government" (Pirke

Avot). Concepts first evolved when Jews were under Roman rule, still permeate the Israeli psyche. Israeli Jews will have to learn that their government should be an instrument for serving them, rather than a force for making them servile.

Peace will undoubtedly bring about a major realignment of political parties, encouraging an emphasis on domestic social and economic policies, rather than the almost exclusive focus on foreign affairs. In this realignment, the capacity of the religious parties to wield influence far beyond their proportional representation may weaken. The non-Orthodox population will not be so willing to compromise in favor of the rabbinate and the religious parties when the consequences do not affect policies of war and peace.

Even under the present conditions, the last two governments have resisted the demands for a revision of the Law of Return, which would have prohibited State recognition of conversions performed by non-Orthodox rabbis abroad. The reason? Recognition that Diaspora Jewry has a stake in these matters and that some weight should be given to the voice of Jewish pluralism.

Peace will intensify the pressures on the rabbinate to forsake the *shtetl* mentality which prevents any liberalization of problems of *ishut* (personal status) conversion, the *agunah* (wife of a missing husband), prohibited marriages such as a *Cohen* and a divorcee, *mamzerut* (illegal children born of certain forbidden relationships) and a host of other matters where traditional *halacha* does not conform with contemporary social attitudes. Either the rabbinate will be able to discover remedies within the framework of *halacha*, or the government will discover secular ways of finding redress. No democratic society can tolerate total indifference to the changing mores regarding the rights of women; the developments concerning abortion in countries with strong Church influence such as France and Italy, clearly demonstrate the inevitability of such changes.

Implications of peace

Peace will necessitate a revision of attitudes toward non-Jews. The recent passage of an aberration called the Missionary Law — a law medieval in character, impossible to implement, inflicting severe damage on Israel's image, and undermining the political support of Israel's position among Christian groups — is characteristic of the attitudes of Jews living as a small defenseless minority in an oppressive society, rather than as a majority in a democracy that must learn to accommodate divergent systems of belief in the course of preserving civil liberties for all.

With the dissipation of the siege mentality, new institutional patterns and values will emerge. The fundamental question remains — will these changes be in the direction of affirming or negating the purposes of Jewish survival? Almost a century ago, Achad Ha'am in his essay, *Avdut betoch herut* (Slavery in freedom) posed the question in relation to the Diaspora: The Jewish people has demonstrated its capacity to survive under the pressures of discrimination and persecution; can the Jews in the Diaspora survive under freedom? Now the question will be posed in relation to the State of Israel: The Jewish state has been established despite recurrent war and constant attack; can it thrive under conditions of peace? Once the borders will have been fixed, can the state expand the frontiers of the Jewish spirit?

The Diaspora

The response to this question will have bearing not only for Israel, but for the Diaspora. For even as Israel has been kept unified by external pressures, so has the Diaspora been united by the inner compulsion to sustain the state and plead its cause. The aura of exhilaration and inspiration surrounding Israel after the Six-Day War is fast dissipating. The Diaspora Jews who come in close contact with Israel are more sober in their expectations and more sophisticated in their criticism. Diaspora Jewry is beginning to look upon the Jewish State as more than a response to the Holocaust. Israel must have intrinsic value for its own sake, not only as a symbol of victory over mankind's evil impulse.

Similarly, life in the Diaspora must have value in and of itself. Emil Fackenheim's oft-quoted statement that the Jewish people must survive if for no other reason than to deny Hitler his final solution, may be good theology, but it is not good psychology. In and of itself, it is not a sufficient motivation for an individual Jew to preserve his Jewish identity. We must recognize that the

Holocaust theme cannot forever serve us as a kind of *zechut avot* (hereditary title) — that traditional Jewish tradition which beseeches God to look with favor upon the descendants of Abraham, Isaac, and Jacob — not for their own merits, but for the sake of the sacred deeds of the Patriarchs. The memory of the victims of the Holocaust fortifies us, but we cannot live only to preserve their memory. If I sense correctly, the Jews of Europe are somewhat weary of being looked upon as victims of the Holocaust. Indeed, now that almost two generations have passed, it is time that we universalize the Holocaust. The deceased belong to all of us. All of us are the sufferers, and to single out contemporary European Jewry as the victims is neither valid nor constructive. We should not cripple them psychologically by imposing on European Jewry, as distinct from other Jewries, the appelation of victims, nor should we permit them to look upon themselves as cripples who lean on the Holocaust as a crutch to rationalize their own shortcomings.

Jewish tradition has learned how to deal with profound sorrow. We have our *Tisha Be'Av* and our *Yom Hashoa* (Holocaust Day) but we know how to rise to celebrate our *shalosh regalim* (the three annual aliyot to Jerusalem). *Yom Hazikaron* (Day of Remembrance) is followed the very next day by *Yom Ha'atzmaut* (Independence Day), for our celebration of life enriches our commemoration of tragedy.

Against the negation of the Diaspora

Of late, a spate of demographic studies have forecast a precipitous drop in Jewish population. Intermarriage, assimilation, a high mortality rate, the low fertility rate, lower even than the dwindling birth rate in the general population, are foreboding factors. The most widely publicized forecast, by Professor Eliyahu Bergman, is that by the year 2076, the tricentennial year of America, the population of American Jewry will comprise at a maximum, fewer than one million Jews, and possibly no more than 10,000 Jews. Other studies have prognosticated the virtual disappearance of European and Latin-American Jewries. There are those who view these statistics as corroboration of classic Zionism and its concept of *shlilat hagalut* (the negation of the Diaspora), the theory that eventually the Diaspora will wither away, if not through anti-Semitism, then through assimilation.

I have been a life-long Zionist, but I have never accepted and I do not now accept the concept of *shlilat hagalut*. Our contemporary history has demonstrated that no political theory has ever borne up completely under the test of time. Capitalism, communism, socialism, liberalism, have all had to readjust their early premises when confronted with new realities. Political Zionism of the nineteenth century is no different. Herzl was able to predict a Jewish State, but one prediction he could not make — what impact that state, once created, would have on the Jews of the Diaspora. If today there is a future for the Diaspora, it is in no small measure because of the existence of the Jewish state.

Just as the Diaspora cannot exist without Israel, so Israel cannot exist without the Diaspora. Rather than bemoan the statistics and permit them to become a self-fulfilling prophecy, our task is to work with Jews where they are, recognizing that "where they are" is bound to change drastically under the impact of the current socio-economic revolution. Given the present trends toward the internationalization of big business, the frequent transfer of executive personnel, and the acceptance of Jews into professional and corporate positions formerly closed to them, the transiency of Jews is bound to increase. Jews are on the move, from cohesive Jewish neighborhoods in large cities to communities with no Jewish institutional framework. This transiency, which will be manifest in Jewish population transfers across national borders, is bound to weaken the demographic base of the Jewish communal pattern. The challenge will be to develop new institutional forms and new ideological foundations for Jewish perpetuation in the Diaspora.

Progressive Judaism's task

Here we come to the task confronting Progressive Judaism. Progressive Judaism is the prototype of integration, and, despite our critics, has demonstrated that it is also a movement of survival. Our recent efforts to "Zionize" our movement, to root it firmly in the Land of Israel, to restore to our movement an *halachic* approach (as distinct from a return to the *halacha*) have served as a corrective.

We now have credibility in the eyes of *Klal Yisrael,* and as we strengthen our movement in Israel by establishing more kibbutzim, congregations, schools, and a national youth movement, and participating more actively in the political process, we shall have even greater credibility.

At the World Zionist Congress, the resolution on pluralism and rights for non-Orthodox movements in Israel won the vocal support of the major movements in the Jewish world. The passage of the resolution attests to our newly won acceptability. We stand in and for two worlds — the Diaspora and Israel. We are not apologetic about our Diaspora stance, as are other religious movements with a different theological orientation. We are not hypocritical about our religious demands. We do not insist in an authoritarian manner that Jews adhere strictly to a ritual code, which we know in advance they will reject in practice. We do not compartmentalize our value system. For us the imperatives of social and personal ethics are as relevant as the ritual demands of Judaism. We have a positive approach. We take people as we find them, and we encourage them to do more for themselves. In sum, we have both the ideological and psychological perspective that can serve as the spearhead of perpetuation.

Long before the State of Israel was established, Martin Buber posed what he called "the real dilemma of Jewish existence ... the struggle between nationalism which denies the spirit of the people, and assimilation which denies the body of the people." (*Israel and the World* [Schocken Books, 1948] p. 199). Progressive Judaism, as I would like to see it today, is the prime movement that has the potential of integrating the spirit and the body of the people.

A movement based only on spirit eventually becomes assimilationist. That is the lesson we learned the hard way; tragically it took the Holocaust to teach us. I contend that we have not yet applied the lesson fully. We have formulated theories in the laboratory of rabbinic and lay conferences, but we have insufficiently applied these theories to life. We are still high on spirit and short on body. Our black friends, who have rediscovered their ethnicity, have learned that soul is music and food and language and a host of common experiences. If we indeed believe that Jews are a people, and that a people has a special soul, then that soul has to touch us, even as we touch it. We have to intensify those components of our Jewish existence that enhance our soul in every sphere — ritual, ethical, cultural, and experiential.

The challenge of the Hebrew language

Take, for example, our approach to the Hebrew language. The Frankfurt rabbinical conference in 1845, a formative meeting in the history of Reform Judaism, adopted a resolution that the use of Hebrew in prayer was not required, although it was desirable to retain some occasional portions in Hebrew. Zechariah Frankel seceded from the Conference and founded what came to be Conservative Judaism, when his motion to declare Hebrew indispensable was defeated. In retrospect, I assume most of us would now support Frankel's position, for our revised liturgies show that we have rejected the early reformers' view that the Hebrew language is not integral to a universal faith.

In this age of a renascent Jewish culture, modern Hebrew is not just another language, merely a vehicle for the communication of thoughts and value. Knowledge of Hebrew is a value in and of itself. As much as the Jew has revived Hebrew, Hebrew has revived the Jewish people. If this is so, then our educational objective should be to make modern Hebrew a second language for Diaspora Jewry. Does this idea sound far-fetched? Not as far-fetched, I assure you, as when Eliezer ben Yehudah first proposed Hebrew as the language of the future Jewish State one hundred years ago. Is it revolutionary? Yes, for if we were to take the objective seriously, we would have to create a vast and costly system of *ulpanim*, schools and camps in the Diaspora, provide more extended learning experiences in Israel, as well as on-going experiences at all age levels in Jewish communities and homes throughout the world. Is it controversial? Quite, because the very process of formulating the objective would force us to rethink the nature of our existence in the Diaspora. Is it worth it? Yes, because the Hebrew language can serve as the bridge between the soul and the soil of *Am Yisrael*. And we need sturdy bridges, bridges to our heritage and to our fellow Jews.

I have purposely selected a proposal that would appear radical to most of our leadership. I could have selected others. I want to demonstrate that we have to begin to think in radical terms. Time is not on our side. Less than thirty percent of Jewish children in the world receive any kind of Jewish education, and for most of those children the education is inferior and superficial. Under such conditions we have to attack our problems as a united people.

The idols of the nineteenth and twentieth centuries have proven false. In and of themselves, humanism, rationalism, liberalism cannot save mankind. They did not even make the effort to save the Jews in Auschwitz. We Jews are blessed more than any other people on earth, for our existence is not dependent on an ideology that history can declare invalid. Distinctions between secular and religious Jews, Orthodox and Reform Jews, Diaspora and Israeli Jews, Zionists and non-Zionists, all prove insignificant when as a people we are put to the test of perpetuation. We are one people, with one task — to give meaning to life.

A response to the Holocaust

For me, the symbol of perpetuation is to be found in an experience my wife and I shared during Sukkot 1969, on a trip to the Soviet Union in the period prior to the comparatively large-scale emigration that began two years later. We had gone to the Soviet Union to meet our courageous fellow Jews, and to give them moral support in their struggle to leave the Soviet Union. The Jews we met were risking their lives and livelihoods at that time, without even the hope that their efforts would reach fruition. While in Riga, we met three young men, who had taught themselves Hebrew — all of whom are now, incidentally, in Israel, who took us to a clearing in the woods a distance of seventeen kilometers from the city. The place is called Rumbuli. There, in 1941, the Nazis rounded up 36,000 Jews and in two days — November 30 and December 8 — sent them with characteristic precision to a mass grave. Several kilometers away, the Nazis had maintained a concentration camp at a place called Salaspils.

After the war, the Latvian government established Salaspils as a national shrine of memory, with no mention of Jews. Rumbuli remained unmarked, the woods covering over any semblance of what had transpired. In 1963, at a commemoration of the Warsaw Ghetto Revolt which the Jews in Riga observed secretly, a woman rose to tell the story of Rumbuli. She had been wounded and left for dead when the Nazi firing squads, working with dedication all day, had lost strength to hold their rifles.

Inspired by the story, the Jews of Riga then and there determined to erect a monument in memory of their brethren. They turned to the government to ask for assistance and for the heavy equipment needed to clear away the vegetation and clean the graves. When the government refused, they decided to do the work themselves by hand. As they worked, at first on their own and in secret, they uncovered bones, to which they gave proper reburial. Slowly, the project became a consecrated task in which large numbers of people were involved. After the project was complete and the graves had been resanctified, the Jewish community requested permission from the government to erect a stone monument. The government gave permission, but insisted that the only words to appear on it were to be "Victims of Fascism," in the Russian and Latvian languages, refusing repeatedly to permit any reference to Jews. Finally, after years of persuasion, permission was granted to add the words in Yiddish: "Karbonos fun Fascism," victims of fascism.

Except for the sign, Rumbuli bears no reference to Jews, but this cemetery has become a meeting place for young Jews who go there to care for the graves and, following their work, gather for study of their Jewish heritage. Rumbuli has become a driving force uniting the Jewish community and inspiring them to study Hebrew and Jewish history; and after their study they sing Israeli songs and dance. Thus, the mass grave of Jews killed almost forty years ago has become a source of inspiration for a new generation committed to the perpetuation of the Jewish heritage.

Shall the young Jews of the Soviet Union endure danger to achieve what we in lands of freedom can have for the asking? Is not theirs the only possible response to the Holocaust? "Son of man, these bones are the whole house of Israel; behold, they say: Our bones are dried up and our hope is lost; we are clear-cut off. Therefore prophesy, and say unto them: Thus saith the Lord God: Behold, I will open your graves, O My People ... And I will put my spirit in you, and you shall live, and I will place you in your own land, and you shall know that I the Lord have spoken and performed it, saith the Lord" (Ezekiel 39:11, 12, 14).

From the WZO Quarterly *Forum, Fall 1978, No. 32.*

APPENDIX

NAME INDEX

SUBJECT MATTER INDEX

For part II, "Taking a Stand", the reader should first consult table of contents.